Studies in Spanish American
Population History

About the Book and Editor

Studies in
Spanish American Population History
edited by David J. Robinson

Each of the contributions in this book sheds new light on key elements in the changing size, structure, and distribution of the Spanish American population during the colonial period. Several authors provide new source materials, while others manipulate well-known data in innovative ways to provide new insights into the past. In several of the essays the authors give information on regions and localities that hitherto have lain beyond the frontier of historical knowledge. Particularly important is their search for the broadest significance of their findings, whether investigating an entire region or a specific city, parish, or even family.

David J. Robinson, associate professor of geography at Syracuse University, is the author of several books on Latin America. He has served on the advisory board of the *Journal of Latin American Studies* and is currently general editor of the Dellplain Latin American Studies series.

DELLPLAIN LATIN AMERICAN STUDIES

PUBLISHED IN COOPERATION
WITH THE DEPARTMENT OF GEOGRAPHY
SYRACUSE UNIVERSITY

EDITOR

David J. Robinson
Syracuse University

EDITORIAL ADVISORY COMMITTEE

David A. Brading
University of Cambridge

Daniel Raposo Cordeiro
Syracuse University

William M. Denevan
University of Wisconsin

John H. Galloway
University of Toronto

John Lynch
University of London

William Mangin
Syracuse University

Studies in Spanish American Population History

edited by David J. Robinson

Dellplain Latin American Studies, No. 8

Routledge
Taylor & Francis Group

LONDON AND NEW YORK

First published 1981 by Westview Press, Inc.

Published 2019 by Routledge
52 Vanderbilt Avenue, New York, NY 10017
2 Park Square, Milton Park, Abingdon, Oxon OX14 4RN

Routledge is an imprint of the Taylor & Francis Group, an informa business

Library of Congress Catalog Card Number: 81-68379

ISBN 13: 978-0-367-28905-8 (hbk)
ISBN 13: 978-0-367-30451-5 (pbk)

For

WOODROW BORAH

who for so long
has pointed the way

Contents

x

Tables

Figures

Preface

Six of the ten essays in this collection (Lombardi, Villamarin, Chance, Greenow, Robinson, and Cook) were originally presented at a Special Session during the 43rd International Congress of Americanists, held in Vancouver during August, 1979. Jointly organized by David J. Robinson and Juan Villamarin, the session was designed to bring together a group of individuals who had been working on the changing population of colonial Spanish America from various disciplinary perspectives, to facilitate an exchange of information and ideas, and to promote the further investigation of significant research questions. The paper of Brian Evans was presented at the same Congress, in another session, but given its purpose and content it was thought to provide an ideal complement to several papers in the present collection.

Two other papers (Lovell and Lutz) were initially presented in a "Seminar in the Historical Demography of Highland Guatemala," part of the 27th Meeting of the American Society for Ethnohistory, held in Albany, N.Y., during October, 1979; Linda Newson's essay has been specially prepared for this volume, and is part of a larger forthcoming study of Central American population history. She also participated in the discussions following the presentation of most of the Americanistas papers. It will be clear from a reading of these three papers that the authors are addressing topics that could equally have found a place in the Americanists discussions, and they thus here provide an important Central American dimension to the debate on population change. One of the benefits of hindsight is the possibility of re-assembling a group of persons who should have been together in the first place!

Only those who have ventured beyond the oral presentation stage of conference papers will understand the full significance of my sincere thanks to all of the contributors to this volume for their patience and kind assistance in revising various drafts of their papers.

xx

Multidisciplinary research sounds exciting, but it can too easily founder on a few unanswered letters and missed deadlines.

I owe a personal debt to Juan Villamarin, whose energies and contacts made the task of organizing a special session at the Americanistas much easier than it might otherwise have been.

Almost all of the maps and diagrams were prepared by Valmor Philp of the Syracuse University Cartographic Laboratory, and to him we extend our special thanks. Jane McGraw typed the entire manuscript in its many drafts, as well as all of the inevitable correspondence that such an enterprise involves, with her inimitable speed and good humor, and I am thus even deeper in her debt. Both the typing and cartographics were funded from the Dellplain Latin American Geography Program at Syracuse University, and I would like to thank Robert G. Jensen, Chairman of the Geography Department, for his unfailing support in that regard.

David J. Robinson
Syracuse, New York

Contributors

John K. Chance	Department of Anthropology, University of Denver, Colorado
N. David Cook	Department of History, University of Bridgeport, Connecticut
Brian M. Evans	Department of Geography, University of Winnipeg, Manitoba, Canada
Linda L. Greenow	Department of Geography, Syracuse University, New York
John V. Lombardi	Department of History, Indiana University, Bloomington, Indiana
Christopher H. Lutz	Centro de Investigaciones Regionales de Mesoamérica, Antigua, Guatemala
W. George Lovell	Department of Geography, Queen's University, Kingston, Ontario, Canada
Linda A. Newson	Department of Geography, King's College, University of London
David J. Robinson	Department of Geography, Syracuse University, New York
Juan and Judith Villamarin	Department of Anthropology, University of Delaware, Newark, Delaware

Introduction

David J. Robinson

This brief introduction will serve to place each of the essays within the wider context of Spanish American population history. Limitations of space preclude a detailed bibliographical and historiographical treatment, and in any event, the reader will find in the notes that accompany each of the essays a large number of citations that provide ample evidence of the advancing state of the art. Each of the contributions sheds new light on key elements in the changing size, structure, and distribution of Spanish American population during the colonial period. While some range over centuries to monitor temporal sequences, others adopt a cross-sectional approach to specify the precise conditions at a convenient historical viewpoint. Several authors provide new source materials, while others manipulate well-known data in an innovative manner to provide new insights into the past. In several of the essays information is provided for regions and localities which have hitherto lain beyond the frontier of historical knowledge.

Equally important is the fact that all of the authors share a multidisciplinary approach to their problems, a characteristic that has long enriched the demographic approach to Latin America's past. Without examining the authors' departmental affiliations it might be difficult to separate the historians from the anthropologists and the geographers. And so it should be, for all of the essays address questions that extend beyond the bounds of any one narrow academic focus. The types of evidence, the methods, the techniques, as well as the interpretations, demand a familiarity with a range of often difficult substantive fields.

It is also good to note that even when an individual city, parish, or even family is being investigated, the author is at pains to search for a wider significance for his findings. The typical, the aberrant, the statistically significant, the example, the sample--all the problems that make historical research as exciting as it is

1

exacting--are to be found throughout this collection.

While population provides the authors with the means of analyzing Spanish America's past, it is not viewed as an end in itself; the numbing that comes from too many numbers is pleasantly absent. First, the populations studied here are usually large and diverse enough to allow one to approach the mass of socialized individuals that comprised the majority of colonial society. Second, the very mode of counting and classifying such persons allows one to appreciate the cultural perceptions, images and prejudices that were the hallmark of intercultural relations over more than three centuries. Third, the contextual arrangement of people in families, clans, neighborhoods, cities, hinterlands, and the like, permits one to monitor not only demographic trends, but since those same persons were workers and consumers, landlords and peasants, residents and migrants, colonists and conquered, changes in their relative numbers and interrelationships provide one with a singular interpretative opportunity. The populace in this sense was the colonial society. When numbers increased or decreased within significant socio-ethnic groups, the repercussions could be ideological as well as economic. When persons became mobile, political as much as social tensions could be produced. Real people belonged (or were ascribed) to racial groups and social classes, and discerning trends in subtle cultural transformations is no easy task. In this respect the mundane census returns, tribute lists, and parish registers, offer surprising avenues of insight.

THE AFTERMATH OF CONTACT AND CONQUEST

Our knowledge of the demographic ramifications of the arrival of Europeans in the New World is still imprecise. Some scholars are prepared to utilize the scanty (and mostly Spanish) sources of the sixteenth century to extrapolate a relatively large pre-contact population for some major regions, with densities approaching those of the modern period.[1] Others deny the probabilities of such situations, stressing what they believe to be the ecological limits of the areas under consideration, the socioadministrative capacity of the pre-Hispanic cultures involved, the varied epidemiology of the diseases involved, and the suspect Spanish documentary record.[2] While this debate will doubtless continue, as more regions and records are investigated, it is important to note that in several respects there are major weaknesses in the evidential basis of the debate. We know, for example, very little of the detailed ethnohistory of the contact cultures: how their settlements were spaced, how their subsistence systems operated, how they coordinated

the management of diverse ecosystems, how balanced were
their diets, how prepared they were to react to a major
cultural intrusion.

Similarly, though ecology is often adduced as a key
factor affecting population carrying capacity as well as
potential rate of change, we know little of the ecotones
of the contact and early colonial New World. And where
detailed work has been undertaken, the results have been
more than a little surprising. In many areas, mid-
twentieth century vegetation and soils have been recognized as poor indicators of earlier conditions.[3] In
others, the colonial palimpsest has all but obliterated
the traces of what might otherwise be susceptible to site
catchment analysis and other rigorous techniques of ecological evaluation.[4]

Another geographical factor that finds a place in
the agenda of favored explanations is the role of altitude as it allegedly controlled the variable incidence of
diseases. Exactly what were the differential probabilities of death in the tropical and sub-tropical lowlands
as opposed to the colder climes of the Andean chains and
Mesoamerican plateau is still very unclear. Evidence is
scant, and climatic controls on disease vectors still undetermined. The crude highland/lowland dichotomy per-
sists only as an epidemiological assumption. Within such
large units the contemporary micro-environmental variations are little understood even after a century or more
of study.

But beyond the initial and drastic reduction of Indian population (and few would deny it to have been less)
in the sixteenth century lie two hundred or more years of
continued population fluctuation. Whereas for central
Mexico the sixteenth century witnessed the primary shock
of demographic change, in other more peripheral regions
it was in the seventeenth and eighteenth centuries that
god-fearing, gold-hunting and disease-carrying aliens
arrived, to disrupt the local economy, to redesign the
cultural landscape and to restructure social relations.
In the colonial core regions too socio-economic evolution
produced an ever-changing balance between births and
deaths, between stable and unstable circumstances, and
between conquerors and conquered. Within this parabola
of episodic decline and recovery several of the present
essays contribute new data and opinions.

For two distinctive Guatemalan regions Lutz and
Lovell provide evidence to parallel that of central
Mexico and Peru: early rapid decline and slow recovery.
Both their studies, as well as that of Newson who sheds
much new light on the Honduran experience, also demonstrate the problematic nature of the data base, the difficulties of standardizing population segments used to
derive totals, the unspecified diseases, the spatial
shifts that often compounded the problems and still

confound the modern researcher. In a similar vein, but
for the seventeenth and eighteenth centuries, Villamarin
and Cook examine the potential of tribute lists and parish registers to elucidate changing population patterns.
The synchronicity of fluctuations among the Chibcha settlements of the Sabana de Bogotá illustrates the usefulness of the regional approach, though Villamarin is careful to note the difficulties of reconciling changes at
the regional level with those operating at the level of
individual communities. Multi-level causation is still
beyond reach, a fact which Cook implicitly accepts when
he sets the Yanque details against the backdrop of Peru
in general. How many Yanques make up Collaguas? And for
the Andean core how far may we extrapolate? All of the
authors demonstrate that a combination of types of documentation is required if the full story is ever to be
told, and yet tantalizingly few places have such extant
sources.

One solution to the problems confronting the historian of past populations would be an escape to the simpli-
fying assumptions of simulated models of change: the
clear counterfactual held up to the blur of historical
"reality." If it is possible to examine the probabilities of transpacific contacts,[5] why not a computer simulation of disease diffusion? In that way the settlement
net, the density of population (by various types) and the
rate of infection could be measured from selected "outbreak" points of specific diseases.[6] Of course bold assumptions would have to be made, but they can always be
modified in a controlled manner--and far more easily than
in the uncontrolled world of the documentary past. To
dismiss recent advances in demographic analysis beyond
the context of colonial Spanish America is to ignore a
set of powerful investigative tools.[7]

POPULATION ON THE MOVE

Besides appearing (births) and disappearing (deaths)
from the scene human populations have another character-
istic--that of physically moving, and this aspect of
Spanish America's past is highlighted in several of the
present essays. Population movement is a characteristic,
however, of varying significance, for not all persons behave alike, and the range of factors known, or assumed,
to affect the decision to move is immense. Equally important (and here all of the present essays are perti-
nent) those who did not move are of significance, for in
studying their patterns much may be learned of the reasons for immobility.

Within the larger frame of colonial Spanish America
it is clear that from an early situation in which mostly
sedentary Indians were disrupted by a highly mobile

Spanish minority, the pattern inexorably shifted to one
with an increasing number of spatially stable persons of
non-Indian origin, with Indians and certain mixed groups
becoming increasingly mobile. Indeed one might posit a
"mobility transition" in colonial Spanish America that
paralleled the shifts from encomienda to hacienda, from
Indian to peasant, from urbanite to urbanized, and from
patrias chicas to proto nation-states.[8]

As Lombardi argues there was an assumed propriety of
place embedded in the Spanish colonial mentality, which
may have been either a consequence of cultural development, or an artifice of imperial control. People should
be of a place, and attached to that place, and those who
were not were suspect. Transients were (as elsewhere)
almost always suspect, for a lack of belonging was
equated with a lack of caring--either for the law, or for
social customs.

The reasons for moving, be it to the next village,
the nearby town, or the next province, varied in both
time and space. A persistent secular threat to land and
livelihood could push Chibchas out of their homelands
(Villamarin); an avaricious clergy demanding services in
cash or kind could loosen the kin and territorial ties of
Yucatecan Mayans (Robinson). With migrants escaping beyond Spanish control from Peru (Cook) to Mexico (Greenow),
it is not surprising that new census categories were designed to isolate and calculate the flow which threatened
to become a flood (Evans); forasteros, ausentes, vagos
and the like needed to be repatriated for the good of
all.

To identify the currents of migration in Spanish
American colonial populations is no easy task. Just as a
migrant could escape tribute or obvención by moving the
effective administrative jurisdiction, so too by leaving
his parish of birth or marriage he escapes the modern researcher (Greenow, Robinson). Unless one can locate a
census that specifies the origins of individuals or family heads (Evans, Cook), one's only recourse is to the in-
terlinkage of birth, marriage and burial records.[9] If
individuals did not behave "properly" and be born (i.e.
baptized), married (i.e. in a church ceremony) and die
(i.e. be buried), then they evidentially did not exist.[10]
We must therefore realize that millions of individuals
will fall completely outside of our historical knowledge:
we can only hope that their more "proper" neighbors offer
some clue as to their unrecoverable feelings and behavior. And if one is to become worried about such "nonexistent" population, one's anxieties are hardly quieted
when one realizes that ethnic and class biases in reporting and recording clearly affect the extant documentation. For every one person who could afford a lawyer or
priest, how many do we count who could not? Whether it
be the men of Cajamarca,[11] or the nuns of Guadalajara[12]

we know that our record is uneven, and suspect.

Yet the fact that much can be gleaned from the records of conscientious parish priests who knew their flock intimately, gives cause for hope. Geobiographies can trace some persons and families through time and space (Robinson), and when aggregated into statistical populations can tell us much of local and regional interaction (Greenow).[13] Extensive multi-stage migration makes nonsense of notions of the closed corporate communities, and those who counterpose a stable past against the mobile present belie the facts as they were so assiduously recorded. It is too easy to assume that Spanish American destabilization of population came, as with Europe and Anglo America, during the nineteenth and twentieth centuries. There was always much in the Spanish American world from which to flee, or to which one could be attracted. Only the complexities of the details of such spatial relocation have yet to be elucidated; these essays contain some clues.

THE COLONIAL CITY AND ITS HINTERLAND

Of the range of institutions that reflected the changing population history of colonial Spanish America, two are of especial significance: the family and the city. While the former provides an opportunity to examine the intrusion of Spanish social organization upon a diverse aboriginal base, the latter allows one to examine the articulation of not only the socio-economic sphere, but also the operation of colonial authority and the developing tensions between those with access to power and those marginalized by the colonial process.[14] The patrilineal nuclear family was promoted as a normative feature of society (Villamarin), and the values of the hierarchical household become evident at every turn of the documentary record. One's place in society was usually reflected at the microcosmic level of the household. In that sense, census becomes symbol, and registration required behavior (Lombardi).

But of the higher level entities which structured social interaction and the relations of production among the larger groupings of ethnic and class divisions, the city was of key significance. As the locus of power and the focus of economic activity it embodied colonial rule. To live beyond the reach of the city extended--outside its hinterland--was to exist outside of the colonial realm.[15]

The urban network provided the Crown with a hierarchical system of population reporting, albeit by the seventeenth century too cumbersome to allow much of the data collected to be efficiently utilized (Lombardi). The urban system, about whose systemic relations so little is known, provided a range of socio-economic opportunities that greatly affected migration patterns (Greenow, Cook). Major changes in population structure may have been directly related to the disruptive effects of the urban economy (Villamarin, Newson, Robinson).

In spite of the quickening pace of research on the internal structure of the Spanish American colonial city, much has yet to be learned. In that respect detailed ecological analysis of social relations in a selected city is to be welcomed (Chance). Though some may express concern over the appropriateness of applying a methodology grounded in twentieth century social relations, when physical distance is a useful proxy for social distance, the fact remains that the patterns produced by such ecological approaches are most useful discriminants of inferred social behavior.[16] As in the nineteenth-century city, one's position in the city was often a reflection of one's position in society.

Of course classificatory problems persist, as they are likely to do so for some time. But the question of how to isolate a lower class group (Chance) is no different from the task of deciphering ethnic and other labels (Evans, Lombardi). One clear signal from recent research is that an approach to population history that uses multiple sources is often very rewarding. Whether it be age data, kin structure, household composition, stage migration, or population decline, the combination of records provides invaluable clues.

If this collection stimulates further research on these and other issues, it will have served its purpose.

NOTES

1. The best introductions to this extensive literature are the three volumes of S. F. Cook and W. Borah, Essays in Population History, Berkeley, 1971-1979. Both the essays and the extensive bibliography in W. M. Denevan, The Native Population of the Americas in 1492, Madison, 1976, provide extremely useful summaries of the various positions.

2. See for example R. A. Zambardino, "Mexico's Population in the Sixteenth Century: Demographic Anomaly or Mathematical Illusion?," Journal of Interdisciplinary History, Vol. XI, 1980, pp. 1-27; also his review of the third volume of Cook and Borah's Essays in Population History, in Annals of Association of American Geographers, 1980, Vol. 70, pp. 583-585. Also D. Henige, "On the Contact Population of Hispaniola: History as Higher Mathematics," Hispanic American Historical Review, Vol. 58, 1978, pp. 217-237.

3. Remote sensing by satellite has recently identified major water-management networks in the Yucatán, which strengthens the views of those who have recently argued for major historic-ecological

8

changes in that region. For an excellent analysis of soil capacities in the Amazon basin as it relates to historical populations see Nigel J. H. Smith, "Anthrosols and Human Carrying Capacity in Amazonia," Annals, Association of American Geographers, 1980, Vol. 70, pp. 553-566.

4. For a description of the technique, see M. R. Jarman, C. Vita-Finzi and E. S. Higgs, "Site Catchment Analysis in Archaeology," in P. J. Ucko, R. Tringham and G. W. Dimbleby, Man, Settlement and Urbanism, London, 1972, pp. 61-67. For an excellent study of the utility of the archaeological approach to colonial sites see David M. Jones, The Archaeology of Haciendas and Ranchos of Otumba and Apan, Basin of Mexico, Research Report No. 2, Mesoamerican Research Colloquium, University of Iowa, 1980.

5. M. Levison, et al., "A Model of Accidental Drift Voyaging in the Pacific Ocean," Proceedings, International Federation for Information Processing, 1969, pp. 1521-36.

6. Such studies would be much easier if the records are available for a dense network or points. For the available Mexican data see D. J. Robinson, Research Inventory of the Mexican Collection of Colonial Parish Registers, Vol. 5 of Finding Aids to the Microfilmed Collection of the Genealogical Society of Utah, Salt Lake City, 1980.

7. For an excellent account of what may be done with microsimulation see E. A. Hammel et al., The SOCSIM Demographic-Sociological Microsimulation Program, Institute of International Studies, Berkeley, 1976. For an excellent series of case studies see K. W. Wachter, et al., Statistical Studies of Historical Social Structure, New York, 1978. An outline of approaches is provided in B. Dyke and J. W. MacCluer (eds.), Computer Simulation in Human Population Studies, New York, 1974.

8. See the classic article of W. Zelinsky, "The Hypothesis of the Mobility Transition," Geographical Review, Vol. LXI, 1971, pp. 219-249.

9. See for example D. J. Robinson, "Córdoba en 1779: Ciudad y Campaña," in Raul C. Rey Balmaceda (ed.), Homenaje a Federico A. Daus, Buenos Aires, 1979, pp. 279-312. Also L. L. Johnson and S. Migden Socolow, "Population and Space in Eighteenth-Century Buenos Aires," in D. J. Robinson (ed.), Social Fabric and Spatial Structure in Colonial Latin America, Ann Arbor, 1979, pp. 339-368; and M. M. Swann, Tierra Adentro: Society and Settlement in Colonial Durango, Ann Arbor, 1981.

10. A general overview is provided in D. J. Robinson, "The Spanish American Family in the Eighteenth and Nineteenth Centuries," Proceedings of the Third World Conference on Records and Family History, Vol. 5, Salt Lake City, 1980.

11. J. Lockhart, Men of Cajamarca: A Social and Biographical Study of the First Conquerors of Peru, Austin, 1972.

12. A. Lavrín and E. Couturier, "Dowries and Wills: A View of Women's Socioeconomic Role in Colonial Guadalajara and Puebla, 1640-1790," Hispanic American Historical Review, Vol. 59, 1979, pp. 280-304.

13. See for example S. Migden Socolow, "Marriage, Birth and Inheritance: The Merchants of Eighteenth Century Buenos Aires," Hispanic American Historical Review, Vol. 60, 1980, pp. 387-406.

14. Excellent overviews are provided in R. M. Morse, "The Urban Development of Colonial Spanish America," in the Cambridge History of Latin America, Cambridge, 1981; W. Borah, "Latin American Cities in the Eighteenth Century: A Sketch," paper presented at the 43rd Congress of Americanists, Vancouver, 1979.

15. Two excellent recent studies of city-hinterland relations are E. Van Young, Hacienda and Market in Eighteenth-Century Mexico: The Rural Economy of the Guadalajara Region, 1675-1820, Berkeley, 1981; and Linda L. Greenow, Spatial Dimensions of the Credit Market in Nueva Galicia, 1721-1820, unpublished Ph.D. dissertation, Syracuse University, 1980.

16. A good review of the problems is to be found in D. W. G. Timms, The Urban Mosaic: Towards a Theory of Residential Differentiation, Cambridge, 1971. Two useful cautions are sounded in B. S. Morgan, "Social Distance and Spatial Distance: A Research Note," Area, Vol. 6, 1974, pp. 293-297; and R. I. Woods, "Aspects of the Scale Problem in the Calculation of Segregation Indices," Tijdschrift voor Economische en Sociale Geografie, Vol. 67, 1976, pp. 169-174.

1
Population Reporting Systems: An Eighteenth-Century Paradigm of Spanish Imperial Organization

John V. Lombardi

Most historians approach colonial Spanish-American demographic materials with an interest in the number and composition of local and regional populations. We evaluate these documents in terms of their completeness and accuracy of enumeration, we compile elaborate data sets based on this material, and in the end, if our labors are rewarded, we can provide detailed descriptions and analyses of colonial populations which we hope provide insights into the conditions of life throughout the Spanish colonies. Such a sequence of research is admirable, and many important contributions to Spanish-American history have been achieved in this fashion.[1]

But as recent research has shown, these census materials can tell us more than the numbers and composition of populations. Because of their central place in Spanish imperial philosophy, these documents can be made to reveal much about the Spanish colonial self-image, about imperial priorities, about local understanding of social structure, and a host of other non-numerical topics. Although the inferences required to extract these notions may sometimes stretch the historical imagination, the exercise makes us more appreciative of the richness of these documents.[2]

DATA AND POLICY

Even though the census system of Spanish America is relatively well-known to most students of the empire, a review of its major characteristics may be helpful. By defining the term census rather loosely, we can include all those Spanish colonial reports commenting in a more or less systematic fashion on population numbers. These could include such varied sources as missionary accounts of conversions, conquerors' chronicles, baptismal and burial records, lists of merchants, passenger manifests, and the remarkable eighteenth-century annual censuses.

11

Other documents such as special surveys, relaciones geográficas, plantation accounts, and public registry documents also yield considerable demographic detail. To be sure, the demographer will find much of this data too imprecise and unsystematic to justify detailed technical analysis. But even so, the vision of America provided there is especially valuable.[3]

Because the Spanish empire was organized around highly rational principles, Spain's imperial bureaucrats never doubted the importance of abundant, unbiased data for the elaboration of colonial policy. And their preoccupation with population data was exceeded only by their obsession with financial data. This pragmatic and rationalist Spanish colonial administration operated on two levels simultaneously, supported by an information system requiring two kinds of data corresponding to the management of human resources both as aggregates and as individuals. To plan properly, colonial administrators needed to know what population aggregates could be deployed at various tasks throughout the empire. How many Indians in an encomienda, how many slaves in the colonial trade, how many people resettled to the mines? Similarly, Spain needed to have good data on the individuals who would direct the activities of the aggregates. Thus, the colonial planners wanted to know whether Gómez was married, whether Jiménez had descended from a conqueror, whether Mendoza had been a good viceroy, and whether Tovar had illegitimate grandparents.

To satisfy the demand for aggregate information the Crown ordered surveys, relaciones geográficas, and regular and irregular population counts. To satisfy the need for individual information, the parishes kept baptismal, marriage, and burial records; houselists were prepared; and especially, dossiers or hojas de servicios y méritos were required. This mass of documentation, of which these few examples are but a token, came from a reporting system so prolific it soon overloaded the bureaucracy's ability to assimilate. Nevertheless, in spite of the widely recognized difficulty of processing the data, Spain not only continued to require it, but Crown officials invented more sophisticated data gathering machinery as time went on.[4]

Because this preoccupation with population information so pervades Spanish colonial administration, its origins deserve some comment. Surely the careful attention to numbers and characteristics of the colonial population formed part of the fundamental plan of the colony, responding to a major problem in Spanish colonial administration. Perhaps it may seem elementary, but there is no harm in reviewing the principal dilemma at the outset of Spain's American enterprise. The problem in America in the early years when the basic elements of the reporting system were established was never a lack of natural

resources to exploit but the availability of human resources to do it. And because Spain could not provide
this human capital, the Amerindian was quickly identified
as America's strategic resource. Without Indian labor
all the wealth of Potosí and Mexico would have been
wasted, locked in the ground awaiting the advent of a
technology capable of extraction without a large number
of human workers. The principal controversy of the early
colonial period involved the encomienda and the treatment
of Amerindians because the Spaniards had quickly identified Indian labor as the sine qua non of success in America. And of course, to deal with the controversy the imperial bureaucracy had to develop some information
sources.

As often happens in such cases, the Indian problem
was well on the way to solution before the bulk of the
information could be generated, but the close connection
between the numbers and characteristics of population and
the production of wealth in America remained a constant
theme of colonial administration. Both in surviving instructions and the texts of documents such as relaciones
geográficas and special population surveys, this notion
emerges. And so it is no wonder that Spain's colonial
administrators pursued data on population so relentless-
ly.[5]

THE URBAN CONNECTION

The above topic could be examined in more depth but
that is for another time and place. Instead, let us
examine another dimension of the Spanish colonial information system that can be seen through the complex of
demographic data included in parish books, houselists,
and regular censuses. Within the carefully kept parish
registers and equally painstaking houselists and censuses
lies the principal Spanish notion about proper social organization. As clearly as in any other source, these
documents demonstrate the central function of the urban
place, the town in Spanish-American society. It is, of
course, a commonplace of Spanish-American history to discuss the urban character of Spain's conquest and settlement of America. But what receives less emphasis is the
continuing and pervasive nature of this urban focus. It
is not just in the sixteenth-century conquest that towns
proved important to the Spanish colonial mission, but
right through the Hapsburg and Bourbon periods as well.
Eighteenth-century colonials were as eager to register
their children's baptisms, marriages, and burials and
validate their urban connection as any first-generation
conquistador.[6]

Through the population records of the empire emerges
a vision of colonial Spanish America that sees the human

landscape through towns. Everyone had to be connected to
a town, and while one could have official residence in
one place and live in another as a visitor or transient,
the distinctions were rather well kept. Moreover, people
not connected to the town network were regarded for the
most part as vagrants, outcasts, or worse.

While this urban-centered social and political arrangement has been much studied, it is important to emphasize the significance of the population accounting
system for its maintenance. Because the token of legit-
imacy and propriety in Spanish-American society came in
the form of properly registered vital events, contracts,
and legal proceedings in the towns and cities, most
people wanted to be recorded in the parish books and
identified with an urban place. As a result, these documents have a consistency and completeness remarkable for
their time. To be sure, some significant, if difficult
to estimate, number of people existed outside the urban
matrix, or at least unrecorded by the parish registers.
And a fascinating study could be done by comparing court
records, parish books, and houselists for the same place
and time to determine the convergence of these sources
around individual names.[7]

SOCIAL NORMS AND RESIDENTIAL PATTERNS

In evaluating the social context of the population
records, the houselist or matrícula provides considerable
insight. Not only do these remarkably complete inventor-
ies of families and individuals permit the location of
people on the town map, they indicate how the clerical
bureaucracy viewed the social composition of households.
While it is not clear how representative this priestly
view of household arrangements might have been, there is
enough consistency among differing list-makers to indicate the presence of a set of norms. For example, the
lists show us households in which every effort is made to
identify a head of household, to place the remaining members of the household in descending order by age and
status and to preserve in the list the subordinate family
organization of slaves, servants, and other dependent individuals.

The houselists are only now beginning to be analyzed,
and the preliminary results so far have been very promising. Although there is still much to be done in this
regard, a paradigm of Spanish-American social and residential structure can be constructed on the evidence contained in these documents plus the data available in the
regularized census reports of the last quarter of the
eighteenth century.[8]

The first principle of this norm of social organization has already been mentioned, the people of the empire

should be identified in the first instance through their connections to urban places. This principle permitted the subsequent development of the rest of the norm, for it attempted to guarantee that individuals could be traced and their activities verified through the document trail left in the urban network, thereby increasing the efficiency of scarce colonial managers. From what we can tell from the research completed to date, Spanish Americans moved about the empire frequently. While every town and village had a core of persisting residents, substantial numbers of individuals changed their residence or simply travelled from place to place within the empire. Given the importance of human resources in this imperial design, the urban, parish-based population recording system existed to provide reference points for the identification and location of highly mobile individuals.

Equally obvious, the careful attention paid to the recording of baptisms, marriages, and burials testifies to the social, political, and economic significance of such documents. Were Spanish America a stable, sedentary society with long traditions of land holding and minimal social mobility, these records might not be quite as interesting. But because the Spanish empire was so large, so new, so changeable, and because one generation's landowner and tenants could well be different from the next generation's, the parish books took on increased importance as the touchstones of stability in an everchanging social and economic environment. Furthermore, the combination of short life spans, long communication times, and extended geographic space encouraged even the most unprepossessing members of society to participate in the parish registry system, thereby guaranteeing the greatest possible sense of permanence and continuity within the Spanish world.

From this principle of primal location of vital events in the parish register we can look to the houselists for a more sophisticated vision of the aggregate society of Spanish America. This urban place where Spaniards ought to be located was ideally organized into a clearly defined and delimited space complete with boundaries, jurisdictions, and activities also located and specified according to plan. The Spanish norm in America did not conceive of the city as an environment in which the growth of commerce, industry, and services would define the characteristics of urban space. Instead, this space was to be organized and, in effect, filled with the proper activities. The houselists can be thought of as individualized representations of this ordered sense of the urban landscape. And it is this normative uniformity that permits us to reconstruct the towns and cities, identify the neighborhoods, chart the ethnic arrangements, and calculate household composition, as well as

compare these characteristics over time. Other evidence,
of course, validates this notion, especially the records
of the ayuntamientos where the day-to-day maintenance and
administration of the urban norms were carried out.[9]

The houselists also tell us something about the
ideal internal arrangements of households. The list-
makers expected to find an individual who could be identified as the household head, and except for a few cases
they were able to find such a person. Contrary to much
popular wisdom about Spanish-American society, there was
apparently not much reluctance to identify women as
household heads, even where there was a husband present.
The rest of the household, according to the norm, appeared to be defined in reference to the household head,
not in reference to some standard applicable uniformly
across the city. That is, the status of an agregado or
servant in one household cannot be construed as lower in
socio-economic terms to the status of household head in
another residence. For the purpose of the houselists,
each household was a social microcosm, a self-contained
unit with its own hierarchy and set of relationships not
easily compared to those existing outside.

This internal hierarchy is not easy to categorize,
for the internal evidence in the household does not seem
sufficient to support an unequivocal hypothesis. But for
the sake of the argument we can propose a tentative paradigm. These Spanish-American houselists show us a residential unit composed of at least a primary unit and frequently one or more secondary units. The primary unit
always included the head of household and was structured
to show the relationship of the primary unit's individuals to the head: such as son of, daughter of, wife of,
etc. Secondary units were more complex, for a household
could have individuals or families as secondary units.
Clearly, the norm provided that a family group (husband
and wife with or without children) not including the head
of household appeared as a secondary unit. Servants also
appeared as secondary units, as did slaves. Some people
listed in the household had ambiguous status, such as unmarried adults not part of a family unit but nevertheless
residing in the household and presumably under the nominal authority of the household head. These individuals
could have been single relatives of the household head
or of other household members, retainers, or other
hangers-on.

These arrangements often became rather complex, but
the general principle of organization seems fairly stable.
Furthermore, these documents emphasize the hierarchical
structure of households, with household head in charge.
The primary unit had the highest status, the unmarried
slaves the lowest status. The lists carefully arranged
the rest of the household in descending order of status
by unit and within units: for example, father, mother,

older sibling, younger sibling.

Because this is the norm to which the list-makers tried to fit reality, the actual houselists show many exceptions and anomalies, but not enough to seriously compromise the norm. Of course, these documents give little indication of how the households actually managed their affairs. Nevertheless, the consistency and care with which these documents were prepared indicates an effort to apply the norm and a sense that the exercise was important. Especially noteworthy, as has been mentioned before, these lists place careful emphasis on location on the urban map. List-makers followed the same route year after year and took particular notice of empty or abandoned or ruined houses. Such concern indicates the close connection between the notion of personal identity as expressed in the named lists and the identity of place as demonstrated by the parish priests' concern that each house appear in its proper place along the street and that the structures without people also be included so that the urban space described by the houselist be an accurate representation.

RACE, MARRIAGE, AND AGE

Three other characteristics of the population concerned the data collectors of the Spanish empire: race, marriage, and age. These three, of special interest to modern demographers and social historians, give the most difficulty in attempting to apply modern demographic and statistical techniques because the categories themselves seem to have variable meanings and the consistency of reporting leaves much to be desired. But even so, this technical weakness in the data can be helpful in the analysis of social phenomena.

Most population material for the Spanish colonial system includes data on race. And there has been considerable work done on the legal implications and the folklore of racial categorizations in Spanish America. From the earliest days of conquest and settlement, race and the status of racial categories proved to be topics of primary interest to settlers, lawyers, clerics, and social theorists. The earliest classification systems identified the three primary types: white, Indian, and black. These designations helped Spain transpose the peninsular preoccupation with racial-social plurality (Christian, Jew, Moor) into a new key for the new world. And part of the durability of the racial classification can be traced to its theoretical neatness.

Whites (read Christian Spaniards) from the dominant caste functioned as governors and managers of the production of wealth. Indians, that charmingly simplistic consolidation of a wide range of cultural levels, existed to receive the faith and produce the wealth. Blacks, those aliens brought from outside the Spanish sphere, carried a special legal status and lived forever with the color that marked their origin.

Given these simple definitions of the caste society, it proved easy enough to invent tripartite legislation providing for the functions, responsibilities, and rights of the individuals within each group. But the population materials collected over the years of the empire clearly indicate the impracticality of this system. While other sources also show this, especially litigation over the application of racial labels, they have the difficulty that they are almost always particularistic or polemical or both. The population records, however, tend to be broad-gauged efforts by more or less disinterested clerics to apply the ideal types to reality. And the priests' discomfort with the labels is manifest. Whether we see the problem in the parish books where one son of a marriage is classified pardo and the next one negro or where an individual is baptised as pardo and married as white, the sense of inconformity between the ideal and real is palpable. Similarly, if we read the official interpretations of words like pardo and negro we might believe that those classified as negro were simply darker versions of those classified as pardo. But the population records for some regions show too few negros for this to have been so and suggest the hypothesis that in practice, in at least one corner of the empire, negro may have come to mean an ex-slave rather than a darker-than-pardo. Or perhaps the hypothesis itself is too simple, perhaps negros were labelled on the basis of color and distance from slavery. Or perhaps the category was required on the form and the census-taker filled in the blank space relatively arbitrarily.

Some census districts make distinctions between indios and mestizos, some find that subtlety unnecessary. And here too, this disparity, this deviance from colonial uniformity should lead us to continue our reexamination of the empire's practice of racial and social labelling.[10]

The census documents also confirm the difficulty Spanish clerics had with collecting information on marriage. Because marriage only included church-sanctioned unions, the data gatherers were precluded from recording data on consensual unions, although other sources clearly show the widespread existence of such living arrangements. Obviously this informal marriage pattern, of great significance for the analysis of Spanish-American social organization and function cannot be approached through the population data. What is not clear, however, is whether the houselists, with their careful breakdown of living units, list common-law couples as independent singles within the household. A comparison of the sources might yield this useful information. But in any

case, it should be evident that as complete records of
biological unions and pairing customs, the bulk of population records do not serve.[11]

Finally, there is the demographically critical question of age. Whether looking at those few houselists
that include age or the censuses with age-based categories, the Spanish conception of age as a crucial social
variable emerges rather clearly. Age apparently had
significance only at certain transitional points in an
individual's life history. At least insofar as systematic reporting was concerned, Spanish officials thought it
important to distinguish the population under and over
age seven, the supposed age of reason. And in many surveys there was an understandable interest in the fifteen-
year milestone as the age eligible to begin bearing arms
in defense of the realm. While there is evidence that
bureaucrats in Spain saw some utility in age-based data,
the record of collecting such information is poor indeed.
Where such data exists, they tend to be unreliable, un-
believable, partial, or some similar combination, render-
ing the information unusable for most demographic purposes.

But for the student of social paradigms, these incomplete records can be fascinating for they reflect both
the individual's perception of his own age and the
census-taker's evaluation. Analysis might reveal what
ages were good ages and which ones undesirable. And
this, in turn, could provide insight into the Spanish
colonial perception of youth, maturity, and aging.[12]

DATA, INFORMATION, POLICY

Throughout this discussion Spanish colonial population data has been discussed as if they were designed,
collected, and used with a modern preoccupation with demographic techniques. But of course that was not so.
Parish registers, houselists, and censuses formed a part
of Spain's information system, and as happened with other
parts of the imperial design, the population data served
individuals and permitted society to insist on its concern with origin and lineage. It is only in retrospect
that these materials are being made to yield important
demographic information.

The houselists carry the notion of location one step
forward by displaying in one place an ordered set of
names that form an analogue to the distribution and arrangement of the population. These lists, because they
were compiled in a systematic and regular pattern, approximate the procedures of a modern census, but because
there was so much attention to social and residential
hierarchy instead of age the demographic value of the
records is limited. The final step in this evolution

brought the aggregate censuses of the last quarter of the
eighteenth century. These materials, while clearly and
explicitly designed to yield demographic data in a use-
able way, drew their materials from the same sources
using similar procedures as earlier efforts, and the results share some of the same defects. One of the key
difficulties in these Spanish imperial population accounting efforts can be traced to the traditional unwill-
ingness of the Spanish bureaucracy to create single-
purpose officials, bureaus, or offices. The peculiarly
holistic philosophy of government employed by Spain in
America provided little comfort for self-contained bureaucratic domains. Not only were officials given multiple functions and responsibilities, but their domains
tended to overlap. The benefits of such a system in
terms of control and cost, as well as the disadvantages
in terms of efficiency and responsiveness, have been extensively studied elsewhere. But from our narrow interest in extracting quality demographic indices from the
population materials, the confusion of purposes and goals
evident in the records inhibits their usefulness.

This exploration of the context that produced
Spanish-American colonial population records could be extended much further, but I would prefer to close with two
observations. With the exception of the parish registers, most of the systematic population accounting information was apparently never used for policy purposes.
Although there is some indication that gross totals and
racial percentages became part of the bureaucratic information pool, the detailed houselists and regular censuses of the eighteenth century languished unexploited
until today. The problem, of course, was not that Spanish officials lacked the ability to add, but that the information processing capabilities of the system proved
inadequate to cope with the volume and complexity of the
population data.[13]

And it is this mismatch between the theory and philosophy of government on one side and the bureaucracy's
skills to implement it on the other that symbolizes the
decline and collapse of the Spanish empire. Spain's inability to develop a management system equal to the size
and complexity of the empire is clearly visible in the
history of the colonial population reporting program and
can stand as a paradigm of the general failure of Spanish
bureaucracy and public management in the late-eighteenth
and early-nineteenth centuries.

NOTES

1. For an outstanding review of the recent literature on population and geography with special attention to social and spatial themes see David J. Robinson, "Introduction to Themes and Scales," in Robinson (ed.), Social Fabric and Spatial Structure in Colonial Latin America (Ann Arbor, 1979), pp. 1-24.

2. The collection of essays cited above provides a comprehensive sample of the growing sophistication of research on the social, demographic, and spatial dimensions of Latin American colonial populations. In contrast to other fields of Latin American history, the high quality of monographic work on these themes has led to relatively few overall analyses of the Spanish American or Brazilian social condition. This may be the result of the growing awareness of the complexity and variability of social and demographic conditions throughout the continent. Ironically, while there is considerable variation displayed in the details of microcosmic Latin American conditions, recent research as summarized in Robinson, Social Fabric, tends to support the view that the Latin American phenomenon, including Brazil, is as we expected all along cut from the same cloth according to a remarkably standard pattern.

3. Of course, the standard survey of Spanish American population is Nicolas Sánchez Albornoz, The Population of Latin America: A History (Berkeley, 1974).

4. For a survey of these data types see John V. Lombardi, People and Places in Colonial Venezuela (Bloomington, 1976); and Woodrow W. Borah, "The Historical Demography of Latin America: Sources, Techniques, Controversies, and Yields," in Paul Deprez (ed.), Population and Economics (Winnepeg, 1970).

5. Numerous sources reflect this preoccupation and many scholars have looked at the Indian question. See for an example of recent work on the item by Juan A. Villamarín and Judith E. Villamarin, "Chibcha Settlement under Spanish Rule, 1537-1810," in Robinson (ed.), Social Fabric. The classic controversy over the black legend and the treatment of the Indians exemplified by the works of Lewis Hanke provide a nonquantitative ideological focus on the same imperial complex. For a survey of the demographic interpretations on this subject see William Denevan (ed.), The Native Population of the Americas in 1492 (Madison, 1976).

6. The flowering of Latin American demographic studies in the last decade has produced an extraordinarily rich harvest of specialized studies emphasizing sophisticated techniques. The registry and household data, once relatively neglected, is now being carefully analyzed for insights on social, spatial, and demographic themes. While no comprehensive listing of this literature is possible here, a few examples will indicate the quality of the genre. See especially Stephanie B. Blank, "Patrons, Clients, and Kin in Seventeenth Century Caracas," Hispanic American Historical Review, Vol. 54 (1974), pp. 260-283; Kathy M. Waldron, A Social History of a Primate City: The Case of Caracas, 1750-1810 (Ph.D. dissertation, Indiana University, 1977); Michael M. Swann, "The Spatial Dimensions of a Social Process: Marriage and Mobility in Late Colonial Northern Mexico," in Robinson (ed.), Social Fabric. Also see Elizabeth Anne

Kuznesof, "Clans, the Militia and Territorial Government: The Artic-
ulation of Kinship with Polity in Eighteenth-Century São Paulo," and
Lyman L. Johnson and Susan Migden Socolow, "Population and Space in
Eighteenth-Century Buenos Aires," both from Robinson (ed.), Social
Fabric.

7. Because of its methodological difficulty, nominal record
linkage between such sources is relatively rare in Spanish-American
studies. But some scholars have had success with the technique, although not for precisely the purpose mentioned here. See, for example, the Blank, "Patrons and Clients," and Swann, "The Spatial
Dimensions," cited above for their discussion of sources and problems.

8. The Joint Syracuse-Oxford Population Project managed by
David J. Robinson is the most ambitious and interesting effort to
collect and process the late eighteenth-century houselists and associated documents. That effort has already produced a number of
significant studies, some of which are reflected in Robinson (ed.),
Social Fabric. See also Kathy Waldron, A Social History.

9. While the Spanish American houselists for various areas of
the empire display some obvious differences in compilation techniques, these do not appear to be sufficient evidence of any different conception of what the function of household and urban space
should be. Most of this discussion is based on a close examination
of the houselists for the Bishopric of Caracas (Archivo
Arquidiocesano de Caracas) and a comparison of these documents with
the results of the new work currently appearing on other areas of
Latin America as cited above.

10. The literature on race and class in Latin America is vast.
Some of it focuses on the intellectual perception of racial termi-
nology and the preoccupation with complex mixtures and picturesque
nomenclature, especially in the Mexican case. See the classic survey by Magnus Mörner, Race Mixture in the History of Latin America
(Boston, 1967). Also very helpful is Swann, "Spatial Dimensions."
Other more quantitative studies attempt to analyze the composition
and changes in the characteristics of aggregates bearing explicitly
racial labels. See Lombardi, People and Places. But all of these
works have to deal with the extreme difficulty of knowing what the
real life referents for racial designations might have been and
whether over any extended period of time these referents were stable.
The very complexity of the naming system by the eighteenth century
and the wide variations in usage throughout the empire make the
utility of many racial categories for comparative purposes less than
overwhelming. Slave, of course, being a legally recorded condition,
was a much more consistently defined category than, for example,
pardo or mestizo. For a discussion of the difficulties in using the
category slave for analytical purposes see Lombardi, "Comparative
Slave Systems in the Americas: A Critical Review," in Richard Graham
and Peter H. Smith (eds.), New Approaches to Latin American History
(Austin, 1974).

11. Much very sophisticated demographic work has been done on
marriage and the results have given us exceptionally useful insights
into Spanish American social and family structure. The technical
competence and historical value of these studies should not obscure

their inability to reach a significant portion of the male-female pairs whose lives were married in everything except the parish books. The best of these studies demonstrate an awareness of this difficulty as in Swann, "Spatial Dimensions."

12. Most students of colonial Spanish American populations have treated age-data with great circumspection. Not only do most scholars think detailed age reporting mostly unreliable, but few colonial documents provide really useful data except in isolated cases covering small geographic areas. Furthermore, the best age information, painstakingly derived from the vital events recorded in the parish registers, has only just begun to be evaluated. While it is quite possible to get reliable age profiles for segments of the upper half of the social strata from such sources, estimates for the lower half tend to be rather approximate at best. There is some consensus that the south model life tables are in some cases a fair representation of Spanish colonial reality, but most scholars who use them surround their calculations with such tentative qualifiers that the exercise is mostly proforma. See for example Lombardi, People and Places. Critical demographic indices for infant mortality and the like are almost impossible to come by except for very small selections of the elite.

13. Studies of Spain's imperial bureaucracy abound, and their analyses have shown the incredible complexity of this system as well as emphasizing the inability, in case after case, of the government bureaucracy to manage its information flow. The classic introduction to Spanish American government is Charles Gibson, Spain in America (New York, 1964).

2
Census Enumeration in Late Seventeenth-Century Alto Perú: The Numeración General of 1683–1684

Brian M. Evans

The count of all the Indian population of Alto Perú held in 1683/84 under the auspices of Viceroy La Palata offers the demographic historian a rich mine of information. Yet, with the exception of the works of Sánchez-Albornoz,[1] the materials have been little used or researched, and very many basic questions concerning this "Numeración General" remain unanswered. For example, although there is clear evidence that the census was held in all the provinces of the Viceroyalty of Peru, from Quito to the confines of Tucumán, and while supposedly five copies were made of the returns,[2] those so far discovered cover only part of Alto Perú and are today to be found in Buenos Aires.[3] These surviving returns are in a varied state of preservation, do not follow any fixed format, and are of uneven quality. The most detailed of them cover the provinces of Larecaja, La Paz, Sicasica, and Pacajes (for locations see Figure 2.1). Those for Paria and Carangas are difficult to use because of their extremely bad state of preservation. The returns for Cochabamba, Porco and Chayanta are well preserved but provide in general less detail, while those for Yamparaes, Omasuyu, Chichas, and Tarija are of only limited use for demographic purposes, because of the generalized and unsystematic way in which they were compiled.

The aims of this paper are to give a brief account of the reasons for holding the census, an outline of the ways in which it was organized and carried out, and of the controversies which followed. The paper also presents some preliminary generalizations on the demographic value of the returns, and finally discusses some possible lines of future research.

The original reason for the count was the continuous and drastic fall throughout the seventeenth century in the number of repartimiento Indians available for the mita in the silver mines at Potosí. As originally established by the Viceroy Don Francisco de Toledo in the 1570s, all tributary Indian males from sixteen provinces

25

26

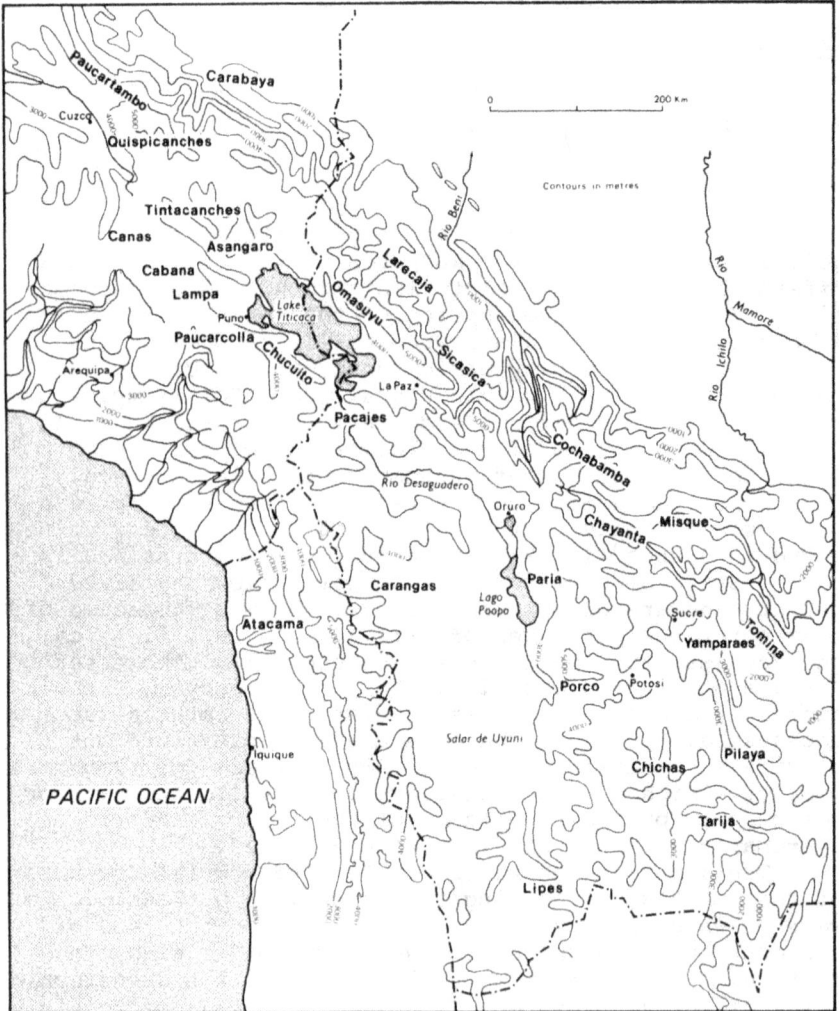

Figure 2.1 Location of Seventeenth-Century Provinces in
Upper Peru

or corregimientos were liable to the mita. The "affected provinces" were (1) Quispicanches, (2) Tintacanches, (3) Canas, (4) Cabana y Cabanilla, (5) Asangaro y Asillo, (6) Paucarcolla, (7) Chucuito, (8) Pacajes, (9) Omasuyu, (10) Sicasica, (11) Paria, (12) Carangas, (13) Cochabamba, (14) Chayanta, (15) Porco, and (16) Tarija. In theory in any year one seventh of all tributaries were to be drafted to Potosí, and once there, a third of the group were to present themselves each Monday for their week in the mines, after which they were allowed two weeks for recovery. Until the 1630s the weekly total available fluctuated at around 4,000.

The Indians, with ample justification, regarded the mita with fear and horror. Many died during their terms of labor, others remained in Potosí as mingas or voluntary labor, while still more abandoned their native villages and lands, (and frequently also their wives and children), and fled to those provinces not liable to the mita, there to try and establish themselves as newcomers or forasteros. As such they often ended up as squatters or peones on Spanish owned haciendas.

This process of course, merely served still further to increase the mita burden on the remaining population, who, despite all, had stayed tied to their villages and ayllus of origin. By the middle of the seventeenth century, there were constant complaints that this originario population, had so decreased that tributaries were being forced to mita, not every seventh year, but every fifth, or even third; thus of course causing a still steeper deterioration. By 1660 the weekly total of available laborers had fallen to below 2,000.[4]

Endless contradictory debates and commissions ensued over the next twenty years concerning the correct solutions to be sought; debates which are in themselves an excellent illustration of the paralysis of late Hapsburg colonial policy.[5] Fundamental was the absolute contradiction between the need to maximize silver output and the need to "protect" the Indians. While there was no agreement as to whether the total Indian population was decreasing, there was agreement that (a) many Indians had apparently fled to provinces free of mita, and (b) even within the sixteen provinces many Indians had won exemption through becoming personal servants to Spaniards (yanaconas), or by seeking work on Spanish owned or occupied lands, where they were protected from the draft (yanaconas de chacras). Therefore if any new general census were to be held--and none had been attempted since the Toledo's "Repartimiento General" a century earlier-- it would have to take these changed circumstances into consideration.

By 1680, Madrid had made up its mind, and decided to hold a general census not only of the sixteen affected provinces but of fourteen other provinces which had

hitherto been free of obligation. These comprised
(1) Cuzco (city), (2) Paucartambo, (3) Carabaya,
(4) Condesuyo de Arequipa, (5) Larecaja, (6) La Paz
(city), (7) Atacama, (8) Mizque, (9) Lipes, (10) Tomina,
(11) Oruro, (12) Pilaya y Paspaya, (13) Yamparaes de
Chuquisaca, (14) Potosí (city). The new viceroy desig-
nate, Don Melchor de Navarre y Rocafull, Duque de la
Palata, was charged with making this census one of the
main tasks of his administration.[6] The Duke was a force-
ful character.[7] Almost immediately upon his arrival in
Lima in November 1681, he set the wheels in motion, and
decided after consultations that the census should be
held not merely in the thirty provinces named, but
throughout the Viceroyalty "en todo el reyno desde Quito
hasta Tucumán."[8]

The line of reasoning behind this momentous decision
seems to have been that most of the problems concerning
Indian tribute throughout the Viceroyalty--and not merely
the issue of the Potosí mita--could be explained by the
fact that there had not been a full demographic survey
since Toledo, despite the common knowledge that in the
meantime there had occurred both depopulation and much
internal migration.[9]

Even at this stage arguments and controversy continued as to the necessity, feasibility and even possibility of holding a census of such magnitude. By and
large La Palata's advisors, experienced, as he was not,
in the complexities of Peruvian administration, were far
less sanguine as to the worth of this project than was
the Viceroy.[10]

However, arrangements for the "Numeración General"
proceeded steadily, and in general terms it was agreed
that the count should be organized along lines suggested
by an earlier commission which had reported in 1679, and
had been summarized by Dr. Francisco de Valera in a
Propuesta, copies of which had been dispatched to Spain,
where they had been discussed by La Palata and the Council of the Indies before the Viceroy had departed for
Lima.[11]

By early 1683 the preparations had been completed.
On April 7 the Viceroy sent a letter to all the Bishops
ordering the local priests (curas) to make a list of all
parishioners, men, women, children, originarios, and
forasteros, so that every parish would have an up-to-date
total to remit to the Corregidores. This was followed on
July 24th by a printed proclamation bearing the title
"Instrucción que han de guardar los Corregidores en la
Numeración General que se ha de hazer de los Indios, cada
uno en su jurisdicción."[12]

The content and form of these instructions merit
careful attention, since, had they been fully and consci-
entiously followed, the Numeración General would have essentially been a comprehensive census of modern type.

The fact that the instructions were frequently misunder-
stood or ignored however was to be at the root of the
criticisms which were to be heaped on the census and
which eventually led to the annulment in 1692 of its financial and tributary provisions by Viceroy Monclova, La
Palata's successor in office.

It must be admitted that the instructions are ver-
bose, repetitive, over detailed and ambiguous. However,
they clearly required that:

1. Everybody was to be enumerated on one chosen day
   (set as 1st October 1683).
2. All Indians, and not just tributary males, were
   to be listed with the following information:
   (a) name, (b) age, (c) civil status, and (d) place
   of origin, if different from the place of residence on the day of registration.
3. The local lists were to be those compiled by the
   priests and caciques with the assistance of parochial records of baptisms and funerals.

The prime purpose of the census was stated as the
need to count people where they actually resided in order
to force the forasteros to assume equal burdens with the
originarios. Yet the format recommended almost guaran-
teed some of the problems which it specifically desired
to avoid. Thus, over half of the instructions devote
themselves to complex and contradictory statements on
just how and where the various types of non-tributary Indians should be listed. The originario population was to
be registered by ayllu. But by the 1680s the ayllu system had severely decayed. Population losses had caused
many to become extinct; in other cases several small
ayllus had merged to form a new unit, whereas in other
cases the survivors of small ayllus had joined pre-
existing structures. Most important of all, the majority
of forasteros and yanaconas no longer remembered or recognized their original ayllu affiliations. The instructions made elaborate provisions for the enumeration of
such classes as (a) absentees whose return home was expected, (b) absentees whose whereabouts was known but who
were not expected to return, (c) forasteros who still
recognized their native pueblos and paid tribute there.
These classes were to be registered in their place of
origin. Clearly, however, this risked some double counting especially of classes (b) and (c) who might also be
counted in their place of actual residence.

The provisions for enumerating the forastero population who no longer paid tribute in their native pueblos,
were still more complex. If this group had places of
origin within the same province as their actual residence
they were to be counted as members of their native villages. This again led to double-counting, since they

were frequently also listed in their new locations. If
they had moved into other provinces, forasteros who did
not wish to return home were to be counted "in situ."
Most forasteros, of course, had fled their native villages years, or indeed generations previously, and some
no longer knew what their home provinces had been, let
alone had any desire to return to them. In addition the
forasteros were to be distinguished from such legal
classes as yanaconas and mitimaes who were to be counted
separately. Originally these two latter groups had been
reasonably easy to define, but by the 1680s many forasteros had sought yanacona status in order to avoid tribute. Hence many individuals were registered twice, first
as forasteros and separately as yanaconas. If this were
not sufficiently confusing, the instructions proposed a
distinction between "yanaconas del Rey," and "yanaconas
de estancias, de chacras, y de obrajes." Just how the
corregidores should make these distinctions was not made
clear. If possible all yanaconas too, were to be investigated as to place of origin, the length of time they
had been living in their present location, and their
claims to be regarded as yanaconas.

Now to have expected the machinery and personnel
available to have provided such a mass of detail over so
vast an area was a forlorn hope.

The Instructions themselves were subsumed under no
less than thirty headings, and called for the returns for
each province to be arranged in eight books (cuadernos).
In theory they were to be arranged as follows, and contain the following information.

Book 1. Originarios actually present in their pueblos on the day of registration. Men, women, and children were to be arranged by ayllu and family. This book
was also to include those temporarily absent for specific
reasons and whose prompt return was expected.

Book 2. Originarios absent on day of registration
and whose imminent return was not expected, but whose
whereabouts was known. They were to be arranged with
their families by ayllu. If possible the date and reasons for their departure were to be provided.

Book 3. Originarios who were absent, and whose
whereabouts were not known. These too were to be listed
by family and ayllu. In some cases, however, the tributaries in this class had fled without their families,
while in other cases the whole family had disappeared.

Book 4. Forasteros who "recognized" their pueblos of
origin. This book, as has been suggested seems to have
given the enumerators their biggest problems. Quite
apart from the problems of whether forasteros still recognized or even knew their places of origin, it is obvious that the local authorities had grave problems with
this class in obtaining ages and details of family.

Book 5. Yanaconas del Rey. In general the

corregidores seem to have regarded this class as an amalgam of various classes of Indians who had become detached from pueblo and ayllu, and who were indeed in many cases little more than vagabonds. It was the intention to reduce them to a permanent location and status by attaching them to ayllus in those pueblos where they were resident in 1683. This frequently proved impossible.

Book 6. This was to include mitimaes, who after being enumerated were to be added to the appropriate "padron" and ayllus in their provinces of origin. In theory, this count was to be checked against Book #2. In fact, it proved impossible since most of the mitimae settlements dated back to Inca times and memories by the 1680s were blurred.

Book 7. Yanaconas de estancias, de chacras, y de obrajes. An examination of the actual census returns suggests that to most corregidores this group consisted essentially of forasteros who no longer knew their places of origin and who were therefore quite "irreducible," but who had--unlike the yanaconas del Rey--a specific function. They worked directly for Spaniards or Criollos, on the rapidly developing privately owned haciendas, which, as the seventeenth century advanced had taken over, by one means or another, much Indian land.[13] The yanaconas in general were the source of much anxiety as by one means or another, they had frequently escaped paying tribute altogether--in which they were often aided and abetted by the landowners for whom they worked. The census returns indicate that in Alto Perú, the corregidores frequently had trouble distinguishing yanaconas from forasteros, and that again it was difficult to obtain accurate information on family ties and structure.

Book 8. The last book was to be reserved for the "Yanaconas de iglesias, conventos y comunidades." At first sight this might have appeared as being a straightforward group, but the instructions go on to warn that all these yanaconas claim to be "del Rey." However, they were to be separated from those listed in Book 5, as an accurate check was required of the real needs of the churches and communities. Clearly there was a suspicion that many of the yanaconas de iglesias were surplus to the actual requirement.

So much for the actual instructions. As to the way in which they were actually carried out we have two sources of information. The first is clearly the surviving returns themselves; the other is the correspondence which ensued between the corregidores, and the other officials involved, in Lima, and Spain, as to the progress and accuracy of the undertaking. Let us now examine this second line of evidence.

Presumably the Instructions cf 24 July 1683 did not reach many of the corregidores until September. If then they had questions or doubts about the exact procedures

they were instructed to follow, they would not have time
to correspond with Lima before the census date which had,
as we have seen, been set for 1 October 1683. We do not
in fact know how general a count was made on that date,
for there is a peculiar gap in all documents and correspondence relating to the progress of the "Numeración General" until 1685. When the record commences, there is
already a marked dichotomy: on the one hand defending the
progress of the census; whilst on the other hand is a
mounting chorus of doubt, disillusion and dissent. From
all of this one point very clearly emerges; the operation, so to speak, had not "gone to plan" and many--
indeed perhaps most--corregidores had either failed to
follow the "instrucciones" altogether, or had interpreted
them in widely different ways.

First, let us examine the record from the Viceroy's
standpoint. On 10 June 1685 the latter wrote to Spain[14]
announcing that the enumeration was now completed in all
provinces except for some areas especially around Quito.
He added that he had placed extra officials on the work
of examining and ordering the lists (padrones), because
otherwise the work would take years to complete for all
83 provinces.

The year following, on 6 April 1686, La Palata wrote
to the King informing him of the progress of the enumeration and its problems. He claimed that few of the difficulties people had forecasted had actually arisen. He
estimated that the total cost would be in excess of five
thousand pesos, and as a sample, enclosed a list (padrón),
of part of the province of Vilcashuaman which had cost
160 pesos.[15] This particular return is of some interest.
It had been completed on 23 October 1684, and seems to be
the only actual census return which has survived in
Seville. It is quite different in form to the volumes in
Buenos Aires, and is limited to male tributaries only.
Then on 11 October 1687 the Viceroy wrote[16] that the work
had run into no insuperable difficulties, and that the
cost would not be excessive, although he admitted the
work was uneven, yet it was better than one might have
expected:

> esta se ha hecho a muy poco costa, y aunque no se a hecho
> con entera fidelidad, porque no han sido de igual satisfac-
> ción ni inteligencia las manos por donde ha pasado que son
> los corregidores, todavía a quedado en mayor estado de lo
> que nunca se pudo esperar.

Lastly, in the file of letters between Viceroy and
Spain on the enumeration is one dated 18 February 1689
praising the work of Don Joseph de Villegas, and Don
Antonio del Castillo "contadores de retasas," for the
census, and asking royal favors for them.[17]

To the very end La Palata defended both his record

and the enumeration. In his "Relación" of 16 August 1689,
although admitting that the census finally took six years
to complete, rather than the one year initially antici-
pated (sections #845, 846 & 847), he went on to justify
his actions, and his decisions about the work at some
length.[18]

Long before he left office, however, it was apparent
that the enumeration was giving rise to the most serious
problems; problems indeed which were eventually to cause
Palata's successor--Viceroy Monclova--to abandon the new
taxes and tribute totals which had been based on the 1683
count.

The first major rumbling of discontent emerged in
June 1685. On the 12th of that month, Joseph de Villegas
drew up a lengthy report (Papel de dudas) of doubts and
difficulties which he saw with the enumeration and its
progress.[19] As the official concerned was in command at
Lima and specifically charged with the collation of the
work, none could have been in a better position to make
an accurate evaluation.

His report contained eight general points, most of
which were individually serious. In order they are:

1. Especially in Upper Peru (las provincias de
arriba), there had been innumerable, complex and confusing changes in the names and boundaries of pueblos,
and in settlement patterns generally.

2. Despite all attempts at standardization of format,
the corregidores had not observed the procedures set
forth in the "Instrucciones" of 24 July 1683. Each had
gone his own way; the results were very difficult to compare and collate. Few had consulted the parochial books
of baptisms and burials.

3. Especially dubious were the statistics in regard
to sex and ages. Many corregidores had just given summary statements on the number of women and children, and
this was not sufficient to judge whether the population
was increasing or decreasing, and for what reasons.

4. Other major problem areas concerned the lists of
those absent, and the lower and upper age groups on the
lists of tributaries. This was because the lists had not
been updated between visitations, and the caciques had
been anxious to maximize the number of tributaries. The
Indians he states frequently lie about their ages. He
quotes examples where fathers aged 20 have sons aged
eight or ten.

5. The changes in population numbers and distribution over the last century meant that the relationships
between the number of Indians and the size of the doc-
trina were now much out of line.

6. Regulation #18 of the "Instrucciones" which required that all forasteros should be asked for their home
provinces and ayllus had been generally ignored. Usually
only the native provinces had been given and this was

insufficient. It had proved impossible to check the list
of forasteros in one place with the lists of absentees in
their original homes.

7. In need of special attention was the task of
checking the absentee lists of each province with those
of the Indians residing permanently in Potosí.

8. There was no agreement between provincial, repartimiento, and ecclesiastical boundaries. Some lists used
one system, some another. In addition there was a specific difficulty involving boundary problems between Paria,
Cochabamba and Chayanta.

The document also details three major problems directly related to the Royal Orders which followed from the
holding of the census:

1. It had proved impossible to get Indians to return
to or live in their original homes.

2. Many forasteros had been forced to pay tribute
twice, and there was enormous confusion over the new
tribute totals in general.

3. The decision not to include Indians living in
mining settlements within the classes liable for mita had
given rise to much dispute.

All in all these criticisms by themselves are so
serious that it is difficult to see how the Duque de la
Palata could have remained so sanguine about his enterprise.

Worse, however, was to follow. Between 1685 and
1692 there were sufficient difficulties, allegations,
charges and counter-charges arising from the enumeration,
and more especially its tribute and financial reassessments, that the correspondence today fills three large
bundles at Seville.[20]

To deal with these controversies in detail is not
the prime purpose of this paper, but before evaluation of
the actual returns, some discussion is in order. The
major complaints may be summarized as:

1. There had been gross overcounting in the enumeration, especially of the forestero class who frequently
had been counted twice or even thrice—usually in their
place of origin and where they actually resided.

2. Because of the over-registration the new tribute
totals were unrealistically high.

3. Most forasteros and yanaconas were grievously
poor and could not meet their tribute payments.

4. Because of the two previous problems (2 and 3),
Indians had fled from their homes in unprecedented numbers, thus adding to the difficulty of finding the increased tribute sums demanded. Thus the Numeración
General had resulted in an exacerbation of the very problems it had been intended to solve.

The complainants were certainly able to amass a good
deal of evidence to support their charges, and they included letters from most corregidores, many local clergy

and caciques, through to the Archbishops of Lima, Cuzco, La Paz and Chuquisaca, and into the Real Audiencia itself. Interestingly, nearly all the complaints come from, or deal with, conditions in Alto Perú, both from the sixteen provinces originally affected by the mita, and by the fourteen to which La Palata had extended the obligation. By the end of 1689 official protests had been received from Larecaja, Pacajes, Misque, Pilaya, Tomina, Yamparaes, Porco, Paria, Carangas, Chayanta, Cochabamba, Lampa, Asángaro, Chucuito, Omasuyu, Sicasica, Paucarcolla, Canas y Tintacanches, Quispicanche, and from Potosí itself.

Even La Palata was forced to admit the justice of some of the complaints for, on 29 April 1689, in one of his last acts as Viceroy he issued a consulta reducing the tribute on forasteros by 50%, except for Cochabamba, Porco, Tarija, Tomina, Pilaya, and Sicasica, where, as forasteros were especially numerous, the reduction was to be only 25%. However, he defended the charge that the Numeración had grossly overstated numbers by claiming that "possible" overcounting in one province was matched by undercounting in others.[21]

His successor, Viceroy Monclova, had no vested interest in his predecessor's work, and no great faith in the desireability or necessity of the mita, his previous experiences in Mexico having predisposed him to the system of voluntary mine labor which had there proved successful. On 16 December 1690 he established a junta of seven experts to collate the complaints and investigate their seriousness.[22] This first junta held 32 meetings, and its successor set up on 19 May 1691 held a further 51, during which time they do indeed seem to have conducted quite detailed investigations, primarily however in regard to the new tribute totals, and only secondarily upon the demographic accuracy of the returns, although the junta did accept the charges of frequent double counting as having validity.

Their final decisions called for a return to the system which had preceded La Palata's reassessment. Monclova accepted their judgement and issued two proclamations which officially brought most of La Palata's innovations to an end.[23]

So the Numeración General was officially annulled, apparently discredited, and was quickly forgotten. It had cost the Real Hacienda over 15,000 pesos,[24] which at first sight appears a modest sum for so large an undertaking, but the main time, trouble and effort had of course been borne by the curas, caciques and corregidores at the local level and without special renumeration.[25]

It is my belief however that a study of the surviving returns of Alto Perú would seem to indicate that the sweeping condemnations of the Numeración General, had frequently been motivated by special pleadings, and that at least some of the provincial corregidores had made very conscientious efforts to gather as full and accurate information as possible.

The remainder of this study is therefore devoted to an examination of, and commentary upon, the surviving returns.

THE SIZE OF THE TOTAL INDIAN POPULATION OF
ALTO PERU IN 1683

For the provinces of Omasuyu, Larecaja, Sicasica, Pacajes, Cochabamba, Yamparaes, Paria, Carangas, Porco, Chayanta, Tarija, and the cities of La Paz, Potosí, and Oruru, the Numeración General recorded a total of 55,946 tributaries.[26] Tributaries were defined as all liable Indian males from 18 to 50 years old. The "tributary index" (or tributaries as a percent of the total population), cannot be calculated for all provinces and pueblos, but for those where it can, it averages 23.7%. Thus one may assume that the total recorded Indian population of the above listed provinces and towns was about 236,000 or say between 220,000 and 250,000.

This clearly represented a considerable decline since the Repartimiento General of Toledo especially in the Altiplano provinces. Nor did the new census "find" the allegedly high numbers in those provinces which had been reported as having over 20,000 tributaries, and Yamparaes over 4,000.[27] However, the real totals were revealed as 7,133 and 1,415 respectively.

Indeed time after time in the legajos of complaints, there are admissions that, whatever its shortcomings, the enumeration had clearly revealed that the supposedly large numbers of Indians who had managed to avoid tribute and mita obligations, simply did not exist. Potosí had been alleged to have been harboring at least 25,000 potential tributaries, the census recorded but 5,557; Cuzco's supposed 30,000 tributaries, were in reality only 3,320.[28]

If indeed the Numeración had tended to inflate the real numbers then depopulation had been very marked not only on the Altiplano, but equally in provinces hitherto unaffected by mita obligations. Thus, the widespread belief that the depopulation of the Altiplano had been caused by flight to the Yungas, and that growth had therefore occurred in the receiving provinces, was not supported by the evidence. Direct comparison is difficult but since Toledan times the population overall had decreased at least 30%. It would seem, however, as though the bulk of the decline had occurred prior to the 1630s, since Chinchon's repartimiento in 1633 generally listed numbers of tributaries very comparable to those found by La Palata.[29]

THE DISTRIBUTION OF THE INDIAN POPULATION IN 1683

The provinces for which returns have survived fall into two basic groups in terms of natural environment (Table 2.1).

TABLE 2.1
Distribution of Altiplano and Yungas population, 1683

Provinces of the Altiplano:	Number of Tributaries	Percent Originario	Provinces of the Yungas:	Number of Tributaries	Percent Originario
Omasuyu	4,903	26.41	Larecaja	7,113	11.00
Pacajes	3,615	68.24	Sicasica	4,494	24.18
Paria	2,748	80.20	Cochabamba	6,466	6.18
Carangas	2,579	90.61	Yamparaes	1,415	24.94
Porco	5,775	54.85	Chayanta	7,732	63.89
			Tarija	1,325	54.11

(plus cities of: La Paz, 353; Potosí, 5,557; Oruru, 1,851)

Total Number of Tributaries: 27,381 — 48.94%

Total Number of Tributaries: 28,565 — 51.06%

In the 1680s, therefore, over half of the recorded Indian population was to be found in the Yungas, a situation not very different from that recorded in the time of Toledo. However, the status of the population in the two regions was in contrast. With the exception of Omasuyu, the majority of the Altiplano population was "originario," whereas in most of the Yungas, originarios formed a minority, especially in Larecaja and Cochabamba. The first named province, it will be recalled, was not liable to mita, and neither in fact were most of the pueblos of Cochabamba, which had been freed of obligation in order to encourage agricultural production.[30] Clearly then, migration had been of major importance, even though the influx into the receiving provinces had in general not caused an actual population increase. By implication therefore, originario population losses must have been greater in the Yungas than on the Altiplano.

ORIGINS AND DESTINATIONS OF MIGRANTS

Studies were made of the following:

1. The provinces of origin of the 3,306 forasteros resident in Larecaja.
2. The provinces of origin of the 2,950 forasteros resident in Chayanta.
3. The origins of the 1,288 forasteros resident in the town of Oruro.
4. The origins of the 886 forasteros resident in Pacajes.
5. The place of residence of 575 people absent from their homes in Pacajes but whose whereabouts were known.

Of the Larecaja sample, the largest groups had originated in Omasuyu (23.2%), Chucuito (14.6%), Lampa (14.6%), Paucarcolla (12.7%) and Asángaro (11.2%) (see Figure 2.2). Between them these accounted for 76.3% of the total. Another 6.2% claimed origins in La Paz and 3.6% in Cuzco. However, individuals had also come from as far away as Lima and Quito. The bulk though were clearly from the neighboring provinces of the Altiplano.

Chayanta reveals a similar pattern although here there was less concentration and more evidence of longer distance migration. The most frequent provinces of origin were Pacajes (14.3%), Paria (14%), Carangas (12.6%), and Canas (12.5%). Other provinces which accounted for more than 5% were Lampa (8.5%), Chucuito (6.9%), and Omasuyu (6.7%).

In Oruro the majority had come from the neighboring provinces, notably from Paria (20.4%), Pacajes (17.4%), Carangas (15.6%), and Chucuito (12.1%), whilst immigrants from the Yungas were conspicuous by their infrequence.

The Pacajes samples are especially revealing, as the population of this province seems to have been unusually mobile. As we have seen, emigrants from Pacajes were very numerous in Chayanta and Oruro. They also formed one of the largest of the forastero groups in Cochabamba. Yet Pacajes paradoxically was also an area of in-migration, whose percentage of originarios (68.24%), was lower than that of most comparable Altiplano regions. Of the 886 forasteros recorded, the single largest group (22.8%), were natives of Chucuito, the second (17.6%), people who had moved within the province but who had severed ties with their native villages, and the third (15.5%), had moved from Omasuyu. Other sizable cohorts had origins in Sicasica (8.7%), La Paz (7.5%), and Larecaja (4.4%).

Of the out-migrants the major destinations were Sicasica (20.1%), Cochabamba (14.4%), Potosí (12.5%), and La Paz (6.8%). Groups of individuals had, however, moved to places as far away as Tucumán, Cuzco, and Lima.

Clearly migration was a major feature throughout Alto Perú in the late seventeenth century. All told over one third of the population recorded in the Numeración

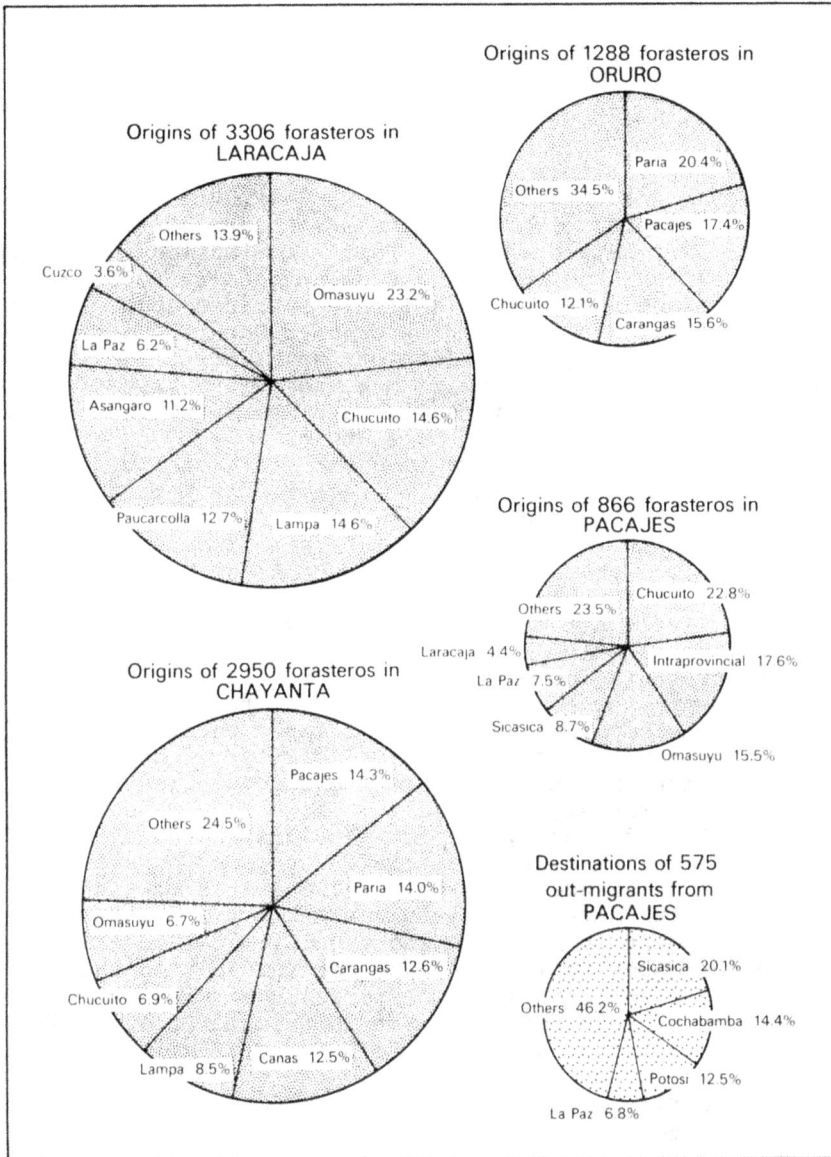

Figure 2.2 Origins and destinations of selected inter-provincial
migrants, Upper Peru, 1683

were no longer living in their provinces of origin.

THE SALIENT DEMOGRAPHIC FEATURES OF THE POPULATION

The statistical accuracy of early censuses and methods of correction are topics of considerable complexity and debate, a discussion of which is beyond the scope of this paper.[31]
The population pyramid for some 23,000 individuals recorded in the 1683 count is shown in Figure 2.3. It is in fact a composite based on the age-counts of fifteen pueblos from the provinces of Pacajes, Sicasica, Larecaja, and Chayanta, whose returns are exceptionally full and well organized, and which in total comprised about 10% of the recorded Indian population of Alto Perú. The sample is thus large enough to smooth out any extreme local variations, and enable one to make some generalizations on the accuracy of age recording and degree of under-registration of the census as a whole.
First--and this is even clearer at the individual level of the pueblos, and in the actual raw returns--the ages are usually approximate at best. Clearly, the "Instrucciones" to the contrary notwithstanding, ages were not in general checked against the books of baptism. There is marked "bunching" at the five and ten year digits, and little attempt or trouble taken over the correct ages of the elderly. The greatest oddity however is the under-representation of both males and females from age ten to twenty. One would have expected this group (especially the boys) to have been of major interest and concern to the Spanish, as the males after eighteen years entered tributary status, and hence under-registration appears at first sight unlikely. There is always the possibility, of course, that the Indians and their caciques might have been especially anxious to have concealed the existence of as many teenagers as possible, but in all the detailed criticisms heaped upon the census, this point is never raised. De Villegas indeed suggested the opposite in his "Papel de Dudas." Another possible explanation is that especially virulent epidemics may have decimated the infant population around 1670, but again the written sources fail to provide confirmation.
For children under ten there is some evidence as a whole of a tendency to under-register females, although in this respect the individual pueblos vary.
Taking the sample as a whole, 40.43% of the population (or 9,419 out of a total of 23,297), were under fifteen. Allowing for the possible under-registration of the children, this indicates that the fertility of the population was extremely high. Yet so was mortality, especially infant mortality. Family size, when it can be

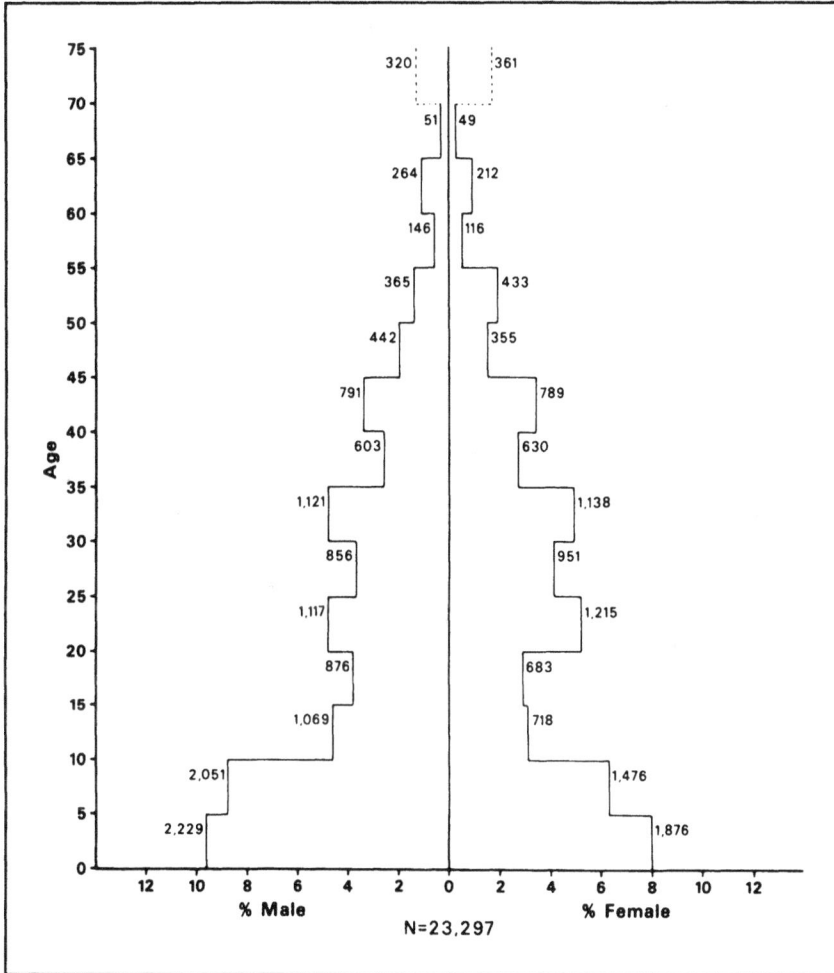

Figure 2.3 Sample age-sex distribution from the 1683 census

reconstructed, was usually small. While the occasional large family with six or more children did exist, it was far more common to have only two or three children living--the irregular spacing of whose ages strongly suggests that many of their siblings had died in infancy. Yet there is also evidence that, despite all hardships and recurrent epidemics, the population had stabilized. The childless families and broken structures, which Cook describes as typical for the period 1570-1620[32] were not frequently encountered. Marriage after age 20 was well nigh universal, and there is clear evidence for the rapid remarriage of the widowed, at least until they reached old age.

Just over 5% of the sample survived to age 60. Evidence from seventeenth century parish registers from Alto Perú which record age at death[33] again tell the same story: nearly half of those born did not survive infancy and childhood, and had died before their tenth year. However the registers record about 15% of deaths at over age 60.

The life expectancy judged from both the "Numeración" and the parish registers was about 25 years or less. With a figure as low as this there could have been little natural increases in population, despite the high fertility.

The adult population shows a fairly normal sex ratio. In the age group 15-50, our sample provides a total of 5,806 males and 5,761 females or 99.2 females per 100 males. This finding is at variance with the usual sixteenth century figures which indicate a far higher survival rate among the Indian female population of both Peru and Mexico, and it too indicates that by the 1680s a new demographic balance had been reached.

CONCLUSION

The holding of the Numeración General was not only as La Palata claimed the greatest single act of his vice-regal tenure, but it has claims to be regarded as the major--indeed virtually the only--attempt to hold a general demographic survey in the seventeenth century Spanish colonial empire. One can indeed but hope that investigators will begin to discover some of the missing returns in the local archives of Bolivia, Peru and Ecuador.

The returns from Alto Perú indicate that in many provinces the returns are sufficiently well-compiled to merit serious and detailed demographic research. Quite apart from some of the topics discussed in this paper, the materials can be used to illustrate various aspects of the social and economic history of Alto Perú, such as the growth and composition of the labor force on the rapidly expanding Spanish owned haciendas, and the

considerable changes that this had involved in the settlement patterns.

The census was a vast and ambitious project. Full
elucidation of its resources will also prove a major
task. It is to be hoped that these remarks may encourage
other scholars to study this particular census, and indeed the generally neglected demography of the late
Hapsburg Empire.

NOTES

1. Nicolas Sánchez-Albornoz, "El indio en el Alto Perú a fines
del siglo XVII," Seminario de historia rural andina, Lima 1973. See
also his Indios y tributos en el Alto Perú, Lima 1978. I.E.P., and
the review of this work by Nathan Wachtel in Annales, Economies,
Sociétiés, Civilisations, Vol. 33, 1978, pp. 1206-1209.

2. "Relación del estado del Peru en los ocho años de su gobierno que haze el Duque de la Palata," Biblioteca Nacional, Madrid
[hereafter cited as BNM] Ms. #3004.

3. Buenos Aires, Archivo de la Nación, Sala XII, Legajos 17.2.3,
17.2.4, 17.3.1, 17.3.2, 17.3.3, 18.1.1, 18.1.2, 18.1.3, 18.4.2,
18.4.3, 18.4.4, 18.6.5, 18.7.4 & 19.7.3.

4. Archivo General de Indias, Sevilla [hereafter cited as AGI]
Charcas 270, ff. 3-67 for a full discussion.

5. AGI, Charcas 268.

6. BNM, Ms. #3004.

7. For a general account, see Margaret E. Graha, "The Administration of Don Melchor de Navarra y Rocafull," The Americas, Vol.
27, 1971, pp. 389-412.

8. AGI, Charcas 272, ff. 194-226. BNM, Ms. #3004, Section 825.

9. "Relación del estado del Peru," BNM, Ms. #3004, Sections
822-830.

10. AGI, Charcas 268.

11. AGI, Charcas 268. "Propuesta del Dr. D. Francisco Valera
al Don Melchor de Liñan," 28 ff., dated 30 January 1680.

12. Several copies of this document are extant in the archives
at Madrid, Seville, Buenos Aires and elsewhere; e.g. AGI, Charcas
270.

13. See for example AGI, Indiferente General 1660, for a detailed survey of this problem in Alto Perú.

14. AGI, Charcas 270, "Expedientes y cartas sobre la Mita de
Potosí 1682-1690."

15. AGI, Charcas 270.

16. Ibid.

17. Ibid.

18. "Relación del estado del Peru," BNM, Ms. #3004.

19. AGI, Charcas 270.

20. AGI, Charcas: much of legajo 270, all of 271 and 272, and
some of 273.

21. AGI, Charcas 271.

44

22. Ibid.

23. AGI, Charcas 273.

24. AGI, Contaduría 1759 B, "Gastos extra-ordinarios de Hacienda."

25. This point is made specifically in points #833-837 of La Palata's "Relación," BNM, Ms. #3004, and in various items of Viceregal Correspondence.

26. AGI, Charcas 271.

27. AGI, Charcas 272, ff. 127-129.

28. AGI, Charcas 272 especially.

29. Figures for Chinchón's repartimiento are supplied in AGI, Charcas 270.

30. AGI, Charcas 271.

31. See for example the discussion and bibliography in S. F. Cook and W. Borah's Essays in Population History, Vol. 1, Los Angeles, University of California Press, 1971, especially pp. 201-299, which deals with the problem of Mexican eighteenth-century censuses.

32. N. David Cook, The Indian Population of Peru, 1570-1620 (Unpublished Ph.D. dissertation, University of Texas, 1973).

33. I have studied those for Puna and Aymaya (both in Chayanta), and Tomahave (in Porco). They are to be found with the Numeración General material in the Archivo de la Nación in Buenos Aires.

3
Colonial Censuses and Tributary Lists of the Sabana de Bogotá Chibcha: Sources and Issues

Juan Villamarin
Judith Villamarin

INTRODUCTION

Although a good deal of demographic work has been done on Indian populations of New Granada, little has been published regarding the Chibcha in the Sabana de Bogotá, one of the colony's most important regions in terms of socio-cultural complexity, population development and colonial organization. The present work will deal with the major sources for study of the area, discussing the available documents on Sabana Chibcha population as a whole, and on tributaries, adult males assessed tribute and labor quotas.[1]

Our approach to the material is primarily socio-cultural; however, we hope that the information presented will be of use to demographers and others interested in population studies. Here as in our other work on the Chibcha, the unit of study is the region and not the province. This insures that we are dealing throughout with a relatively homogeneous ecological background, a matter of importance since the province of Santa Fe in 1592-1595 encompassed a substantial range of altitudes with corresponding differences in climate, soils and other natural resources. The Sabana de Bogotá and Valley of Ubaté, whose communities made up fifty-nine percent of those in the province at that time, are highland basins with elevations of 2,550 m. to 2,650 m., and are surrounded by mountains that ascend to 3,000 m. (Figure 3.1). Almost all other communities in the Province were situated at elevations of 1,000 m. to 2,000 m. in warmer lands (tierra templada) with very different resource

We wish to thank the University of Delaware, whose Faculty-Grants-in-Aid to Juan A. Villamarin provided support for travel and collection of data for this paper. We also thank Professor Peter M. Weil, University of Delaware, for his comments and suggestions on the paper.

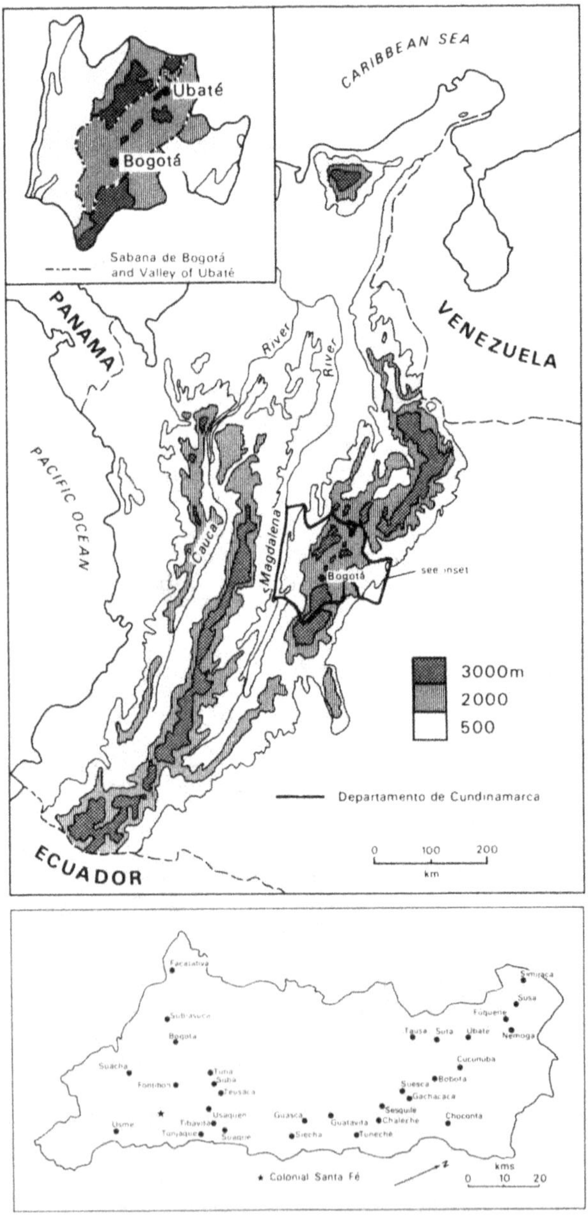

46

Figure 3.1   The Sabana de Bogotá, sample communities

potential.[2]

The Chibcha were a sedentary agricultural people
with local, ranked political hierarchies, and incipient
state formation at the regional level when the Spanish
conquerors arrived in 1537. The Spaniards immediately
drew on the Indians for labor, goods and services after
conquest, but did not make a complete and reliable count
of them in the Sabana region until over half a century
later, by which time there had been great population
loss.[3] The first full, well-documented census of the
Sabana natives was carried out in the years 1592-1595,
when the crown was beginning to consolidate its authority
over Chibcha and Spaniards alike.[4] Altogether, throughout the colonial period there were three major censuses
including the one of the 1590s. The second was taken between 1636 and 1640, and the third in 1758-1759, but reported in 1761.[5] The seventeenth century census, which
was probably terminated for lack of funds before its com-
pletion, does not have population figures for all the
communities in the region.[6]

Between the second and third major censuses, the
most abundant archival information on population is in
tributary accounts. In the Archivo General de Indias
there are lists of tributary Indians in the Sabana which,
with some gaps, cover the period from the middle of the
seventeenth century to the middle of the eighteenth century. Supplementary data for the years between 1740 and
the early 1800s are found in unclassified documents in
the Colombian National Archives in Bogotá.[7]

In the following sections we will discuss the documents available on population, their uses and limitations.
The meaning of the term, tributary, and its relation to
male and total population will be explored; and finally
the tributary accounts will be discussed with regard to
the other data and their contribution to our understanding of population trends.

CENSUS MATERIAL

The Sixteenth Century

One of the earliest documents containing data on
population is a partial estimate that appears to refer to
tributary Indians in some Sabana communities in 1556.*
It includes Indian pueblos within a six league radius of
Santa Fe, and was part of the information submitted by
clergy to the crown as the basis for their petition for
aid in building monasteries.[8] Jiménez de Quesada,

---

*The classification and changing responsibilities of tributaries are
discussed in the next section, "Tributaries."

reporting in the 1560s on the <u>conquistadores</u> who came with him and who had <u>encomiendas</u>, also gave estimates of Indian tributaries.[9] Although there are scattered reports on tributaries and censuses for a few communities,[10] during this period a systematic and general census of all the communities was not made in the region, despite the crown's repeated orders that such information be sent to Spain. The region's powerful <u>encomenderos</u> resisted having the Indians under their control counted, most likely to prevent curtailment of their extraction of goods and services from the natives. Officials cautiously avoided open confrontation with the encomenderos since the crown had not yet established a strong presence in the colony.[11] Although there were two <u>visitas</u> during this period, one in 1560 and another in 1563, neither included a census even though the <u>visitador</u> told the Indians in 1563 that he was coming, among other things, to count them.[12]

Indirect sources of information, such as tribute assessments, which have been useful elsewhere for reconstructing population, cannot be used here with ease, for although there is a fairly complete list of them for 1564 (recopied in 1575) they lack the consistency necessary to make the link between them and tribute-paying men.[13] This is not so of the assessments for Tunja, where it has been possible to derive tributary numbers.[14] Through the early seventeenth century the <u>tasa</u> was levied on communities as wholes; to date documents indicating what it was assumed individuals should have to contribute have not been found. A tribute system based on individual responsibility for payment, with specified taxes per tributary, was instituted in the Sabana in 1625.[15]

From 1592 to 1595 Visitador Oidor Miguel de Ibarra supervised the only complete census of the sixteenth century. He reported it in detail to the crown in 1595, stating that he was accounting for:

> . . . los indios que cada pueblo y encomendero tiene, poniendo el número de caciques, capitanes e indios útiles para pagar demora y los reservados de ella y no se ponen los huidos ni los que se han llevado a la población de las minas de la plata por solo poner los presentes, y asimismo de todas las indias y muchachos poniendo los indios de por si y las indias y chusma de por si . . . .[16]

Ibarra recorded the number of males, females and children (<u>chusma</u>), but did not give the number of tributaries per se. Instead they were included along with Indian officers and <u>reservados</u>, men who did not pay tribute because they were too old. As a result the exact number of tributary Indians is known only for a very few communities. The census does have each community's total population,

which can be used for general comparison with figures
available for later in the colonial period. In our opin-
ion any calculation of sixteenth century Sabana population must be based on this census, and not on earlier
figures which were, essentially, estimates that sometimes
were based on secondary and impressionistic information.[17]

The Seventeenth and Eighteenth Centuries

There were two visitas carried out in the early seventeenth century, from which population figures on a few
communities are available. One was done in 1600, and has
very little on population as such aside from the infre-
quent mention of numbers of indios útiles (tributaries).[18]
The other was carried out in 1603-1604, and has a breakdown of population, distinguishing tributaries from other
categories of natives, but covering a very limited number
of communities.[19]

In 1593, as the crown asserted greater control over
the colony, the office of corregidor was established in
the Sabana. Incumbents were ordered to keep updated
lists of tributary Indians, each year adding on those who
had reached seventeen years, the age of tribute payment,
and subtracting those who had passed fifty-four or had
died.[20] Each community was responsible for paying the
tribute, which was calculated on the basis of ninety percent of its tributaries. The ten percent allowance for
the community was most likely initiated with the Visita
of 1603-1604, and was given in order to take into account
absentee Indians and emigrees.[21] In reality ten percent
appears to have been a maximum figure; the number of
tributaries in each community's deduction was arbitrary,
as one can see in Table 3.1, which is based on figures
from the few communities for which numbers of both the
total tributary population and the assessed population
are available in the early seventeenth century.

The real audiencia revoked the ten percent discount
on 6 March 1625, ordered that the corregidores make censuses of the tributary Indians (indios útiles) and that
tribute be collected from each one.[22] The head tax system, based on the idea of payment by individuals rather
than by communities as wholes, remained in effect for the
rest of the colonial period. From 1625 on males categor-
ized and listed as tributaries were only those who actually paid (or were supposed to pay) tribute. As we
will discuss below there were other able-bodied men who
stayed in the communities but were exempt from payment.

There were two more visitas during the seventeenth
century, the one of 1636-1640 and a very limited one in
1670. On the basis of the first, population was reported
in a document which, in spite of physical deterioration,
gives a fairly comprehensive account of the numbers of

TABLE 3.1
Tribute Deductions in the Early Seventeenth Century

| | Tributaries Resident in Community | Number of Assessed Tributaries | Deduction | |
			Number of Tributaries	Percentage of Total
Chocontá	571	514	57	9.98
Fúquene-Nemoga	276	270	6	2.17
Guasca	300	300	0	0
Nemocón-Tasgata	133	122	11	8.27
Sesquilé-Gachacaca	200	190	10	5.00

Sources: AHNC, Miscelanea: Vol. 8: fol. 555r (Chocontá); Visitas de Cundinamarca: Vol. 6: fol. 812r (Fúquene-Nemoga); Vol. 7: fol. 751r (Guasca); Vol. 12: fols. 762r-762v (Nemocón-Tasgata); Vol. 10: fol. 365r (Sesquilé-Gachacaca).

tributaries in the Sabana and New Granada.[23] Total population figures are available for about half the Sabana communities in visita documents and in later references to it based on parts no longer in existence.[24] In the visita of 1670 the Indian population was reported in several different categories (útiles, reservados, officials, etc.); however, the number of communities covered was very small.[25]

The next large scale, comprehensive census was carried out in 1758-1759 by Oidor Joaquin Aróstegui y Escoto. In his general report of 1761 Aróstegui y Escoto gives an account of tributaries and total population. In the individual visitas (of which only a small number are extant) a more detailed breakdown (útiles, officers, ausentes, etc.) is provided.[26] This is the last complete set of figures for the colonial period. There is some population information in a partial visita of 1778-1779, and reports on some communities' tributaries and/or total populations in the early nineteenth century, containing data that can be compared with earlier figures and which are utilized in the graphs in this paper.[27]

Finally, there is the series of accounts of tributary Indians in the Archivo General de Indias, extending from 1660 to the 1740s. The series is unique for the area in being the single longest-run set of figures for a given segment of the population. With some qualifications the accounts provide information on trends of the Indian population during that time. The data for these lists was supposed to be compiled by corregidores on the basis of head counts carried out with the aid of local priests.[28] Some records suggest that the lists may not always have been done this way. Corregidores may have made one or two lists (descripciones) during their tenure by actual counts, and then used them as bases for their subsequent reports, taking into account changes in the number of Indians paying tribute each time.[29] The series is fairly complete. From the seventeenth century on, tribute was paid in two installments, one in June (tercio de San Juan) and the other in December (tercio de Navidad). Both sets of figures are found in the documents. For the graphs in this essay we have used the tercio de San Juan accounts because they appear to be more complete. We will return to a discussion of the graphs after exploring the effects on census taking of Indian post-conquest social organization, the use of the term, tributary, and the relationship of tributary counts to other population figures in the Sabana.

TRIBUTARIES

"Tributary" (tributario, indio útil, indio de demora) was a Spanish administrative concept employed for the

collection of money and goods from the Indians and allocation of their labor. The Chibcha had a broadly based
system of labor and goods allocation with respect to native political hierarchies, which the Spaniards drew on
but modified according to their own concepts and needs.[30]
  From 1539 to the end of the sixteenth century, a
period of encomendero dominance, Spaniards considered
tributaries to be adult males, and their estimates of
them in official documents included only men. During
this time, however, women also may have served in providing encomenderos with gold, goods and services.[31] Tributary classification was formalized toward the end of the
sixteenth century and beginning of the seventeenth by a
much strengthened colonial government. From then until
1740 in the Sabana, it included married and unmarried
adult males between the ages of seventeen and fifty-four,
who had to pay tribute in money and goods, and who were
also liable to serve in labor quotas (forced labor--
repartimiento).[32] Tribute and labor assessments were
determined and managed by crown officials. The establishment of repartimiento made the Indians accessible to
other Spaniards in addition to the encomenderos. Change
from a community-assessed tribute to a head-tax type in
1625 did not change the form of tributary classification
established in the early 1600s, nor did it alleviate the
Indians' work load.[33] Between 1740 and 1810 tributaries
continued to be classified as described above, and to pay
tribute, but labor quotas were abolished.[34]
  How the tributary category is to be viewed within
the context of total Chibcha population is influenced by
data on native organization on the one hand and Spanish
classification on the other. We shall discuss first Indian factors--kinship, territoriality and emigration--
that may have affected the accuracy of tributary and general census counts, and second the Spanish systems of
categorization of adult males.[35]

Chibcha Kinship and Territoriality

  Implicit in the Spanish use of the term, tributary,
was that such men were heads (or potentially heads) of
individual nuclear families who traced descent patrilin-
eally and were patrilocal in mode of residence.[36] In
fact the Indians had matrilineal descent with patrilocal
residence during the father's lifetime, and eventual
preferential residence in the mother's brother's territory (avunculocal residence). Along these lines natives
moved from one community to another, especially in the
sixteenth century. Crown officials were aware of the
situation and utilized the concept of matrilineal descent
in solving problems of conflicting claims for Indians by
encomenderos and caciques.[37] Baptismal documents

sometimes recorded the mother's community or section of
it.[38] None of this, however, was reflected in the censuses, despite the continued importance of matrilineal
ties among the Chibcha in the sixteenth and seventeenth
centuries. The counts specify individuals present at the
time, but not their final community affiliation. Sixteenth century parish records are scarce, but those that
remain might provide some indication of the extent of
movement based on matrilineal bonds in selected areas.

Although the Spanish model implied the idea of mo-
nogamous nuclear families, it appears that polygyny,
which had been mainly the pre-conquest nobles' preroga-
tive, was also practiced by individuals of lesser rank
after the conquest. In the visita of 1563 the visitador
ordered that in the Sabana:

> . . . que agora e de aqui adelante cada uno de ellos no
> tengan mas de una mujer propia y no se casen con las
> hermanas de las mujeres que hubieren tenido y se les
> hayan muerto.[39]

Other documents suggest the existence of polygyny after
the conquest, but its extent is difficult to assess.[40]
The Indians seem to have been aware of Spanish prejudice
against the practice and may have attempted to conceal
some of the women and children from census takers. Generally the size and composition of Indian households is
not known and does not appear to have been of great importance to Spanish officials. This may have had an effect on the accuracy of censuses, and makes it difficult
for modern investigators to formulate ratios of total
population to tributaries.

By the early seventeenth century Spanish clergy were
established permanently in rural communities to oversee
native life and enforce church rules. Polygyny may have
declined partly as a result of active intervention by
them and crown officials, and partly of other effects of
conquest such as diminished economic capability of adult
males to take more than one wife, population upsets
caused by disease, emigration and forced labor, as well
as other factors that disrupted traditional organization.

Toward the end of the sixteenth century permanent
records based on baptism, death and marriage began to be
kept by priests. Individuals could turn to these in order to make claims of community membership, and converse-
ly, communities could use such records on which to base
their cases for the return of natives who had left.
Priests, who soon became important members of rural society, also influenced Indian inheritance patterns by
writing wills for them with a patrilineal bias. Patri-
lineality and patrilocality became more widely practiced
by the Chibcha in the late colonial period, but did not
completely replace matrilineal inheritance of land,

making it possible for an individual to claim membership
in one community on the basis of land he might have in-
herited via the Spanish patrilineal model, or in that
which he had rights to by the Chibcha matrilineal system.[41] The overlapping of Spanish and native systems
probably enhanced opportunities for mobility, contributing to the movement of Indians in and out of Sabana
pueblos.

Emigration

    Men, women and children moved from their communities
to others in the region as well as to Santa Fe de Bogotá
and areas outside the Sabana during the entire colonial
period. Although emigration from Sabana pueblos did not
occur on as large a scale as in the early years of colonial rule, it was a constant process, and was important
over the long term. From the middle of the sixteenth
century individuals who took up residence in communities
other than their own became clients or dependents of
other Indians, especially of members of the local political hierarchies.[42] Probably in return they obtained
access to land and other resources. Male Indian immigrants, forasteros, were not reported in census counts
until 1670, and they were not required by the Spanish
authorities to pay tribute on a regular basis until the
late seventeenth century.[43] They may, however, have been
paying some form of tribute all along to Indian authorities in return for the privilege of living in their communities. This practice provided the grounds for con-
flicts among community heads, caciques, who made claims
and counterclaims for disputed subjects. A cacique could
make a demand for individuals who had left his community,
basing his argument on custom, yet resist returning immigrants who were requested by their native caciques in
order to keep enough manpower to meet Spanish demands for
goods and services.[44]
    Probably some of those who left their native commu-
nities were lost to Spanish counts entirely, while others
showed up in the lists of absentees (ausentes) that the
Spaniards made in conjunction with the censuses. Loss of
population through emigration is clear. However, the
gains that at least some communities must have had as a
result of the Indians' movement are much more clouded,
for newcomers were probably not reported if it could be
helped, to avoid taxation. The movement of individuals
points to the fact that there were differences in economic and political conditions in different communities,
drawing (or driving) Indians from one pueblo to another,
a matter we will discuss further in the last section of
this paper. In some cases the Indians left the area entirely, moving to other regions or towns.

Spanish Classification, and Tributaries in Relation to Total Male Population

The tributary category did not cover all adult males. In addition there were reported for each community ausentes (absentee tributaries), Indian officials exempted from tribute payment, and reservados (men exempted because of illness, old age or special jobs). Most of the material that follows is from the seventeenth and eighteenth century documents; there is very little on these categories in the 1592-1595 census.

Ausentes. The absentee adult males discussed in the preceding section were considered by the Spaniards to be potential tributaries. A specific ratio of absentees cannot be established, since the numbers vary so much among communities and even within particular communities over a span of time (Table 3.2). For example in the 1636-1640 census of Chocontá ausentes were 6.8 percent of the total number of potential tributaries for the pueblo; in 1778-1779, 14.1 percent and in 1804/1806, 10.8 percent. In Fúquene-Nemoga in the census of 1636-1640 they made up 8.1 percent; in 1778-1779, 37.7 percent. The percentages in Sesquilé-Gachacaca went from 1.5 in 1636-1640, to 39.0 in 1778-1779, to 11.6 in 1804/1806. The highest proportion of ausentes is found in the visita of 1778-1779, and can probably be correlated with the land problems that the Indians were facing at the time, along with the difficulties caused by massive immigration of non-Indians into their reservations.[45]

Ausentes were not included in the census tallies of 1592-1595. Visitador Oidor Ibarra gave some information on them, but his figures are very difficult to use, since he did not report them by communities, but gave the total number of absentees per encomendero, many of whom had more than one community as a single encomienda during the period.[46] In the censuses of 1636-1640 and 1758-1759 ausentes were included in total population counts. In the individual visitas, however, they were listed separately from tributaries, and their numbers are known for those communities whose documents have survived.[47] The number of extant visitas for 1758-1759, with more than two thirds of the particular accounts lost, is smaller than for 1636-1640. Fortunately total population of each of the pueblos was recorded in the general report.

Ausentes are usually not mentioned in the Archivo General tributary series. In the nineteenth century documents in Bogotá, some reports give an account of them as well as of the tributaries.

Indian Officials and Others Exempted from Tributary Status. A number of able-bodied adult males were exempted from paying tribute. Through most of the seventeenth

TABLE 3.2
Ausentes

	A Number of Resident Tributaries	B Ausentes	 A + B	Ausentes-- Percentage of A + B
	From Visita of 1636-1640			
Bogotá	292	15	307	4.9
Chocontá	345	25	370	6.8
Fontibón	193	8	201	4.0
Fúquene-Nemoga	160	14	174	8.1
Guasca	216	6	222	2.7
Sesquilé-Gachacaca	128	2	130	1.5
	From Visita of 1778-1779			
Chocontá	220	36	256	14.1
Fúquene-Nemoga	104	63	167	37.7
Guasca	102	10	112	8.9
Sesquilé-Gachacaca	89	57	146	39.0
	From Tribute Lists of 1804/1806			
Bogotá	117	12	129	9.3
Chocontá	166	20	186	10.8
Fontibón	46	6	52	11.5
Guasca	67	6	73	8.2
Sesquilé-Gachacaca	76	10	86	11.6

Sources: For 1636-1640--AHNC, Visitas de Cundinamarca: Vol. 8: fol. 205v (Bogotá); Miscelanea: Vol. 8: fol. 597r (Chocontá); Visitas de Cundinamarca: Vol. 12: fol. 938v (Fontibón); Vol. 6: fol. 833r (Fúquene-Nemoga); Vol. 7: fol. 779r (Guasca); Vol. 10: fol. 380r (Sesquilé). For 1778-1779--AHNC, Visitas de Cundinamarca: Vol. 7: fol. 442r (Chocontá); Vol. 10: fol. 924v (Fúquene); Vol. 7: fol. 485r (Guasca); Vol. 7: fol. 461v (Sesquilé). For 1804/1806--AHNC, Tributos: NC #32 (Bogotá, Fontibón 1806; Chocontá, Guasca, Sesquilé 1804/1805).

century these were the native political officials--the
traditional chief of the community, cacique (sijipcua),
and heads of subdivisions, capitanes (sivintiva). The
census of 1592-1595 indicates that they did not pay tribute, but there is very little information on their numbers. In the census of 1636-1640 they made up 2.3 percent to 4.6 percent of able resident men (Table 3.3).
The number of men exempted greatly increased in the eighteenth and nineteenth centuries as people holding specific church and government related jobs came to be excused
from the tribute lists. The proportions of these together with Indian officers rose to between 8.9 and 14.4
percent in 1778-1779, and up to 30.3 percent in 1804/1806
in the communities in our sample. During that time span
they probably outnumbered exemptions for age and illness
(Table 3.4). A great diversity of job-holders had come
to be included --fiscales, alcaldes, sacristanes, church
singers and deputies of the corregidor.

In 1636-1640 capitanes and caciques were reported
separately from tributaries in the visita, while the
sacristan and fiscal were included in the category of
reservados. In the eighteenth century all officers and
church/government job-holders were included in the new
category, reservados por oficio. During the later part
of the colonial period it appears that such jobs were
sought by the Indians purposefully in attempts to gain
exempt status.

Reservados. In most communities there were a number
of adult males who did not pay tribute because they had
passed their fifty-fourth birthday or were sick (Table
3.4). Priests kept Indians' baptismal records, that
could be checked for the purpose of exemption due to age.
One could be classified as reservado for a temporary illness or permanent disability. Individuals had to submit
proofs, and in the latter case were erased permanently
from the lists of contributors. Information regarding
the nature or degree of disability was seldom given.[48]
As has been pointed out, sacristanes and fiscales were
included in the reservados category in the seventeenth
century.

Individuals on this list, whether because of illness
or as a way to escape payment, appear to have been few in
number in the eighteenth and nineteenth centuries, off-
setting the tributary rolls least of any of the non-
paying categories at that time. The proportion of men
considered reservados because of age, in contrast to illness, is difficult to determine, since the two classes
were usually not reported separately. There is some information on this for 1804/1806. In Bogotá, Fontibón and
Guasca, all the men on the reservado list were over
fifty-four years old. In Chocontá fourteen out of sixteen (87.5 percent) were reservados because of age. In

TABLE 3.3
Officials and others exempted from payment of tribute

	A Number of Resident Tributaries	B Number of Officials and Others Exempted[1]	A + B	Officials and Others Exempted-- Percentage of A + B
	From Visita of 1636-1640			
Bogotá	292	14	306	4.6
Chocontá	345	8	353	2.3
Fontibón	193	9	202	4.5
Fúquene-Nemoga	160	4	164	2.4
Guasca	216	9	225	4.0
Sesquilé-Gachacaca	128	4	132	3.0
	From Visita of 1778-1779			
Chocontá	220	26	246	10.6
Fúquene-Nemoga	104	14	118	11.9
Guasca	102	10	112	8.9
Sesquilé-Gachacaca	89	15	104	14.4
	From Tribute Lists of 1804/1806			
Bogotá	117	19	136	14.0
Chocontá	166	25	191	13.1
Fontibón	46	20	66	30.3
Guasca	67	9	76	11.8
Sesquilé-Gachacaca	76	12	88	13.6

Sources: For 1636-1640--AHNC, Visitas de Cundinamarca: Vol. 8: fol. 205v (Bogotá); Miscelanea: Vol. 8: fol. 597r (Chocontá); Visitas de Cundinamarca: Vol. 12: fol. 938v (Fontibón); Vol. 6: fol. 833r (Fúquene-Nemoga); Vol. 7: fol. 779r (Guasca); Vol. 10: fol. 380r (Sesquilé). For 1778-1779--AHNC, Visitas de Cundinamarca: Vol. 7: fol. 442r (Chocontá); Vol. 10: fol. 924v (Fúquene); Vol. 7: fol. 485r (Guasca); Vol. 7: fol. 461v (Sesquilé). For 1804/1806--AHNC, Tributos: NC #32 (Bogotá, Fontibón 1806; Chocontá, Guasca, Sesquilé 1804/1805).

[1]In the Visita of 1636-1640 only caciques and capitanes were included in this category. In the eighteenth and nineteenth centuries, members of the traditional political hierarchy and church/government job-holders were included.

TABLE 3.4
Reservados

	A Number of Resident Tributaries	B Number of Reservados	A + B	Reservados-- Percentage of A + B
From Visita of 1636-1640				
Bogotá	292	16	308	5.2
Chocontá	345	26	371	7.0
Fontibón	193	40	233	17.2
Fúquene-Nemoga	160	17	177	9.6
Guasca	216	19	235	8.1
Sesquilé-Gachacaca	128	2	130	1.5
From Tribute Lists of 1804/1806				
Bogotá	117	4	121	3.3
Chocontá	166	16	182	8.8
Fontibón	46	0	46	0
Guasca	67	1	68	1.5
Sesquilé-Gachacaca	76	16	92	17.4

Sources: For Visita of 1636-1640--AHNC, Visitas de Cundinamarca:
Vol. 8: fol. 205v (Bogotá); Miscelanea: Vol. 8: fol. 597r (Chocontá);
Visitas de Cundinamarca: Vol. 12: fol. 938v (Fontibón); Vol. 6: fol.
833r (Fúquene-Nemoga); Vol. 7: fol. 779r (Guasca). For 1804/1806--
AHNC, Tributos: NC #32 (Bogotá, Fontibón 1806; Chocontá, Guasca,
Sesquilé-Gachacaca 1804/1805).

Sesquilé, however, seven out of sixteen on the list (43.7 percent) were reported to be ill at the time.

Requinteros. As discussed earlier, there were other adult male Indians, classified as forasteros. They were infrequently reported, and not included in the lists of tributaries. These were men who had married into a community other than their own or had immigrated, sometimes alone and sometimes with their families. By late seventeenth century they had to pay a tribute to the crown. The assessment was uniform for them but, in most cases, lower than the amounts paid by natives of the communities in which they lived. The tribute-paying forasteros were called requinteros, and were reported as a separate category. Most likely, for local administrative reasons discussed above, there were many more forasteros than those few reported as requinteros (Table 3.5).

Indian Manipulation of Spanish Classification

Eligible adult males were faced, until the 1740s, with meeting forced labor demands, and throughout the entire colonial period with tribute payments. It appears that some were successful in managing their situation so as to escape classification as tributaries. Exemption due to illness, as would be indicated on the reservado lists, appears to have been difficult to obtain, but may have served as an outlet, however limited, in the seventeenth century. By the nineteenth century it seems to have become the least opted way for exemption. Instead classification as holder of a designated non-tributary job was more common. In the eighteenth and nineteenth centuries the number of men holding such positions in the Indian communities greatly increased, indicating that much greater opportunity was allowed with respect to this work for legitimately avoiding tribute payment while remaining in the pueblo. A certain way of escaping tribute and labor demands was emigration, which was partially reflected in the ausentes figures, and was carried out by Indians during all periods of the colonial era. Some remained in the Sabana as forasteros, and later requinteros, while others were lost completely to the local native population.

Spanish Classification of Tributaries in Relation to Total Indian Population

Given the Spanish classification of tributaries and the Indians' manipulation of the system, one expects that the ratio of total population to tributaries would increase through time. This was indeed the case in the

TABLE 3.5
Requinteros: From Tribute Lists of 1804/1806

	A Number of Resident Tributaries	B Number of Requinteros	A + B	Requinteros-- Percentage of A + B
Bogotá	117	8	125	6.4
Chocontá	166	2	168	1.2
Fontibón	46	3	49	6.1
Guasca	67	2	69	2.9
Sesquilé-Gachacaca	76	6	82	7.3

Source: AHNC, NC: Tributos No. 32 (Bogotá, Fontibón 1806; Chocontá, Guasca, Sesquilé 1804/1805).

seventeenth and eighteenth centuries (Table 3.6). The increments are partly a function of decrease in individuals classified as tributaries, and not of increase in family size, fertility or improvement of the resource base.[49] Unfortunately we do not have the exact numbers of tributaries for the end of the sixteenth century, but must use the total number of adult males as given in the census of 1592-1595. Using these figures we find that at the end of the sixteenth century the ratio of total population to adult males was between 2.2 and 3.8. The data suggest that during this period tributary classification of adult males was offset least by the exemptions discussed above, an interpretation supported by specific information on tributaries in three communities from our sample in the 1590s. In Chocontá the ratio of total population to adult males was 3.4, in Guasca 3.7 and in Suesca 3.0. The ratio of total population to tributaries was 3.6 in Chocontá, 4.5 in Guasca and 3.1 in Suesca.[50]

Ratios of total population to tributaries in 1636-1640 ranged between 3.6 and 5.8. By the census of 1758-1759 the ratios had risen to between 4.4 and 11.3, probably reaching their highest levels at this point. It should be noted that in 1758-1759 absentee tributaries were counted in among the population totals, and that therefore the ratios we have obtained are somewhat high. For example in Guasca, one of the few communities with specific data, the ratio corrected for ausentes would be 7.0 instead of 8.0.

In the early nineteenth century the ratios for seven communities were between 4.3 and 8.9. Four of the six pueblos show increase while two dropped below the 1758-1759 values.

Accounts of tributary Indians have been important for analyzing and calculating total populations and their long term trends in New Granada. In some cases only counts of tributaries have been available and have served as bases on which to reconstruct population curves for whole Indian communities.[51] Calculation of the Sabana communities' population between 1660 and the early 1800s on the basis of the tributary series may be possible, but would pose many difficulties. One would have to interpolate the likely rates of population change relative to men classified as tributaries, while keeping track of changing rates in exemptions as well. Other shortcomings in the data, already discussed, would also have to be taken into account.[52] More precision can be gained by using parish records, which so far have not been utilized extensively in the area. This would be a worthwhile, if painstaking task for an investigator with an interest in demographic studies, and would help us to use what census and tributary material we have with greater accuracy. In the meantime the series, which we will discuss in the following section, can tell us a great deal about the

TABLE 3.6
Ratios of total population to tributaries

Communities	1592-1595* Total Population	Adult Males	Ratio	1636-1640 Total Population	Tributaries	Ratio	1758-1759** Total Population	Tributaries	Ratio	1805 Total Population	Tributaries	Ratio
Bogotá	2,263	673	3.4	1,262	292	4.3	646	110	5.9			
Bosa-Suacha	2,928	1,005	2.9		466	5.0	831	117	7.1			
Chocontá	2,570	765	3.4	1,715	345		1,345	234	5.8	1,176	166	7.1
Cucunubá-Bobota	737	217	3.4		160		563	81	7.0			
Facatativá	872	233	3.7									
Facatativá-Chueca	1,139	307	3.7	1,084	202	5.6	659	91	7.2	570	95	6.0
Fontibón	1,831	507	3.6		193							
Fontibón-Techo	1,927	540	3.6	1,152	218	5.3	827	136	6.1	328	46	7.1
Fúquene-Nemoga	816	282	2.9	920	160	5.8	742	91	8.2			
Guasca-Siecha	1,489	402	3.7	1,037	216	4.8	622	78	8.0	375	67	5.6
Guatavita-Chaleche-Tuneche	1,400***	404	3.5				1,264	221	5.7	1,352	210	6.4
Serrezuela (Subiasuca)	294	82	3.6		65		327	29	11.3	127	30	4.3
Sesquilé-Gachacaca	682	229	3.0	466	128	3.6	708	131	5.4	675	76	8.9
Simijaca	758	235	3.2		176		427	43	9.9			
Suba-Tuna	1,332	428	3.1		172		298	46	6.5			
Suesca	905	306	3.0		241		942	129	7.3			
Susa	756	342	2.2		246		801	83	9.7			
Suta-Tausa	750	199	3.8		122							
Ubaté	2,769	938	3.0		440		1,890	324	5.8			
Usaquén-Tibavita-Teusaca-Tunjaque-Suaque	1,787	505	3.5		166		180	41	4.4			
Usme	800	237	3.4				255	42	6.1			

Sources: For 1592-1595--Ruiz Rivera, Fuentes Para la Demografía Histórica, pp. 23-33. For 1636-1640--AHNC, Visitas de Cundinamarca: Vol. 8: fol. 205v; Miscelanea: Vol. 8: fol. 597r; Visitas de Cundinamarca: Vol. 12: fol. 938v; Vol. 6: fol. 833r; Vol. 7: fol. 779r; Vol. 10: fol. 380r; Gobierno: Vol. 1: fols. 34r-45v. For 1758-1759--AHNC, Visitas de Cundinamarca: Vol. 8: fol. 794v-829r. Rojas, Corregidores y Justicias, p. 523. For 1805--AHNC, Tributos: NC #32.

*Only figures for total adult male population are available in the 1592-1595 documents. See Text.
**Ausentes are included in total population figures in the 1758-1759 column.
***Tuneche is not included in the 1592-1595 figures.

tributary population itself, and also, with qualifications, about the general course that the rest of the Indian population followed. Consideration of the series in
light of other kinds of data can give us insights into
factors affecting both tributaries and the native population as a whole.

TRIBUTARY ACCOUNTS: 1660-1800s AND POPULATION TRENDS

     This discussion is based on the Archivo General de
Indias tributary series that extends from 1660 to the
1740s, on data in eighteenth century censuses and on unclassified documents in the Archivo Histórico Nacional in
Bogotá, which cover the early nineteenth century. The
communities represented in our sample cover most sections
of the Sabana, and at the end of the sixteenth century
made up forty-four percent of the region's seventy-seven
native communities. We selected them for discussion because of the completeness of their data through the entire period dealt with here. All indications are that
data for other communities existed but were lost, or, for
the nineteenth century are as yet unavailable to the public.
     Our treatment of the thirty-four communities in
twenty graphs reflects the Spaniards' reporting and their
resettlement of many native communities together in nucleated zones in the early seventeenth century. Although
in many cases the Indians maintained their traditional
identities and did not remain in the nucleated areas, the
Spaniards consistently treated them in terms of the units
given here for administrative purposes.
     Thirty-six of the seventy-seven Indian communities
mentioned above survived through the late eighteenth century; among these were nineteen of our sample. Nine of
the surviving communities (six of those in our sample)
were then made parishes (parroquias), and although re-
taining their Indian names, became very strongly identified with non-Indian populations. The rest of the communities (including fifteen of those in our sample) disappeared completely or were incorporated as parts of the
remaining ones.[53]

Tributary Counts and Total Population--The Overall View

     Tributary population declined in the seventeenth
century and early eighteenth century far more than would
be indicative of the attrition discussed in the previous
section, suggesting processes that had a bearing on the
population as a whole. The drop was especially marked in
the years between the 1680s and the early 1700s after a
short upswing in many communities, such as Bogotá, Bosa,

Chocontá, Fontibón, Fúquene-Nemoga, Guatavita and annexes, Guasca-Siecha, Simijaca, Suacha, Suesca, Susa and Ubaté, from 1660 to the 1680s (Figures 3.2 to 3.12). A mid-eighteenth century increase can be noted in several communities (Bogotá, Chocontá, Cucunubá-Bobota, Facatativá, Fontibón, Guatavita and annexes, Simijaca, Suba-Tuna, Suesca and Ubaté). At the end of the 1700s and beginning of the 1800s the tributaries dropped to levels far below those reached in the early seventeenth century (for example: Chocontá, Cucunubá-Bobota, Fúquene-Nemoga, Guasca-Siecha, Sesquilé-Gachacaca, Suesca, Suta-Tausa, Susa, Ubaté and Usaquén). Over the long run population also declined, showing no indications of sustained recovery such as occurred in Mexico. We do not have the data that would tell us whether it followed the more specific trends of the tributary population; however, there is some information to suggest that there was a slight growth within at least some communities for a short period in the mid-eighteenth century after which, as with tributaries, decrease again ensued.[54]

The similarities among the graphs of several of the communities in our sample suggest the operation of region-wide processes. With the exception of Guatavita and its annexes (Figure 3.6) all show an absolute decrease in numbers by the early nineteenth century. We have calculated percentage drops for those years in which the data on all the communities are complete (Table 3.7 and Figure 3.13), and found that between 1673 and 1803 the number of tributaries decreased by 51.4 percent. The decline was broken by the two periods of growth mentioned above. During the first, 1660-1680s, there was an increase in tributary numbers in about half of our sample communities, followed by a drop which was especially steep through the 1690s and early part of the 1700s. Again, basing computation only on figures for which there are years with complete data (Table 3.7), we find that after a period of fourteen years of rather slow decline (1673-1687, with a drop of 6.83 percent) a period of rapid decline followed, particularly in the eight years between 1687 and 1695, when the number of tributaries decreased by about a third (33.63 percent). In several communities in the mid-eighteenth century another less sharply defined period of growth took place. Though figures for the eighteenth century are not complete enough to allow one to compute annual percentage losses and gains, it is evident that between 1706 and 1761 there was a growth in total numbers of 13.6 percent, followed from 1761 to 1803 by a drop once again, of some 18.5 percent. We shall return to a discussion of these trends, looking into possible interpretations of the losses and gains after an overview of important differences among the graphs.

66

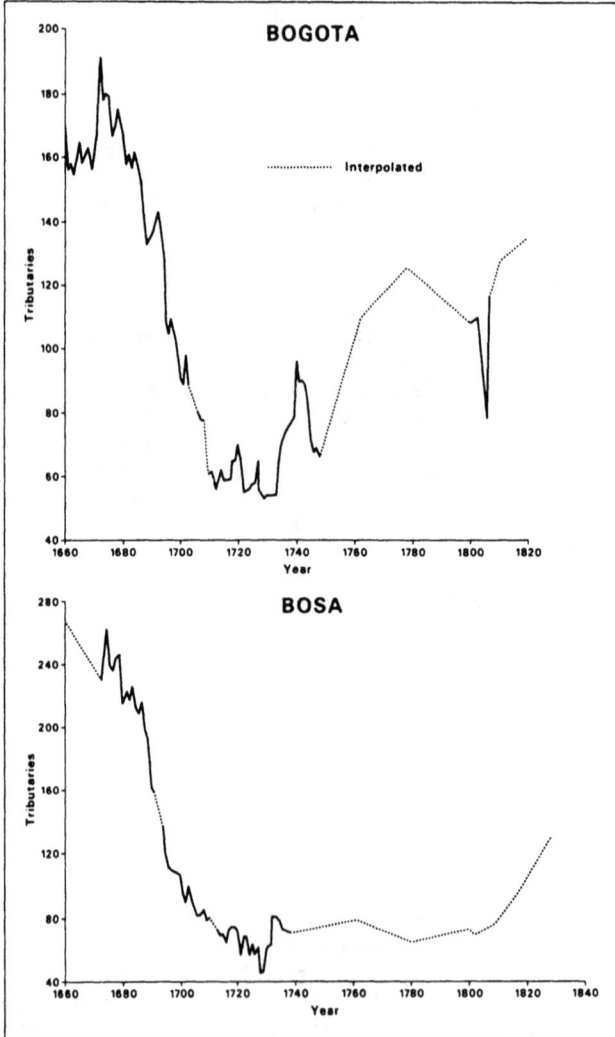

Figure 3.2   Tributary change in Bogotá and Bosa, 1660-1830

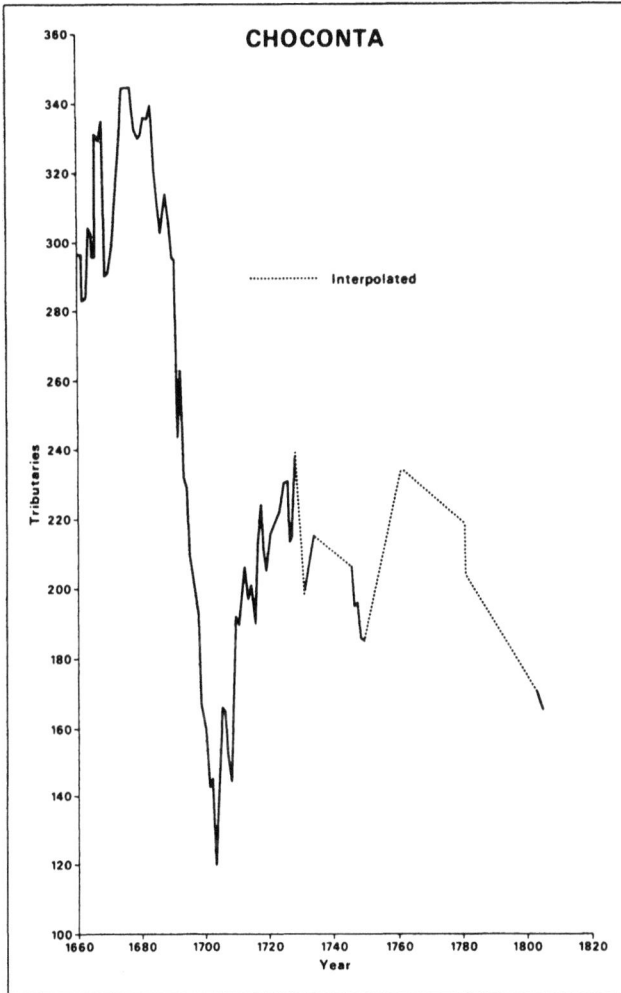

Figure 3.3   Tributary change in Chocontá, 1660-1810

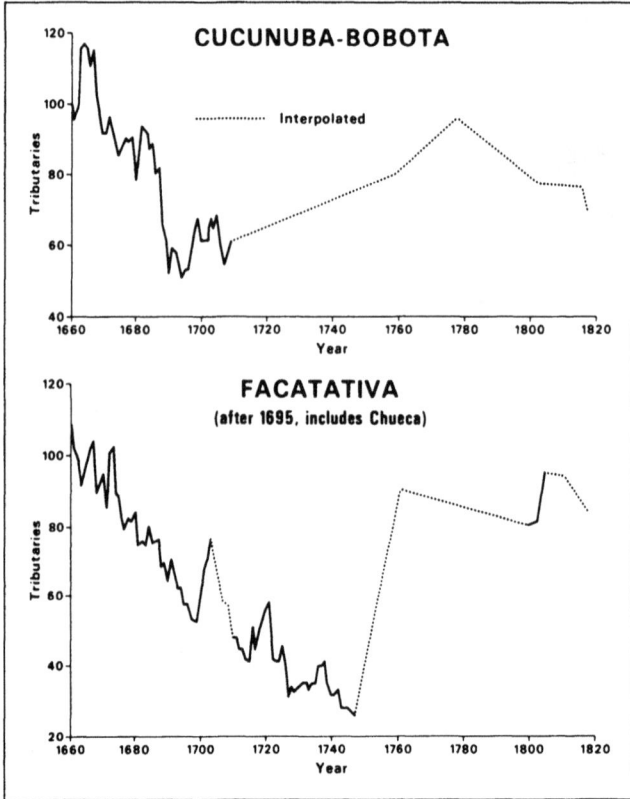

Figure 3.4   Tributary change in Cucunubá-Bobota and
Facatativá, 1660-1820

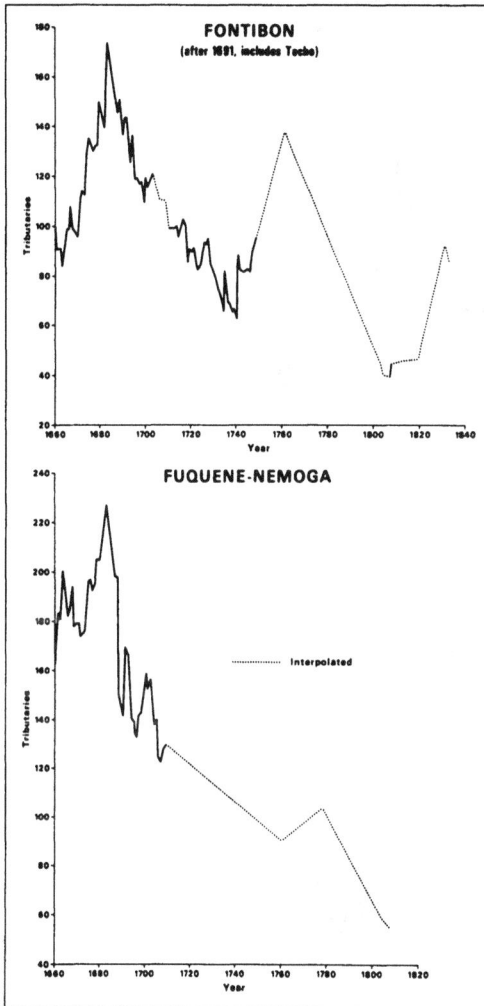

Figure 3.5 Tributary change in Fontibón and
Fúquene-Nemoga, 1660-1830

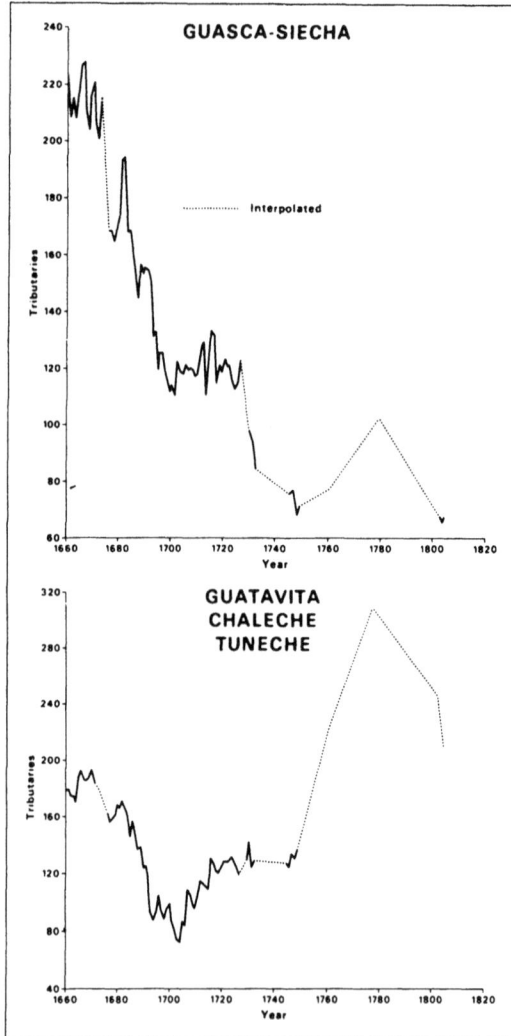

Figure 3.6 Tributary change in Guasca-Siecha and Guatavita, 1660-1810

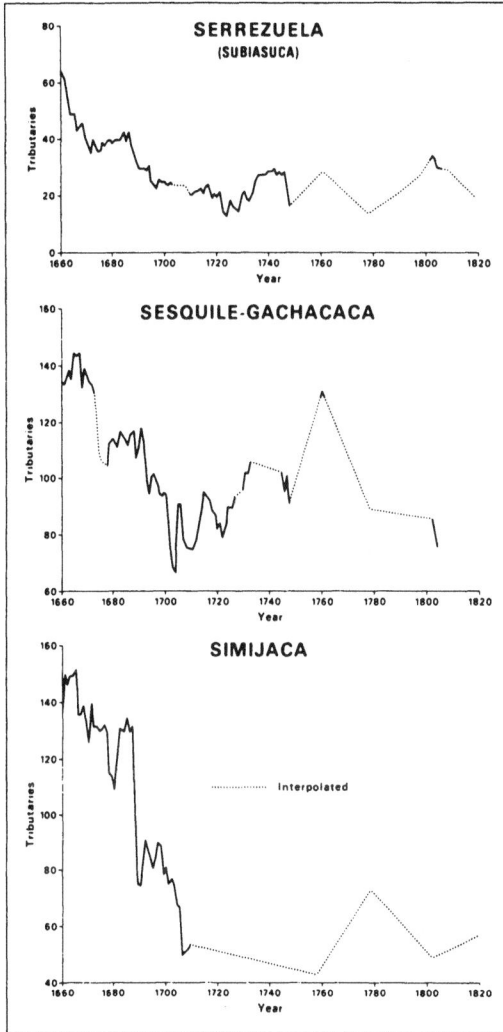

Figure 3.7   Tributary change in Serrezuela, Sesquilé-
Gachacaca, and Simijaca, 1660-1820

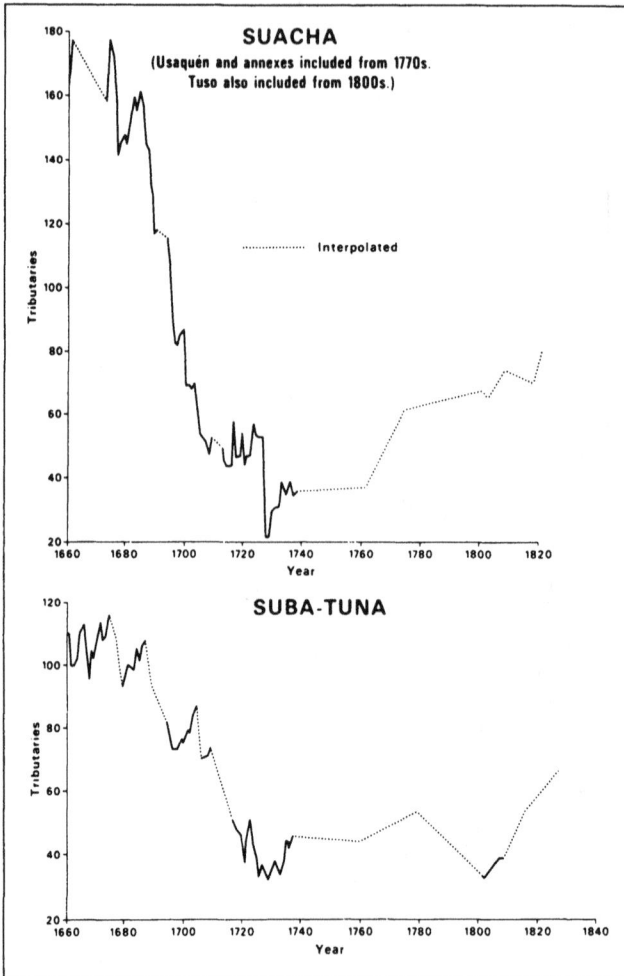

Figure 3.8   Tributary change in Suacha and
Suba-Tuna, 1660-1830

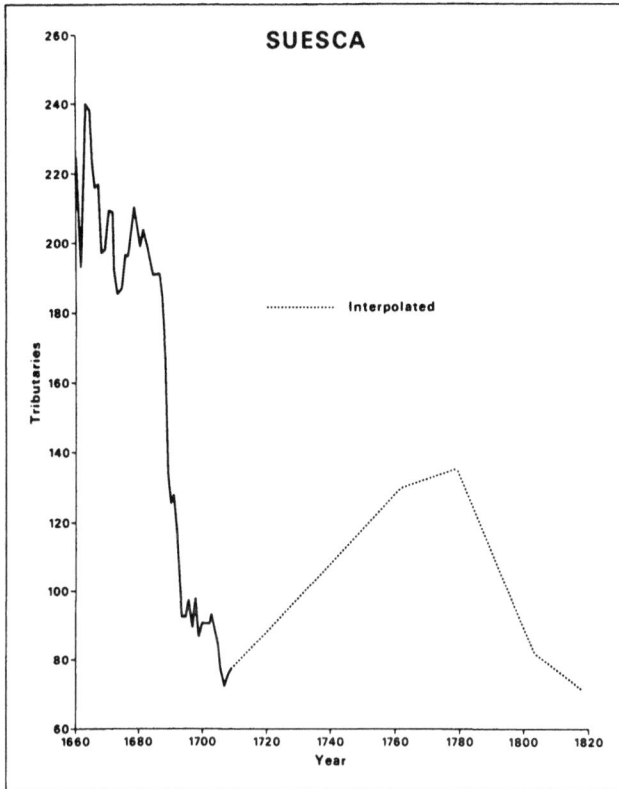

Figure 3.9 Tributary change in Suesca, 1660-1820

74

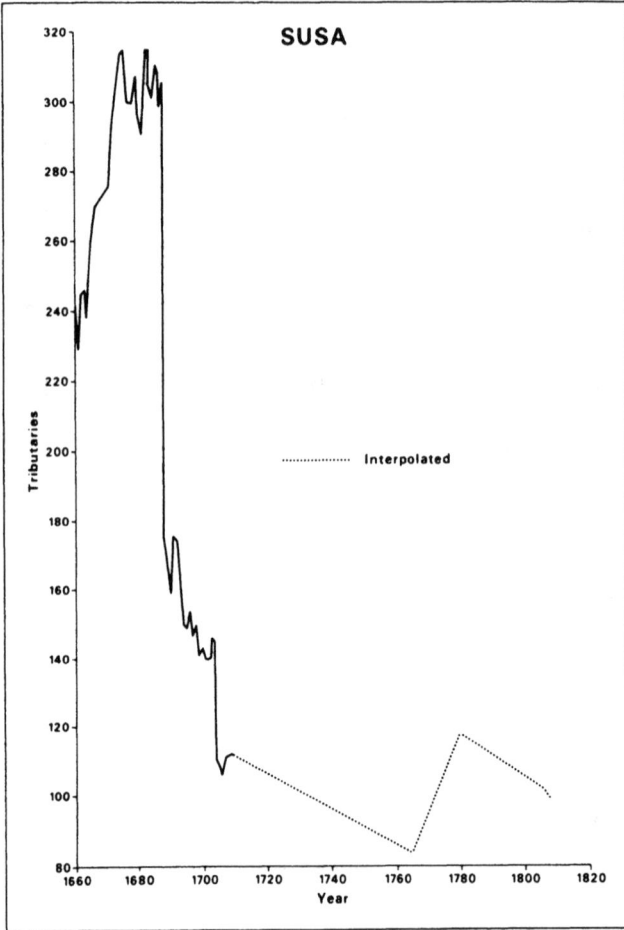

Figure 3.10   Tributary change in Susa, 1660-1810

Figure 3.11   Tributary change in Suta-Tausa, Usaquén, and Usme, 1660-1830

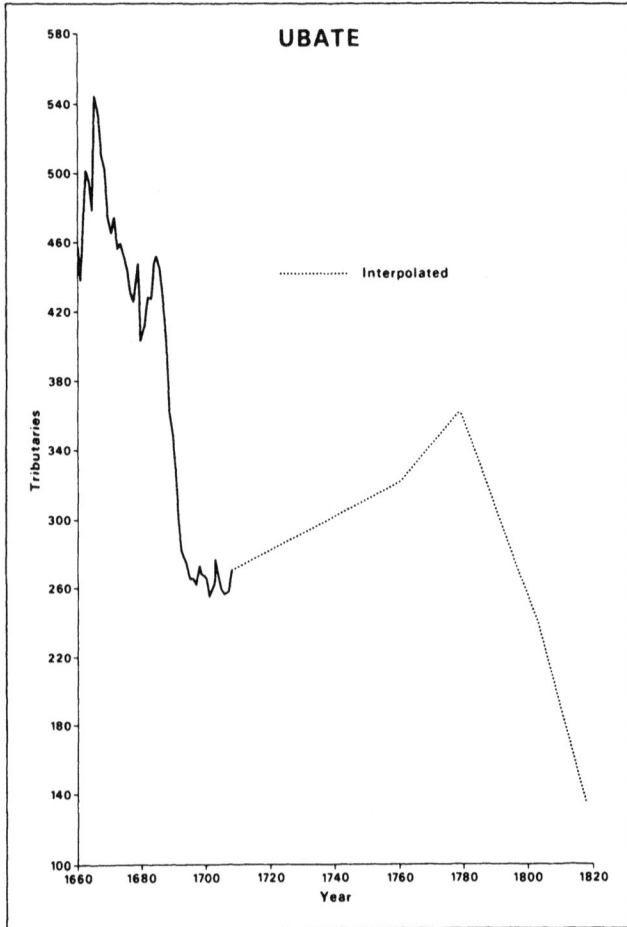

Figure 3.12   Tributary change in Ubaté, 1660-1820

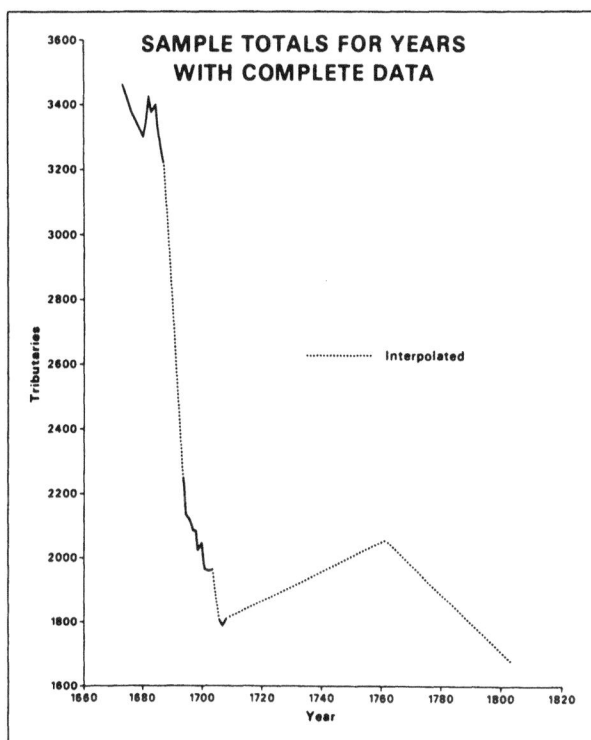

Figure 3.13 Sample tributary totals for years with
complete data, Sabana de Bogotá, 1660-1810

78

TABLE 3.7
Tributary numbers in years with complete data

Year	Tributary Totals	Percentage Change
1673	3,453	
1676	3,376	-2.2
1679	3,326	-1.4
1680	3,299	- .8
1681	3,349	+1.5
1682	3,421	+2.1
1683	3,373	-1.4
1684	3,397	+ .7
1685	3,336	-1.8
1686	3,269	-2.0
1687	3,217	-1.6
1694	2,255	-29.9
1695	2,135	-5.3
1696	2,122	- .6
1697	2,086	-1.7
1698	2,085	-.05
1699	2,028	-2.7
1700	2,048	+1.0
1701	1,966	-4.0
1702	1,965	-.05
1703	1,967	+ .1
1706	1,811	-7.9
1707	1,799	- .7
1708	1,816	+ .9
1761	2,058	+13.3
1802-1803	1,678	-18.5

Sources: See Notes 27 and 28.

Tributary Counts and Individual Communities

Inspected community by community, the tributary counts indicate that there were also variations in patterns. Some are minor, probably reflecting differences in timing of reaction to similar conditions. Bogotá's tributaries began to increase between 1672 and 1675, Fontibón's in 1684, Suesca's in 1663 and Ubaté's in 1665 (see Figures). Other patterns, however, are clearly unique. For example Guatavita and annexes (Figure 3.6) are unlike any other community in our sample in that their peak in tributary numbers for the time span in question, occurred in the late eighteenth century, rather than in the seventeenth. Usaquén, whose annexes had been incorporated into it, was an extreme case in its termination as an independent pueblo in 1770 (Figure 3.11). The smallest communities--Serrezuela and Usme--have profiles that are different from most of the others, not indicating distinct long-term periods of rise or fall. Chocontá and Susa, which are both among the larger communities have fairly similar patterns through the early 1700s, and then diverge, with Chocontá regaining numbers through the middle of the century and Susa losing them until a short upswing around 1780.

An examination of the data demonstrates that the more detailed the census information, the more precision is called for in the qualitative data that is associated with it. Uncovering overall trends still leaves open questions regarding how particular stresses or opportunities affected particular communities, and points out the differences in focus between regional and community approaches to population change. One mode of analysis does not replace the other, but rather each provides a complementary clarification of the issues. Collection of information at the community level beyond that which is found in the National Archives in Bogotá and those in Seville is time-consuming and may be limited in content and extent. But some significant information about communities may be buried in local documents, especially in parish records. Records of pastoral visits may prove to be another source of information. Although most were burned in 1948 during the uprising in Bogotá, some records may remain in the Vatican archives and might have valuable information.

What sort of problems would we be looking to solve in searching for more data in both the local and general archives? Differential effects of three major factors in population decline--disease, labor extraction and limitations on native land use would be among the most important to approach. We know that all of these had negative impact on the population as a whole, but the tributary data in the series suggest some degree of variation in different areas. We shall briefly explore these three factors in light of the tributary series and some of the issues that it raises.

Epidemics

Measles and smallpox continued to be the two most serious diseases among the Indians in the seventeenth and eighteenth centuries. Since an epidemiological study of the colonial period has yet to be done, the information is very incomplete. We do know, however, that there were measles epidemics in 1692 and 1729, epidemics of smallpox in 1693, 1756, 1781-1783 and 1801-1803, and sporadic outbreaks of smallpox in Santa Fe and the Sabana in other years as well. There were also other epidemics of unclearly identified diseases. One was supposed to have come from Japan in 1760; "peste" occurred in 1739, 1793-1794, and "pasa-diez" in 1808. Toward the end of the eighteenth century there are specific references to crop failures and hunger occurring both before and after periods of disease.[55]

Of all the epidemics, that of measles in 1692 and smallpox in 1693 appear to have contributed most to population decline. The number of tributaries in all the communities in our sample fell from 3,217 in 1687 to 2,255 in 1694, a decline of thirty percent. Inspection of the year to year tributary figures suggests that the epidemics intensified a decline that had already begun in the 1680s. They may also have had a delayed effect on tributary numbers, indicating that fatalities occurred primarily among the very young, and pregnant women, eliminating the potential tributaries of the next twelve to fifteen years. Tributary numbers reached the lowest point of the era in 1707. Furthermore the epidemics may have struck earlier in some areas. In Susa, Fúquene, Simijaca and Ubaté, communities that are close to each other, tributary population dropped precipitously between 1687 and 1688; in Susa from 306 to 175, in Simijaca from 131 to 111, and the next year to 75, in Fúquene from 198 to 151, and in Ubaté from 410 to 364 (see relevant Figures). Decline occurred but was less pronounced in the epidemic year of 1692, and the years thereafter. Whether measles or another catastrophic disease occurred first in Susa, Simijaca, Fúquene and Ubaté, remains unknown.

Data on epidemics can be gained through inspection of the yearly differences in burials in parish records. Persistence as well as access to supplementary documentary material will be necessary, however. Sometimes priests made notations in the records regarding disease, but other times not, even when the figures suggest that an epidemic may have been occurring.[56]

Labor

The Indians lost manpower to the Spaniards through
personal services during the early years of colonization
and through the forced labor systems (repartimiento) that
were established by the crown in the early seventeenth
century.[57] In 1657 legislation was implemented to reduce
demands on the Chibcha for labor in the city, rural and
mining areas. The rise in tributary population in many
of the communities between the 1660s and the 1680s may
have developed partially in response to the decreased
labor demands, with adult males possibly less resistant
to being counted. Nevertheless each tributary was still
expected to spend one month every second year in forced
labor in the city, at least one year in every three to
ten years in the mines, between six months and a year
every three years in agricultural work (concertaje) and
at least two months a year in seasonal agricultural work.
Women and children were also called on to do some of the
seasonal work. Wages, set by crown officials for Indians
engaged in forced labor, served mainly to help meet tribute payments and not for purchases.[58]

The phase of increasing numbers of tributaries that
we find in most of the communities in mid-eighteenth century roughly corresponds to an easing of labor demands in
urban areas, the abolition first in the mines and later
in agriculture of forced labor, and the permanent establishment of free labor by 1740.[59] As we have suggested
above, Indian population rose in the eighteenth century,
reaching a peak in the 1760s and 1780s, and then went
into another decline thereafter.

We suspect that some of the Indians' movement within
the Sabana was attributable to variations in labor demands as well as to those in tribute. Information is
available regarding differences in tribute assessments,
but labor needs to be explored further in the general and
local archival records. Both should be looked at in
terms of tributary population data available for the individual communities. Land tenure probably is a factor
to be considered concurrently, since large Spanish estates had access to forced native labor, while farms of
small and medium size did not. There may also have been
variations in labor requirements for work in the mines.
Officials' protection of the tributaries may have varied
from pueblo to pueblo, and finally, varying degrees of
skill in evading tributary classification, and consequently labor drafts, may have contributed to the differences in extant figures.[60]

Land

As a result of the assignment of reservations in the

late sixteenth century, the Sabana Chibcha were left with
access to a maximum of five percent of the land, parts of
it in zones of low productivity. Resettlement programs
also contributed to limitations on the Chibcha's resource
base. Techniques or tools to improve productivity were
not introduced for the cultivation of native staples, nor
were the new sources of protein such as beef or mutton
accessible to them, because of their lack of lands for
pasture and the animals' costs. Even chickens and fish
were destined for the tables of the encomendero, corregidor and priest or for marketing rather than for the Indians' consumption.[61]

Throughout the Sabana native crops were in constant
danger of destruction by livestock that the Spaniards
allowed to graze freely. The Chibcha's use of land was
therefore further reduced by the need to maintain some
distance from non-Indian estates where herds were kept.
The accumulation of foodstuffs or animals appears to have
been difficult for the Indians and perhaps not very attractive, since such goods could be confiscated for payment of tribute and taxes, and later in the eighteenth
century for the supply of Santa Fe. Taxes, resettlement,
land and property appropriations no doubt affected the
Sabana Chibcha's nutrition and fertility as well as material wealth. Toward the end of the eighteenth century
their continued existence in their own pueblos was
threatened by the pronounced growth of non-Indian populations. Poor mestizos, mulattos and whites settled on Indian lands as renters at first, particularly in the nucleated zones which the Indians had been forced to build.
The mixed population, that came to form the most important component of nineteenth and twentieth century rural
population, began to take over Indian land, in some
cases, such as in Usaquén and annexes, completely, and in
others at least partially.[62]

Some of the tributary and general population losses
among the Indians in this period no doubt were due to
mestizaje through marriage and/or acculturation, attractive routes since mestizos were not subject to tribute.
Many other natives opted to leave their pueblos and go to
others where conditions were less onerous, or to the city
or even other regions. In the late eighteenth century
priests, crown officials and others remarked on the apparent ease with which the Indians moved.[63]

The increase of non-Indians on Indian land at the
end of the eighteenth century corresponds to a decline in
both tributary and total Indian population numbers in
most communities in our sample, and in the Sabana in general. More detailed research might indicate whether
proximity to Spanish estates was correlated with greater
loss of tributary population, because of increased demands for labor and chances of crop damage. It would
also be useful to investigate what impact resettlement

attempts by the Spaniards had on both the tributary and general population, the effects of different rates of influx of non-Indians, and the relation between distance from the capital and native decline. Our findings on the last point indicate that the greater proportion of communities that declined by over fifty percent between 1592-1595 and the middle of the eighteenth century were within a radius of twenty kilometers of Santa Fe (Usaquén, Teusaca, Suba, Tuna, Bosa, Fontibón, Bogotá among others); but communities at great distances also lost substantial numbers, Chocontá, Guasca-Siecha, Simijaca and Suta-Tausa among them declining by between a third and a half.

SUMMARY

We have discussed the population material available for the Sabana and pointed out that there are three major reliable censuses of total population--1592-1595, 1636-1640 and 1758-1759--of which only the first and last are fairly complete. For some indication of trends between these dates and afterward, tributary counts can be used, particularly the long series found in the Archivo General de Indias, with supplementary data from the Archivo Histórico Nacional in Bogotá.

We have explored the meaning of "tributary" in relation to male and total populations, and have shown that the increase in population:tributary ratios in the eighteenth and nineteenth centuries had to do with Spanish classification and Indian avoidance of tributary classification rather than with increasing family size, change in fertility or improvement in the resource base. Finally we have inspected the tributary series with regard to population as a whole, population trends in the late seventeenth and eighteenth centuries and differing patterns among the communities. Some of the problems regarding epidemiology, labor and land have been suggested that might be profitably addressed using the tributary series and more detailed local research.

NOTES

1. Archival material for this paper comes from the Archivo Histórico Nacional de Colombia (Bogotá), cited as AHNC; the Biblioteca Nacional--Libros Raros (Bogotá), referred to as BNLR; parish records of Sabana communities; and the Archivo General de Indias (Seville), cited as AGI. María Angeles Eugenio Martínez, Tributo y Trabajo del Indio en Nueva Granada (Seville, Escuela de Estudios Hispano-Americanos, 1977), p. 204, has recently commented on the lack of demographic work for the Sabana.

2. Even within the highland basins there were variations in rainfall, frost and other factors, but these differences were less pronounced than those between areas at different altitudes. S. F. Cook and Woodrow Borah have pointed out the importance of taking altitude (as a determinant of differing natural zones) into consideration in population data analysis. See S. F. Cook and Woodrow Borah, Essays in Population History. Mexico and the Caribbean (2 vols., Berkeley, University of California Press, 1971-1974) Vol. 1, pp. xiii, 79ff., 411-429; and The Indian Population of Central Mexico 1531-1610 (Berkeley, University of California Press, Ibero-Americana 44, 1960), pp. 33-56.

3. Juan A. Villamarin, Encomenderos and Indians in the Formation of Colonial Society in the Sabana de Bogotá, Colombia: 1537-1740 (Ph.D. dissertation, Brandeis University, 1972), pp. 94-108; Villamarin and Judith E. Villamarin, Indian Labor in Mainland Colonial Spanish America (Newark, University of Delaware Latin American Studies Program, Occasional Papers and Monographs No. 1, 1975), pp. 85-89; Villamarin and Villamarin, "Chibcha Settlement Under Spanish Rule: 1537-1810," in David J. Robinson (ed.), Social Fabric and Spatial Structure in Colonial Latin America (Ann Arbor, University Microfilms International, 1979), pp. 29-33.

4. Villamarin, Encomenderos and Indians, pp. 141-161; Eugenio Martínez, Tributo y Trabajo, pp. 204-212; Julian Ruíz Rivera, Encomienda y Mita en Nueva Granada (Seville, Escuela de Estudios Hispano-Americanos, 1975), pp. 27-35.

5. Ruíz Rivera, Encomienda y Mita, pp. 48-57, 351-354 (1636-1640). The visita of the Sabana was done primarily in 1638-1639. A few Sabana communities (such as Guachetá and Lenguazaque) were included in the Province of Tunja, and were visited in 1636. AHNC, Visitas de Cundinamarca: Vol. 8: fols. 779r-836v (1761); this document has information on most of the communities in the Sabana. The 1755-1756 visita of Tunja has population figures for the following Sabana pueblos: Guachetá, Lenguazaque, Simijaca, Susa, Tausa, Zipaquirá and Usaquén. See Ulises Rojas, Corregidores y Justicias Mayores de Tunja (Tunja, Imprenta Departamental de Boyacá, 1963), pp. 522-523.

6. A final, overall report has not been found. There are population figures on a number of communities for which individual visitas have been located in the AHNC. The most complete set of figures are those of tributary Indians, included in a general report on New Granada's tributaries in AHNC, Gobierno: Vol. 1: fols. 4r-78r. This document has also been published in the Anuario Colombiano de Historia Social y de La Cultura, No. 2 (1964), pp. 410-530 (462-485, Province of Santa Fe), transcribed by Alvaro González under the supervision of Jaime Jaramillo Uribe.

7. See notes 27 and 28 below. The communities in our sample are Bogotá,* Bosa,* Chocontá,* Cucunubá,* Bobota, Facatativá,* Chueca, Fontibón,* Techo, Fúquene,* Nemoga, Guatavita,* Chaleche, Tuneche, Guasca,* Siecha, Serrezuela,* Sesquilé,* Gachacaca, Simijaca,* Suba,* Tuna, Suacha,* Suesca,* Suta,* Tausa, Susa,* Ubate,* Usaquén, Tibavita, Teusaca, Tunjaque, Suaque, Usme.* Those marked with an asterisk survived through the early nineteenth century. The others were associated with them administratively, and

ultimately became sections of them, or disappeared entirely. This process and the grouping together of some of the communities in the graphs are discussed in the last section of this study. Examples cited here are taken from the above sample, and are not necessarily exhaustive of the information.

8. AGI, Santa Fe 233, r 1, num. 11. For the communities in our sample we have the following: Bogotá 900 tributaries, Bosa 500, Facatativá 250, Fontibón 800, Serrezuela 130, Suba-Tuna 800, Usme 300. Eugenio Martínez, Tributo y Trabajo, pp. 583-586, also has these figures.

9. Juan Friede (ed.), Fuentes Documentales Para la Historia del Nuevo Reino de Granada. Desde la Instalación de la Real Audiencia en Santa Fe (8 vols., Bogotá, Biblioteca Banco Popular, 1975-1976), Vol. 5, pp. 129-135. According to the estimates Bogotá had 800-1,000 tributaries, Suba-Tuna had 900-1,000, and Usme 200-300.

10. AHNC, Visitas de Cundinamarca: Vol. 1: fols. 813r-838v, 844r-871v; population figures on Cucunubá-Bobota and Simijaca in 1586 when they were being resettled by the Spaniards.

11. Villamarin, Encomenderos and Indians, pp. 31-70. Juan Friede (ed.), Documentos Inéditos Para la Historia de Colombia. Coleccionados en el Archivo General de Indias, de Sevilla (10 vols., Bogotá, Academia Colombiana de Historia, 1955-1960), Vols. 5-10; Fuentes Documentales, Vols. 1-8. Esperanza Galvez Piñal, La Visita de Monzon y Prieto de Orellana al Nuevo Reino de Granada (Seville, Escuela de Estudios Hispano-Americanos, 1974). Ulises Rojas, El Cacique de Turmequé y su Epoca (Tunja, Imprenta Departamental, 1965).

12. AHNC, Encomiendas: Vol. 26: fols. 870r-909v (Bogotá 1560); Vol. 9: fols. 310r-330v (Subiasuca, later called Serrezuela, 1563). It is not known how many pueblos were covered in the two visitas.

13. AHNC, Reales Cedulas: Vol. 1: fols. 192r-195v.

14. See German Colmenares, La Provincia de Tunja en el Nuevo Reino de Granada (Bogotá, Multilith, Universidad de los Andes, 1970), pp. 115ff. Hermes Tovar Pinzón, "Estado Actual de los Estudios de Demografía Histórica en Colombia," Anuario Colombiano de Historia Social y de la Cultura, No. 5, pp. 65-140; Tovar Pinzón has found the following information for the provinces of Tunja and Velez (pp. 121-125):

Tribute

Community	Pesos de Medio Oro	Mantas	Tributaries
Duitama	750	750	750
Sasa	300	300	300
Sutamanga	200	200	200

The correspondence of number of tributaries to tribute, as illustrated above, is found to exist in 93.3 percent (104) of the communities that have information on both factors. In seven communities there are differences as in the following:

Community	Pesos de Medio Oro	Mantas	Tributaries
Tibaquirá	150	150	50
Sora	500	500	450
Pisba	650	650	700

Our data for Sabana communities (see Villamarín, Encomenderos and Indians, p. 60) does not have the internal conformity of the Tunja and Velez material. Tribute assessments on some of the communities in our sample in 1564 were as follows:

Tribute

Community	Pesos de Buen Oro	Mantas
Bogotá	660	330
Chocontá	--	950
Cucunubá-Bobota	--	200
Guasca	400	150
Simijaca	158	100
Suta-Tausa	200	120
Ubaté	--	1,000
Usme	200	120

Eugenio Martínez (Tributo y Trabajo, pp. 251-259) has data showing that in Nemocón-Tasgata (in the Sabana), tribute assessment was 230 pesos and 100 mantas for 201 tributaries.

15. Villamarín, Encomenderos and Indians, pp. 55-63, 218.

16. Julian Ruíz Rivera, Fuentes Para la Demografía Histórica de Nueva Granada (Seville, Escuela de Estudios Hispano-Americanos, 1972), p. 23; see pages 23-33 for census of 1592-1595.

17. Juan López de Velasco, Geografía y Descripción Universal de las Indias (1574, Madrid, Ediciones Atlas. Biblioteca de Autores Españoles, 1971), p. 181; López de Velasco's figures of 40,000-50,000 tributaries for the Province of Santa Fe in the early 1570s have no basis in an actual count, and may have been based on a report on New Granada, now found in the Archivo General de Indias (see Friede, [ed.], Fuentes Documentales, Vol. 5, p. 264). Fiscal Valverde, in a letter of 4 February 1572, says that there were a total of 17,000 tributaries at the time (see Eugenio Martínez, Tributo y Trabajo, p. 207). Neither Eugenio Martínez's search in Seville, nor ours in Bogotá found indications of any extensive count prior to the 1590s.

18. Ruíz Rivera, Fuentes Para la Demografía Histórica, pp. 37, 42-51; Encomienda y Mita, pp. 37-38.

19. AHNC, Visitas de Cundinamarca: Vol. 6: fols. 1r-247v (Tenjo and annexes); fols. 399r-530v (Cajica, Tabio and annexes).

20. AHNC, Caciques e Indios: Vol. 42: fols. 81r-93v.

21. AHNC, Visitas de Cundinamarca: Vol. 7: fol. 145r; Vol. 1: fol. 410r; Caciques e Indios: Vol. 72: fols. 166r-168v.

22. AHNC, Caciques e Indios: Vol. 72: fol. 168v.

23. AHNC, Gobierno: Vol. 1: fols. 4r-78r.

24. On the tributary population also see Ruíz Rivera, Encomienda y Mita, pp. 351-354. For the Visitas of 1636-1640 see AHNC, Visitas de Cundinamarca: Vol. 8: fols. 167r-205v (Bogotá); Vol. 12: fols. 643r-656v (Cajica); Miscelanea: Vol. 8: fols. 559r-597r (Chocontá); Visitas de Cundinamarca: Vol. 1: fols. 235r-241r (Engativá); Vol. 12: fols. 913r-938v (Fontibón); Vol. 6: fols. 815r-833r (Fúquene-Nemoga); Vol. 7: fols. 157r-166r (Gachancipá); Vol. 7: fols. 758r-779r (Guasca-Siecha); Vol. 12: fols. 750r-761r (Nemocón-Tasgata); Vol. 10: fols. 369r-380r (Sesquilé-Gachacaca); Vol. 1: fols. 414r-425v (Sopó-Meusa-Queca); Vol. 13: fols. 606r-610v (Subachoque); Vol. 13: fols. 592r-603r (Tabio-Gines-Chibiasuca); Vol. 2: fols. 576r-583v (Tenjo-Gongotá); Vol. 5: fols. 32r-40r (Usaquén); Vol. 2: fols. 192r-208v (Zipaquirá-Gotaque-Tenemequirá-Suativa).

25. AHNC, Visitas de Cundinamarca: Vol. 11: fols. 535r-554r (Cajicá); Vol. 11: fols. 369r-383r (Cota); Vol. 11: fols. 446r-460v (Gachancipá); Vol. 13: fols. 465r-486r (Sopó-Meusa-Queca); Vol. 13: fols. 361r-381r (Tabio-Chibiasuca-Gines-Subachoque); Vol. 13: fols. 258v-289r (Zipaquirá and annexes).

26. AHNC, Visitas de Cundinamarca: Vol. 8: fols. 779r-836v (1761); Vol. 7: fol. 521r (Guasca).

27. For visitas of 1778-1779 see AHNC, Visitas de Cundinamarca: Vol. 7: fol. 1086r (Bogotá); Vol. 8: fols. 843r-847v (Bojacá-Bobase-Cubiasuca); Vol. 7: fols. 842r (Bosa); Vol. 7: fol. 442r (Chocontá); Vol. 10: fol. 964r (Cucunubá-Bobota); Vol. 10: fol. 924v (Fúquene-Nemoga); Vol. 7: fol. 428r (Guatavita-Chaleche-Tuneche); Vol. 7: fol. 485r (Guasca-Siecha); Vol. 7: fol. 1086r (Serrezuela); Vol. 7: fol. 461v (Sesquilé-Gachacaca); Vol. 10: fol. 945r (Simijaca); Vol. 7: fol. 495v (Sopo-Meusa-Queca); Vol. 7: fol. 842r (Suacha); Vol. 7: fol. 842r (Suba-Tuna); Vol. 10: fols. 973r-973v (Suesca); Vol. 10: fol. 940r (Susa); Vol. 10: fol. 958v (Sutatausa); Vol. 10: fol. 952r (Tausa); Vol. 10: fol. 913v (Ubaté).

For reports on early nineteenth century figures see AHNC, Tributos: NC (Not Classified) #1 (Bogotá, Bojacá, Engativá, Facatativá, Fontibón, Serrezuela, Tenjo--1800); #11 (Bosa, Suacha, Suba 1800-1801; Usme 1817-1818); #13 (Suacha, Suba 1801-1802); #14 (Bosa, Suacha, Suba 1808); #21 (Chocontá, Guasca, Guatavita, Sesquilé 1804-1805; Bogotá, Fontibón, Serrezuela, Tenjo and annexes 1805; Bosa-Suacha, Suba 1809; Bosa 1830); #25 (Cucunubá, Simijaca, Suesca, Suta, Ubaté 1817); #26 (Bogotá, Bojacá, Engativá, Facatativá, Fontibón, Serrezuela, Tenjo 1803); #28 (Usme 1803); #29 (Chocontá, Guasca, Guatavita, Sesquilé 1803-1804; Cucunubá, Fúquene, Simijaca, Suesca, Susa, Suta, Ubaté 1803-1804); #32 (Chocontá, Guasca, Guatavita, Sesquilé 1804-1805; Bogotá, Bojacá, Engativá, Facatativá, Fontibón, Serrezuela, Tenjo 1806-1810, 1818; Bosa, Fontibón, Suba 1828; Fontibón, Usme 1830); #33 (Fúquene, Susa 1817; Bosa, Suacha, Suba 1817; Chocontá, Guasca, Guatavita, Sesquilé 1816-1819--For this period in these communities the figures of 1804-1805 were used by the Spaniards because of their lack of control during the Independence struggle; Cucunubá, Suesca, Simijaca, Suta, Ubaté 1818-1819; Bogotá, Bojacá, Engativá, Facatativá, Fontibón, Serrezuela, Tenjo 1816-1818); #37 (Bogotá, Bojacá, Engativá, Facatativá, Fontibón,

Serrezuela, Tenjo 1802-1804); #40 (Bosa, Suacha, Suba 1806-1807); #41 (Bogotá, Bojacá, Facatativá, Tenjo 1804); #43 (Bogotá, Bojacá, Engativá, Facatativá, Fontibón, Serrezuela, Tenjo 1801). AHNC, Resguardos de Cundinamarca: Vol. 1: fol. 465v (Tausa 1804).

28. AGI, Contaduría, 1341, 1344, 1344A, 1344B, 1345, 1346, 1346A, 1346B, 1347, 1544, 1546, 1554, 1591, 1595, 1596. Sabana communities covered were Bogotá, Bojacá-Bobase, Chinga, Chise, Chitasuga, Chueca, Churuaco, Ciénaga, Cubia, Engativá, Facatativá, Fontibón, Guangata, Serrezuela, Sisativa, Tenjo, Tibaguya--from San Juan 1658 to San Juan 1670; from Navidad 1671 to Navidad 1703; San Juan 1706 to San Juan 1708; and Navidad 1710 to San Juan 1748. Cucunubá-Bobota, Fúquene-Nemoga, Simijaca, Susa, Suesca, Ubaté--from Navidad 1657 to San Juan 1692; Navidad 1694 to San Juan 1709. Chocontá, Guasca, Guatavita, Sesquilé--from Navidad 1659 to Navidad 1673; San Juan 1676 to San Juan 1727; San Juan 1730 to San Juan 1733; San Juan 1745 to Navidad 1749. Cajicá, Chia, Cogua, Gachancipa, Gotaque, Nemocón-Tasgatá, Suativa, Subachoque, Sopo, Tabio, Tenemequirá, Tibito, Tocancipa, Zipaquirá--from San Juan 1658 to Navidad 1681; Navidad 1689 to Navidad 1691. Guachetá, Lenguazaque--from Navidad 1669 to Navidad 1674; Navidad 1677 to San Juan 1731; Navidad 1733 to Navidad 1739. Usme--from San Juan 1665 to San Juan 1688; Navidad 1694 to Navidad 1710. Bosa-Suacha, Teusaca, Tibavita, Tunjaque--from Navidad 1673 to San Juan 1691; San Juan 1694 to San Juan 1704; Navidad 1706 to San Juan 1710; Navidad 1713 to Navidad 1738; for Bosa and Suacha also Navidad 1659 to Navidad 1661. Cota--from Navidad 1673 to Navidad 1678. Suba-Tuna--from Navidad 1660 to San Juan 1691; San Juan 1694 to San Juan 1704; Navidad 1706 to San Juan 1710; Navidad 1717 to Navidad 1738.

29. AHNC, Residencias de Cundinamarca: Vol. 4: fol. 692v (1727); Vol. 5: fol. 90v (1753); Vol. 5: fol. 799r (1641); Vol. 6: fol. 1018r (1655); Vol. 9: fol. 312r (1645).

30. Villamarin and Villamarin, Indian Labor, pp. 82-89.

31. Villamarin, Encomenderos and Indians, pp. 13-93. Eugenio Martínez, Tributo y Trabajo, pp. 185-187, 204-212.

32. Villamarin, Encomenderos and Indians, pp. 141-210; Villamarin and Villamarin, Indian Labor, pp. 2, 18, 85-89. Ruíz Rivera, Encomienda y Mita, pp. 242-244. AHNC, Caciques e Indios: Vol. 55: fol. 634v; both married and single men had to pay full tribute. The ages formally delimiting tributary status differed slightly from province to province. In Tunja they were seventeen to sixty years (Colmenares, La Provincia de Tunja, p. 63); and in Cartago fourteen to fifty years in 1559, fourteen to forty-five in 1568, and seventeen to fifty-four in 1627 (Tovar Pinzón, "Estado Actual de los Estudios," pp. 83-84).

33. Under this system tribute differed among communities but in most cases was uniform for all native males within a given community. Villamarin, Encomenderos and Indians, pp. 153-161, 218-228. Ruíz Rivera, Encomienda y Mita, pp. 224-235.

34. Villamarin and Villamarin, Indian Labor, pp. 85, 88-89.

35. Cook and Borah (Essays in Population History, Vol. 1, p. 17) have pointed out the importance of defining terms, stating: "Use of Indian tribute material for demographic information must be based upon detailed understanding of the tribute system and changes in

classification of tributary." We find in analyzing the Sabana material that it is essential to explore changes in classification,
exemptions and other factors affecting tributary and general population counts.

36. In the censuses nuclear families were used as the basic
units. First the male head of the family was listed, then his wife
and children. Single individuals were reported separately. See
AHNC, Visitas de Cundinamarca: Vol. 6: fols. 412r-440v (1603); Vol.
7: fols. 758r-779v (1639); Vol. 8: fols. 843r-847v (1778).

37. Juan A. Villamarin and Judith Villamarin, "Kinship Organi-
zation and Inheritance Among the Sabana de Bogotá Chibcha at the
Time of Spanish Conquest," Ethnology, Vol. 14 (1975), pp. 173-179.
AHNC, Caciques e Indios: Vol. 57: fols. 685r-720v.

38. Sylvia M. Broadbent, Los Chibchas. Organización Socio-
política (Bogotá, Universidad Nacional de Colombia-Facultad de
Sociologia, 1964), pp. 32-33. Chia, Libro de Bautismos 1 (1720-
1744).

39. AHNC, Encomiendas: Vol. 9: fols. 312v-313r (Subiasuca,
later called Serrezuela, 1563). Also see AHNC, Visitas de Cundinamarca: Vol. 4: fol. 977v (Suta, Tausa, Simijaca) and Encomiendas:
Vol. 12: fols. 222r-222v (Cota 1563):

que agora y de aqui adelante cada uno de ellos no tengan
mas de una mujer propia y no se casen con las mujeres de
sus hermanos aunque esten vivos o esten muertos, ni tam-
poco con las hermanas que ovieren tenido y se les hayan
muerto.

40. AHNC, Visitas de Cundinamarca: Vol. 5: fols. 211v-212r
(Ubaté 1592). In the interrogation of the Indians a question dealt
with this matter. One of the caciques of Ubaté stated that all the
Indians were Christians, ". . . bautizados e casados segun orden de
la Santa Madre iglesia," and that they didn't have, ". . . parientas
con quien use de las cosas que dice la pregunta (concerning sexual
relations) ni que sean parientas unas de otras, ni otras de otras,
que si algunos (indios) tuvieran se vera por la lista que se hiciera
por el señor visitador." In Teusacá, Visitas de Cundinamarca: Vol.
5: fol. 558v (1593), the cacique made a similar statement, but de-
clared that he had six females in his service, "y que con algunas de
ellas, de cuando en cuando tiene parte con ellas carnalmente, y que
esto es de tarde en tarde." Polygyny in the Sabana needs to be further explored, as do other factors affecting marriage patterns and
access to women after the conquest. See also Vernon Dorjahn, "The
Factor of Polygyny in African Demography," in William R. Bascom and
Melville J. Herskovits (eds.), Continuity and Change in African Cultures (Chicago, University of Chicago Press, 1959), pp. 87-112.
Dorjahn discusses some of the census problems associated with polygyny and the socio-cultural, fertility and general demographic ramifications.

41. Villamarin, Encomenderos and Indians, pp. 121-122, 270-271.
Villamarin and Villamarin, "Kinship Organization."

42. Villamarin, Encomenderos and Indians, pp. 243-249, 254-258.
Although it is clear that women and children emigrated during all
periods of the colonial era, quantitative data on their emigration
is usually not available, because the documents are geared mainly

toward reporting tribute-paying men.

43. AHNC, Visitas de Cundinamarca: Vol. 11: fols. 446r-460v
(Gachancipá 1670). Crown officials were trying to collect a tax of
four pesos from each forastero. AGI, Contaduría, 1596 (1671-1673).
AHNC, Visitas de Cundinamarca: Vol. 8: fols. 783r-783v (1761). Visitador Aróstegui y Escoto stated that there were many ausentes, and
that the forastero tribute of 4 p 4 r a year favored Indian movement, because it was lower than what men had to pay in their native
communities. He proposed, and apparently ordered, that forasteros
pay the same tribute as that of the community in which they were
living, but this was not carried out. See AHNC, Tributos: NC #1
(1800).

44. AHNC, Caciques e Indios: Vol. 21: fols. 12r-19v (1585).
BNLR, Manuscrito #181 (1597) Oidor Visitador Ibarra ordered that
caciques and capitanes "no recojan, tengan y escondan en sus pueblos
a ningunos indios que no fueren del naturales, y los forasteros los
embien, y restituyan a su pueblo y natural." There were few dis-
putes among caciques for Indians on the boundaries of their terri-
tories. The number of such cases was small probably because the
Europeans did not break up communities, but followed Chibcha socio-
political and geographical divisions fairly regularly in allocating
encomiendas.

45. Villamarin and Villamarin, "Chibcha Settlement," pp. 67-77.

46. Ernesto Restrepo Tirado, "Lista de los Encomenderos del
Partido de Santa Fe en 1595 (Documentos del Archivo de Indias),"
Boletín de Historia y Antiguedades, Vol. 23 (1936), pp. 116-127.
Ruíz Rivera, Fuentes Para la Demografía Histórica, pp. 23-33.

47. The total figures including ausentes were generally used in
documents. For example Visitador Aróstegui y Escoto referred to
some of the 1636-1640 census in his 1761 report, and when giving
totals used figures that included ausentes. Guasca's total 1639
population is cited as being 1,049 (AHNC, Visitas de Cundinamarca:
Vol. 8: fol. 794v); we know from its visita that there were six
ausentes included in the 1,049 figure (Visitas de Cundinamarca: Vol.
7: fol. 779r). Figures also remain for Chocontá, that had a total
of 1,335 including twenty-five ausentes (Visitas de Cundinamarca:
Vol. 8: fol. 801r; Miscelanea: Vol. 8: fol. 597r); Fúquene-Nemoga
with a total of 934 including fourteen ausentes (Visitas de Cundinamarca: Vol. 8: fol. 803r; Vol. 6: fol. 833r); and Nemocón-Tasgata,
with a 452 total including four ausentes (Vol. 8: fol. 806r; Vol.
12: fol. 761r). In 1758 Guasca's total population was given as 622,
including seventy-six ausentes (Visitas de Cundinamarca: Vol. 7:
fol. 521r); Bosa's was 499 including twenty-eight ausentes (Vol. 8:
fol. 823r; Vol. 7: fol. 633r), and Tocancipá's was 776 including
thirty-six ausentes (Vol. 8: fol. 812v; Vol. 4: fol. 713r). It
should be noted that in visitas there are sometimes small arithmeti-
cal discrepancies between the actual enumeration of people, and the
summing of categories and totals. Usually only totals were referred
to in other documents.

For our Table 3.6 we have been able to delete ausentes from
total population figures of 1636-1640. There is insufficient data
to do so for 1758-1759.

48. AHNC, Miscelanea: Vol. 78: fols. 940r-940v (1669); Vol. 113:

fols. 444r-444v (1672).

49. Juan Friede, "Algunas Consideraciones Sobre la Evolución Demográfica en la Provincia de Tunja," Anuario Colombiano de Historia Social y de la Cultura, No. 3 (1965), pp. 5-19. Friede establishes a ratio of 4.82 for the visita of 1636 in Tunja, and states (p. 12):

Tan alto coeficiente, indicio de familias numerosas, se debe indudablemente al benigno clima de la altiplanicie andina, a su fértil suelo apto para la agricultura y a la carencia de una intensiva explotación minera.

50. Villamarin, Encomenderos and Indians, pp. 245-246. AHNC, Visitas de Cundinamarca: Vol. 8: fols. 794v, 801r.

51. Colmenares, La Provincia de Tunja, pp. 58-69; Historia Económica y Social de Colombia 1537-1719 (Cali, Universidad del Valle, 1973), pp. 60-71. Eugenio Martínez, Tributo y Trabajo, pp. 212-223. Ruíz Rivera, Encomienda y Mita, pp. 94-100.

52. The matter of appropriate ratios for different segments of the colonial era has been addressed by several investigators. Jaime Jaramillo Uribe ("La Población Indígena de Colombia en el Momento de la Conquista y sus Posteriores Transformaciones," Anuario Colombiano de Historia Social y de la Cultura, No. 2, 1964, pp. 239-293) suggests (pp. 244-246) using a coefficient of 3 for the sixteenth century, 4 for the seventeenth century and 5 for the eighteenth century, in contrast to using 4 as a multiplier to calculate Colombian Indian population in all three centuries, as had been done previously. Ruíz Rivera (Encomienda y Mita, p. 98) has established the ratios of 3.12 for 1595 and 3.06 for 1602-1604 in the Province of Tunja. Eugenio Martínez (Tributo y Trabajo, p. 216) is in agreement. Ruíz Rivera also offers the following values for the Province of Santa Fe: 1595:5.53; 1600-1604:4.31; 1635-1640:4.78; 1670-1671:5.53; 1687:7.26; 1690:6.03. It is not always clear how he derives the figures. Also see Colmenares, La Provincia de Tunja, p. 66; and Note 51 above.

There already exist works calculating the population of the Province of Santa Fe. See Eugenio Martínez (Tributo y Trabajo, pp. 204-223) for the sixteenth century; Ruíz Rivera (Encomienda y Mita, pp. 27-61, 89-110) for the seventeenth century. These authors are clear about the shortcomings of the data. Professor Hermes Tovar Pinzón is preparing a detailed population study of the Chibcha area.

53. See Villamarin and Villamarin, "Chibcha Settlement" for more detailed information on the Sabana communities' settlement patterns during the colonial period. The nineteen communities in our sample that remained in existence through the late eighteenth century were Bogotá, Bosa, Cucunubá, Chocontá, Facatativá, Fontibón, Fúquene, Guasca, Guatavita, Serrezuela, Sesquilé, Simijaca, Suacha, Suba, Suesca, Susa, Suta, Ubaté and Usme. The fifteen that did not were Bobota, Chaleche, Chueca, Gachacaca, Nemoga, Siecha, Suaque, Tausa, Techo, Teusaca, Tivavita, Tuna, Tuneche, Tunjaque and Usaquén (Usaquén remained in name but its Indians had been moved to Suacha).

54. Villamarin, Encomenderos and Indians, pp. 247, 250-251.

55. Villamarin, Encomenderos and Indians, pp. 135, 252-253. Major epidemics in the sixteenth and seventeenth century were smallpox (1558, 1588, 1621, 1651), measles (1618) and tobardillo

(exanthematic typhus?) (1630-1633). There were other serious diseases of unknown nature (1568-1569). As stated, smallpox and measles continued to be the most devastating epidemics afterward. On the late seventeenth century through the early nineteenth century, see J. A. Vargas Jurado, "Tiempos Coloniales," in J. A. Vargas Jurado, J. M. Caballero and J. A. deTorres y Peña (eds.), La Patria Boba (Bogotá, Biblioteca de Historia Nacional, Vol. I, Imprenta Nacional, 1902), pp. 13, 45, 52; and in the same volume, J. M. Caballero, "En La Independencia," pp. 93, 99, 102, 108. Also, AHNC, Tributos: Vol. 20: fol. 571r (1782); Miscelanea: Vol. 2: fols. 809v-810r (1782); Caciques e Indios: Vol. 25: fol. 879r (1783); Resguardos de Cundinamarca: Vol. 2: fol. 884r (1783); Caciques e Indios: Vol. 25: fols. 608v-620r (1793-1794); Miscelanea: Vol. 22: fols. 266r-389v (1801); Vol. 33: fols. 379r-398v (1801); Vol. 44: fols. 495r-524v (1801); Vol. 2: fols. 817r-868v; 909r-919v, 930r-1003r (1802-1803); Vol. 3: fols. 269r-280v; 316r-326v (1802-1803).

On the epidemics' coincidence with crop failure and hunger, see AHNC, Tributos: NC #18 (Chia 1780-1781); Tributos: Vol. 20: fol. 571r (Bogotá, Bojacá, Facatativá, Fontibón, Tenjo 1782-1783); Caciques e Indios: Vol. 25: fol. 879r (Cucunubá 1783); Vol. 25: fols. 608v-620r (Bojacá, Engativá, Facatativá, Fontibón, Tenjo, Serrezuela 1793-1794); Tributos: Vol. 22: fols. 738r-764v (Guatavita 1803); fols. 149r-161v (Chocontá 1803). Further work is needed to establish the relations among these factors.

56. Bogotá, Libro de Bautizmos, Vol. 2 (1782, 1783). In 1782 thirty-six deaths were registered, and in 1783, 137; almost all of the latter were cited as having resulted from smallpox.

57. Villamarin, Encomenderos and Indians, pp. 211-214, 228-233, 253-254. Villamarin and Villamarin, Indian Labor, pp. 86-88.

58. Villamarin, Encomenderos and Indians, pp. 212-228. AHNC, Tierras de Boyacá: Vol. 17: fols. 517v-519v.

59. Villamarin and Villamarin, Indian Labor, pp. 88-89.

60. Villamarin, Encomenderos and Indians, pp. 218-228. Juan A. Villamarin, "Haciendas en la Sabana de Bogotá, Colombia, en la Epoca Colonial (1539-1810)" in Enrique Florescano (ed.), Haciendas, Latifundios y Plantaciones en América Latina (Mexico, Siglo Veintiuno Editores, 1975), pp. 335-337. Julian Ruíz Rivera, "La Plata de Mariquita en el Siglo XVII: Mita y Producción," Anuario de Estudios Americanos, Vol. 29 (1972), pp. 121-169.

61. Villamarin, Encomenderos and Indians, pp. 148-151, 263-266, 272-276. Juan A. Villamarin, "Factores Que Afectaron la Producción Agropecuaria en la Sabana de Bogotá en la Epoca Colonial" (Tunja, Ediciones Pato Marino, 1975). Villamarin and Villamarin, "Chibcha Settlement."

62. Villamarin and Villamarin, "Chibcha Settlement," pp. 67-84.

63. AHNC, Visitas de Cundinamarca: Vol. 8: fol. 783v; Tributos: NC #6.

4
The Ecology of Race and Class in Late Colonial Oaxaca

John K. Chance

The use of quantitative sources in studies of colonial Latin American societies has become increasingly sophisticated in recent years. Analyses of census data in particular have provided new insights into social structure and social change, especially in urban areas. A number of recent studies have extended our knowledge of the ecology of the eighteenth-century Latin American city by matching census counts with city plans to plot the spatial distribution of households and individuals.[1] The present paper provides new data on the residential patterns of racial and occupational groups in a late colonial Mexican city, applying to them some statistical indexes of segregation developed by North American sociologists for United States cities.[2] These measures have previously been applied mainly to blacks and whites, though some studies have dealt with a variety of ethnic and socioeconomic groupings.[3] In recent years, some of these measures of segregation have also been applied successfully by social historians to nineteenth-century American cities.[4] It is time, I think, that we try them out in the Latin American context to see if they can bring more clarity and precision to our understanding of colonial urban social structure.

In this paper I am concerned with the case of Oaxaca, Mexico (or Antequera as it was known in colonial times) in 1792. Though it had a population of only 18,000 in that year, Antequera was typical of the highland towns of Spanish America in that it had significant numbers of Spaniards, Indians, and castas (people of mixed racial ancestry), surrounded by a dense and highly developed Indian peasant population. Mining was of minimal significance in the Oaxaca region, and the economy revolved around agriculture, trade (especially in the cochineal dyestuff), and textile manufacture.

The data used in this paper come from the 1792 Revillagigedo military census, which gives a complete house-to-house count of the city's 12,600 non-Indian and

non-slave inhabitants in that year.[5] While this source
has the disadvantage of excluding all Indians and most
blacks, it is fairly consistent in its listing of racial
affiliations and occupations of the rest of the adult
males. But of course, reliable census data are not
enough for the study of social segregation; a map which
permits the placement of particular individuals in households on the grid of city streets is also required. Fortunately, there exists such a map for Antequera: it was
drawn in 1803 and carries the same street names as those
employed in the 1792 census.[6] A sketch of the city with
the street names then in use (all are different today)
appears in Figure 4.1.

By matching up street addresses in the census with
the 1803 map, it is possible to locate each household in
a specific "linear block" consisting of the facing sides
of a block-long street segment. In 1792, Antequera had
303 of these. There is no doubt about the actual street
on which each household in the census was located, though
in some cases where the addresses were unclear I have had
to resort to estimates in order to place households within particular facing blocks. This did not prove to be
very difficult, since the city was laid out in a uniform
fashion and the streets for which complete information is
available contained on the average 10 houses per block,
increasing to 15-20 in the area immediately surrounding
the Plaza de Armas. Breaks between blocks were also
fairly easy to identify in the census because of the frequent presence of corner stores and familiar landmarks
such as churches and government buildings. In any case,
it is doubtful that any errors in placement would be off
by more than a block, and I feel confident that the
matching of the census with the map provides a fairly
accurate model of Antequera's urban ecology at the close
of the eighteenth century. While the segregation statistics discussed below are based on the 303 linear or
facing block units, for the sake of clarity these entities have been aggregated into manzanas ("island blocks")
in Figures 4.2 to 4.11.

The physical plan of the city shows that Antequera
came close to meeting the ideal of the grid-pattern town
that was applied so often throughout Spanish America.[7]
Much as it does today, life revolved around the central
square, the Plaza de Armas, which was bordered on the
north by the Cathedral and on the south by the Casas
Consistoriales and the residence of the Intendente of
Oaxaca. Close by to the southwest of the Plaza de Armas
was the focal point of the city's market, the Plaza de
San Juan de Dios. Excluded from all the Figures (and
necessarily from the analysis in this paper) are the outlying suburban communities where much of the urban Indian
population resided: Santo Tomás Xochimilco to the north,
San Matías Jalatlaco to the northeast, Trinidad de las

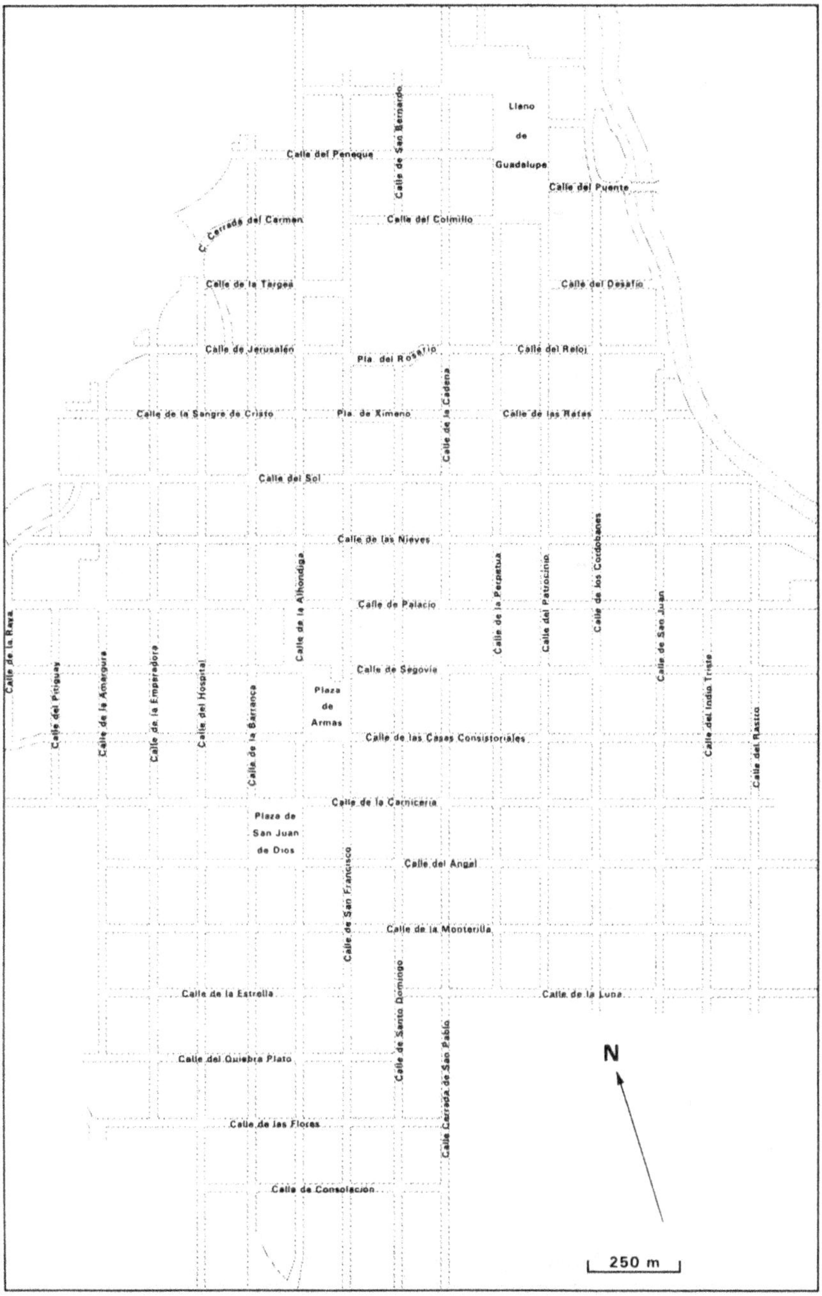

Figure 4.1 Streets of Antequera, 1792-1803

Huertas to the southeast, San Martín Mexicapan and San
Juan Chapultepec to the southwest, and the Villa de
Oaxaca (today part of the city and known as El Marquesado)
to the northwest.[8]

My central concern is the relationship between social distance and geographical space of the major racial
groupings of peninsular Spaniards, creoles, castizos,
mestizos, and mulattoes, and three occupational clusterings which I call Socioeconomic Groups (SEGs): the elite,
preindustrial middle groups, and lower groups. The elite
consisted of the city's leading merchants, high royal
officials, and large landowners (the clergy is excluded
from this analysis because of its atypical residence pattern). The middle groups included the professionals,
high-status artisans, small landholders, and traders,
while among the lower groups were the low-status artisans,
male servants, and those listed as unemployed.[9] I will
refer to these groupings interchangeably as SEGs or
classes.

The analysis of segregation is based on a total of
4,550 household heads for race and 3,246 adult males for
class. For comparative purposes, the indexes for race
have also been computed for the adult males. The basic
hypothesis of this paper derives from the ecological
branch of urban sociology: that the greater the degree of
difference between the spatial distributions of groups
within an urban area, the greater their social distance
from one another. In other words, I am hypothesizing a
general fit between the residential distribution of race
and class on the one hand, and the place of these dimensions within the overall urban social structure on the
other.

In previous work on colonial Oaxaca which relied to
a great extent on the same census material, William B.
Taylor and I have emphasized the utility of a multi-
dimensional approach to social stratification which mini-
mally distinguishes between racial and socioeconomic determinants of social status. We maintain that by 1792,
urban population growth, an expanding capitalist economy,
and a high rate of interracial marriage and "passing" had
considerably weakened the estate-based racial hierarchy--
the sistema de castas--devised by the elite and the official bureaucracy.

> . . . by the end of the colonial period the complexity
> and range of variation within the economic class struc-
> ture were as great as those of the status hierarchy em-
> bodied in the sistema de castas, if indeed the latter
> had not been overtaken in this respect. The city's
> dramatic growth and increased opportunities for trade
> after the Bourbon reforms rendered the sistema de castas
> all but obsolete as a mechanism of status definition.
> More than ever, social honor came to be dependent on

economic considerations as the number of claimants to
white status multiplied.
    Only at the top and perhaps at the bottom of the
socioeconomic scale did racial affiliation correspond
to ethnic identity and class-like behavior.[10]

The basic argument, then, is that caste and racial
estate models are inadequate for the analysis of stratification in eighteenth-century Mexico, at least in Antequera. I find it preferable to posit at least two ana-
lytically separate hierarchies of racial status ("social
honor" in Weber's terms) and economic class, recognizing
that these determinants were frequently working at cross
purposes with each other. If this interpretation is
valid, one would expect the city's residence pattern to
be mixed, with a relative absence of clearly segregated
neighborhoods based on either race or class (with the exceptions of the peninsular-dominated elite and the urban
Indian proletariat). This is the specific hypothesis
that I wish to test in this paper.[11] It should be kept
in mind, however, that Indians, slaves, and blacks are
omitted from the analysis because they were not included
in the census. We know from other sources that many of
Antequera's urban Indians did in fact live in highly segregated barrios on the fringes of the city.[12]

II

I have applied two measures of segregation to the
data. Both were introduced by Otis Dudley Duncan and
Beverly Duncan in 1955 and have become widely used among
North American sociologists.[13] The first measure is the
index of dissimilarity. Given the distribution of two
racial or occupational groups over all the areal units of
the city (in this case, facing blocks), this index measures on a scale of 0 to 100 the degree of spatial dissimilarity between the two groups. To compute this index, it is necessary to calculate the percentage of all
members of each group that reside in each block. The index of dissimilarity between the two groups is then one-
half the sum of the absolute values of the differences
between the respective distributions. This statistic
yields a measure of displacement. A score of 80, for example, would tell us that 80 percent of the people in
group A would have to move to a different area in order
to make their distribution identical with that of group
B. The index of dissimilarity therefore measures the extent to which the observed degree of segregation differs
from a hypothetical state of total segregation. The second statistic, the index of segregation, is computed in
much the same way, except that in this case dissimilarity
is measured between a given group and all other groups in

the city combined. This is a broader, more general purpose index that measures the place of a particular group
in the city as a whole.

Once the statistics are calculated (and with 303
blocks, a computer is indispensable), the question of
course arises as to how to interpret the values. How do
we decide what figures represent high and low segregation
scores? In theory there is no answer to this problem,
but there is a practical solution. Following Nathan
Kantrowitz, it seems reasonable to consider indexes upward of 70 as high, indexes of 30 or less as low, and
variations in level of less than 5 points as unimpor-
tant.[14] These thresholds are, of course, arbitrary, but
they have found some acceptance among researchers, and
until comparative data become available for other Latin
American cities, they may serve as a point of departure.[15]

One final word of caution: the indexes of segregation and dissimilarity, like the concept of residential
segregation itself, are sensitive to differences in size
of the groups being measured. Thus, a group numbering in
the hundreds is likely to exhibit a higher index of segregation, other things being equal, than a group numbering in the thousands. This "distortion" occurs because
the index is partially dependent on the relationship between the size of the total population, the number and
population size of the areal units (blocks), and the number and proportion of group members. This is inevitable,
however, for the whole notion of residential segregation
is dependent on these same variables, and any statistical
measure must have some dependence on them.[16] Given these
limitations, it is highly desirable to supplement these
statistical indexes with maps which plot the actual distribution of different groups within the city. This has
been done in Figures 4.2 through 4.9, which show the distribution of the principal racial and class groupings by
manzana.

III

The indexes calculated for Antequera in 1792 are
presented in Tables 4.1 to 4.6. It should be noted that
the indexes for racial groupings have been calculated
twice with two different data bases. The population of
4,550 household heads in Tables 4.1 and 4.3 is the most
comprehensive and permits comparison of the corresponding
indexes with studies done in North America and elsewhere.
But it is equally desirable to have indexes for both race
and class in Antequera based on the same population, so
in Tables 4.2 and 4.4 the "class" population of 3,246
adult males has been used. Thus by comparing Tables 4.2
and 4.4 with Tables 4.5 and 4.6, we can more accurately
compare segregation by race versus class.

TABLE 4.1
Indexes of segregation for racial groupings, Antequera 1792
(household heads)

Peninsulars (263)	65.7
Creoles (2,417)	29.4
Castizos (107)	64.7
Mestizos (1,015)	34.9
Mulattoes (748)	39.6
Castizos Mestizos (1,870) Mulattoes	30.4
Mestizos Mulattoes (1,763)	30.3

TABLE 4.2
Indexes of segregation for racial groupings, Antequera 1792
(adult males)

Peninsulars (236)	70.0
Creoles (1,572)	33.9
Castizos (132)	60.6
Mestizos (702)	30.3
Mulattoes (589)	43.5
Castizos Mestizos (1,423) Mulattoes	37.3
Mestizos Mulattoes (1,291)	38.5

TABLE 4.3
Indexes of dissimilarity for revised racial groupings, Antequera
1792 (household heads)

	1	2	3	4
1. Peninsulars	-	64.7	70.7	73.1
2. Creoles	-	-	35.2	39.7
3. Castizos and Mestizos	-	-	-	45.6
4. Mulattoes	-	-	-	-

TABLE 4.4
Indexes of dissimilarity for revised racial groupings, Antequera
1792 (adult males)

	1	2	3	4
1. Peninsulars	-	68.0	76.5	76.6
2. Creoles	-	-	40.5	45.5
3. Castizos and Mestizos	-	-	-	47.7
4. Mulattoes	-	-	-	-

TABLE 4.5
Indexes of segregation for SEGs and selected occupations, Antequera
1792 (adult males only; Indians, Negroes, and clergy excluded)

Elite: Total (328)		64.6
Merchants (217)	76.2	
High royal officials (72)	77.1	
Large estate owners (42)	86.3	
Preindustrial Middle Groups: Total (803)		35.1
Professionals (210)	59.5	
High-status artisans (277)	48.5	
Small landholders, sharecroppers, and farm laborers (156)	67.5	
Traders (127)	64.5	
Lower Groups: Total (2,112)		40.9
Low-status artisans: total (1,900)	41.7	
Blacksmiths and farriers (128)	75.4	
Carpenters (133)	72.5	
Hatters (94)	74.2	
Shoemakers (217)	55.4	
Tailors (349)	43.8	
Weavers (284)	55.6	
Male servants (93)	78.7	
Unemployed (102)	65.7	

TABLE 4.6
Indexes of dissimilarity for SEGs, Antequera 1792 (adult males only;
Indians, Negroes, and clergy excluded)

	1	2	3
1. Elite	–	60.0	68.2
2. Preindustrial Middle Groups	–	–	37.2
3. Lower Groups	–	–	–

As an inspection of the maps (Figures 4.2 to 4.6) would suggest, among the racial groups in Table 4.1 we find a fairly high index of segregation for peninsular Spaniards (65.7), and fairly low ones for the creoles (29.4), mestizos (34.9), and mulattoes (39.6). The corresponding values in Table 4.2 are slightly higher because the population represented in that Table is smaller, but the differences are of the magnitude of only about 4.5 points and hence not significant. The one anomalous case (in both Tables) is that of the castizos (offspring of Spaniards and mestizos), who have an unexpectedly high index. The map of their actual distribution in Figure 4.4, however, makes it clear that this high score is due more to their small numbers than to their residential concentration per se. Lumping all of the castas (castizos, mestizos, and mulattoes) together, we get an index of segregation for non-whites of 30.4 (Table 4.1) or 37.3 (Table 4.2). As the maps confirm, there were no discernible "all white" areas of the city. To be sure, there was a clustering of whites in the manzanas around the Plaza de Armas, but even here the castas were well represented (Figure 4.10).

While peninsulars (many of whom were merchants) clustered in the central city, there seems to have been no obvious pattern for the other groups. For example, of the total of 303 facing blocks, 77 percent had three or more white (peninsular or creole) household heads, while 75 percent had three or more castas. Allowing for five or more per block, the respective proportions are 65 percent and 56 percent. Nor were there any particular areas of the city which uniformly contained fewer than five casta household heads per block. Indeed, only one principal street--Calle de Segovia--can be so characterized. It seems, then, that there was a very low degree of racial segregation among the mestizo and mulatto populations of Antequera. The indexes of dissimilarity in Tables 4.3 and 4.4 support this conclusion. While the peninsulars remain spatially distinct no matter who they are compared with, dissimilarity among the rest is noticeably lower. Especially noteworthy is the spatial heterogeneity of the large white creole group, a pattern which fits with their socioeconomic heterogeneity which I have discussed elsewhere. [17]

Turning now to the classes or SEGs in Table 4.5 and Figures 4.7 to 4.9, we find a similar pattern. The elite was highly centralized, with a segregation index of 64.6. Elite residence was densest on the east-west streets of Casas Consistoriales, Segovia, and Palacio, and the north-south street of San Francisco (also the most densely inhabited street in the city). These streets, together with the Plaza de Armas, contained 63 percent of the entire elite group (clergy excepted). Much more dispersed were the middle groups with a segregation index of

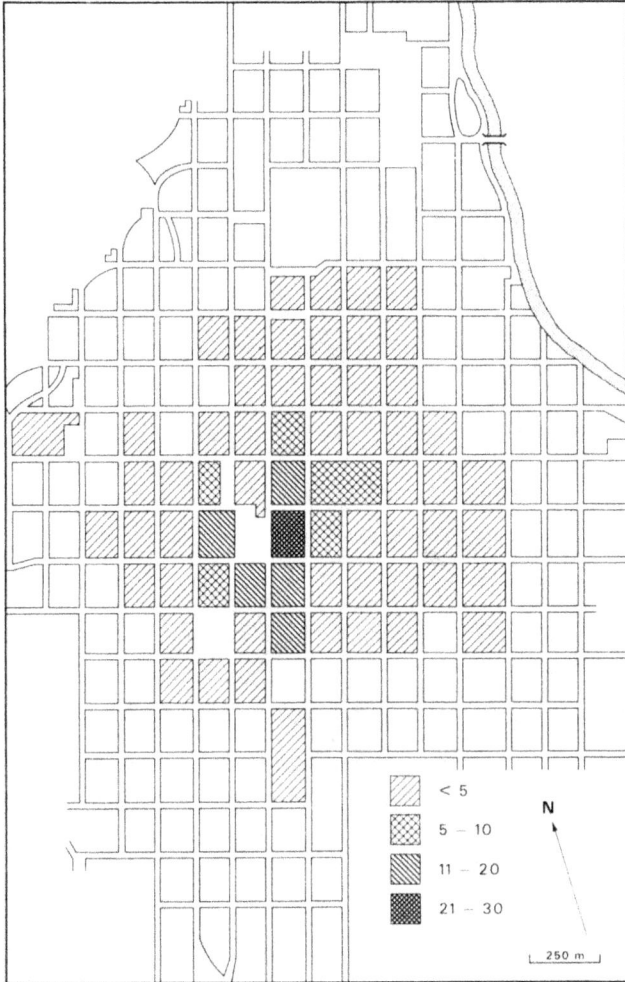

Figure 4.2 Peninsular Spaniards in Antequera by manzana, 1792
(N = 263 household heads)

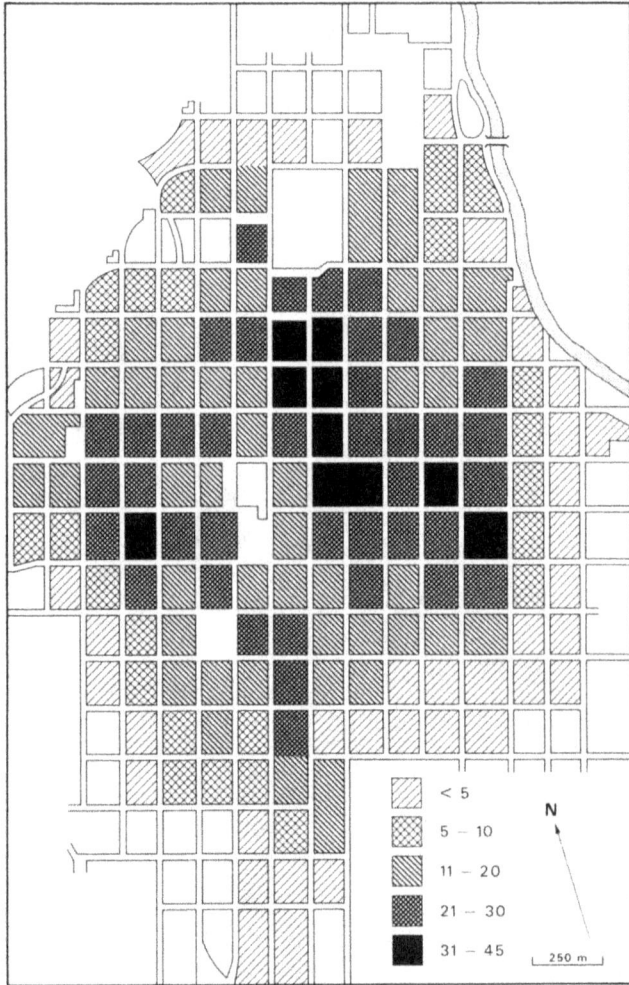

Figure 4.3 Creoles in Antequera by manzana, 1792
(N = 2,417 household heads)

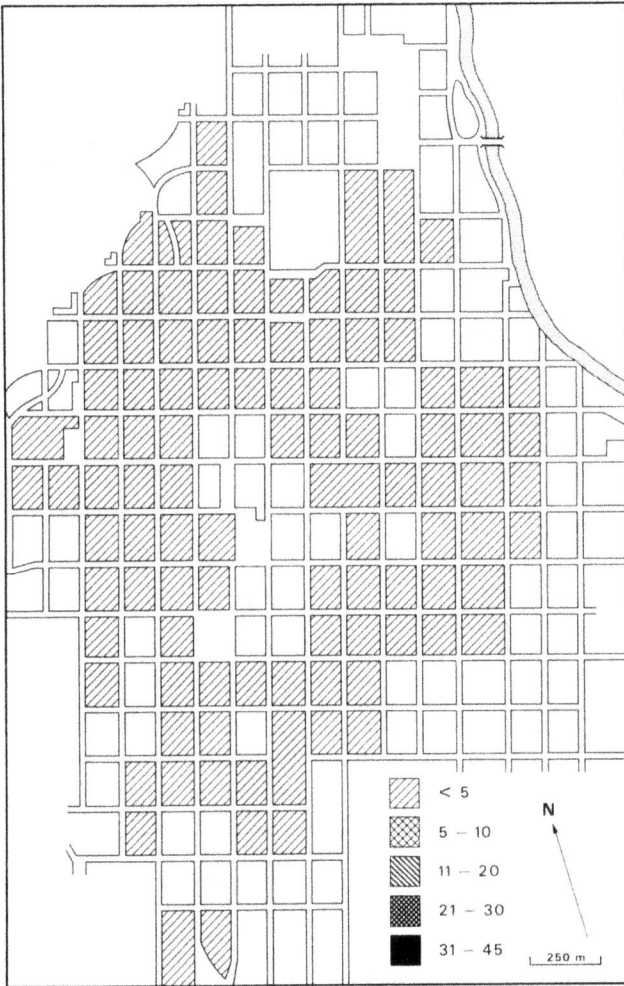

Figure 4.4 Castizos in Antequera by manzana, 1792
(N = 107 household heads)

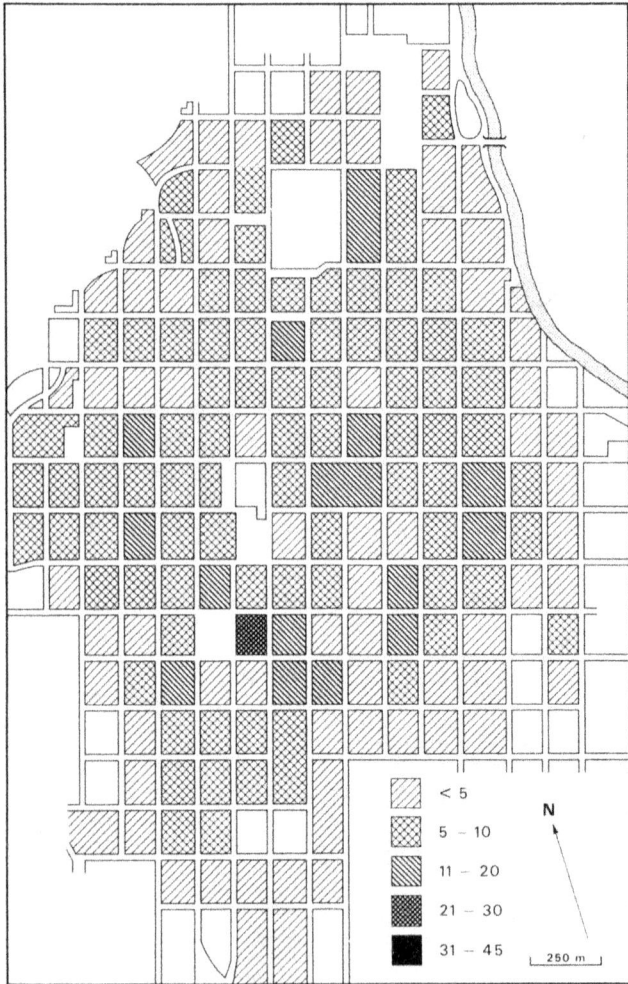

Figure 4.5 Mestizos in Antequera by manzana, 1792
(N = 1,015 household heads)

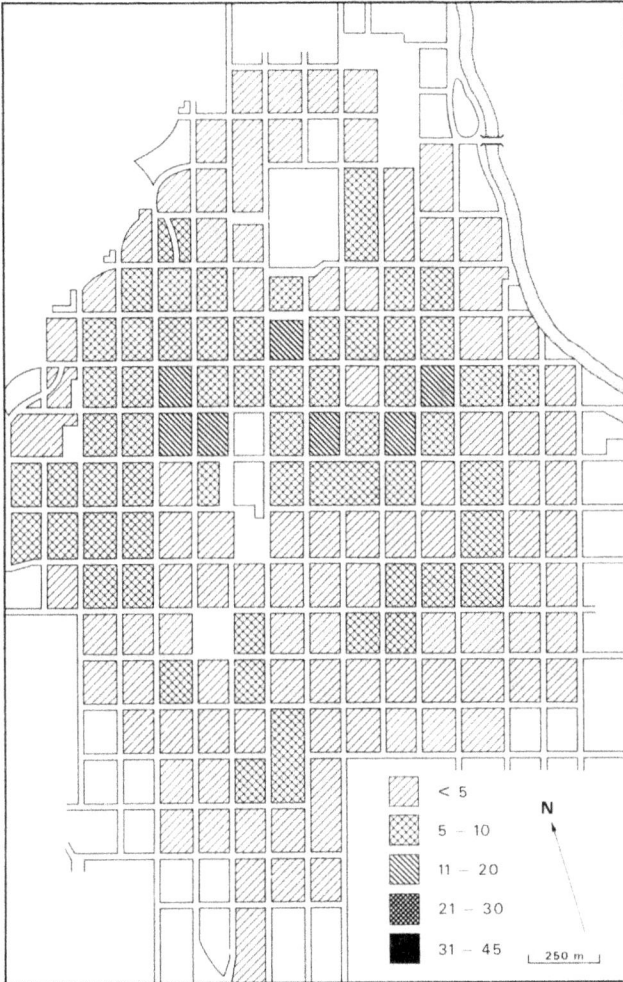

Figure 4.6 Mulattoes in Antequera by manzana, 1792
(N = 748 household heads)

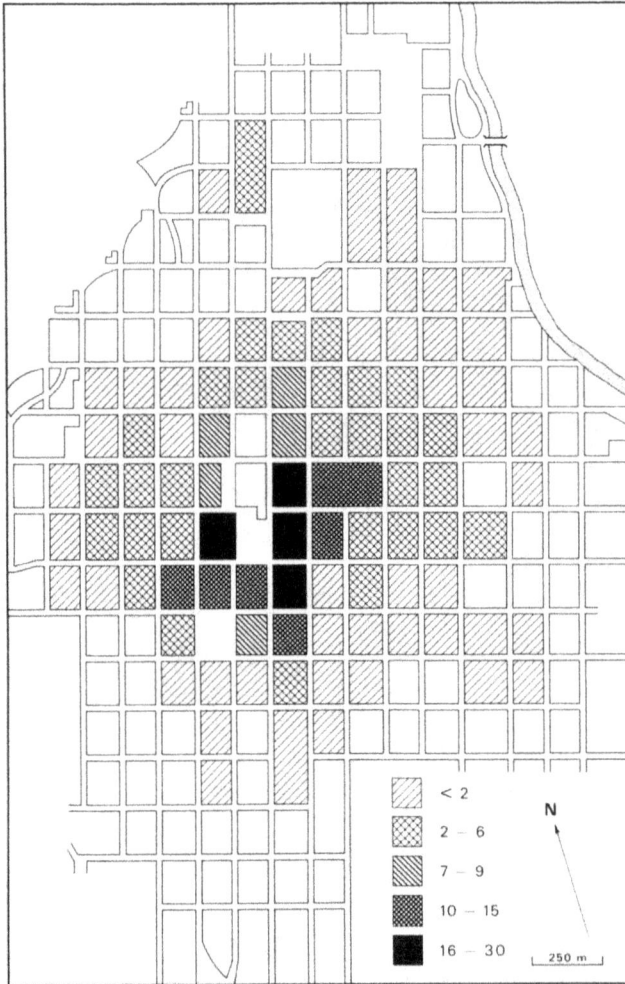

Figure 4.7   The elite of Antequera by manzana, 1792
(N = 331 adult males)

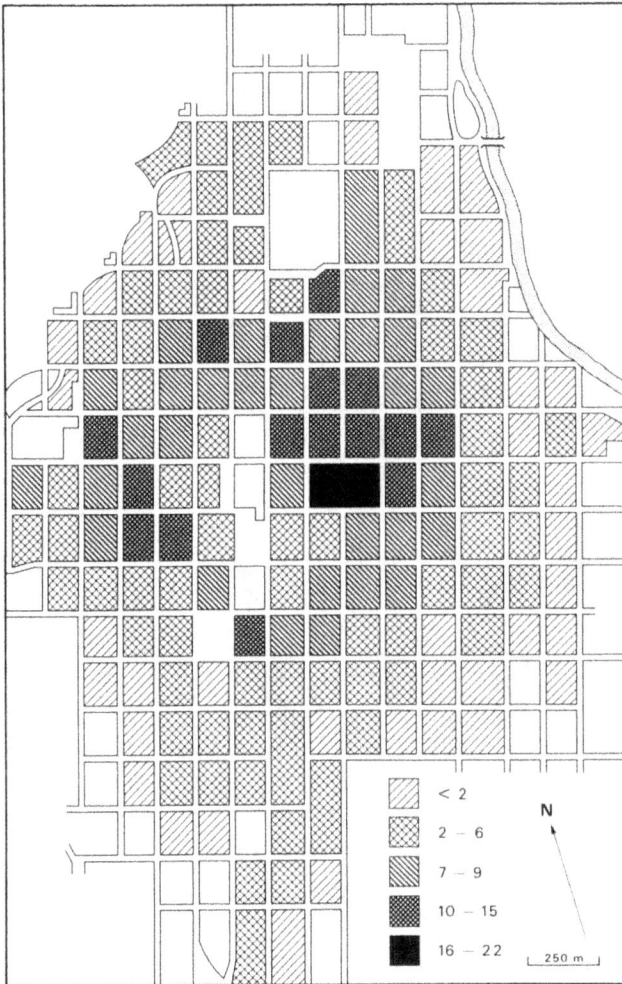

Figure 4.8 Preindustrial middle groups of Antequera
by manzana, 1792 (N = 803 adult males)

110

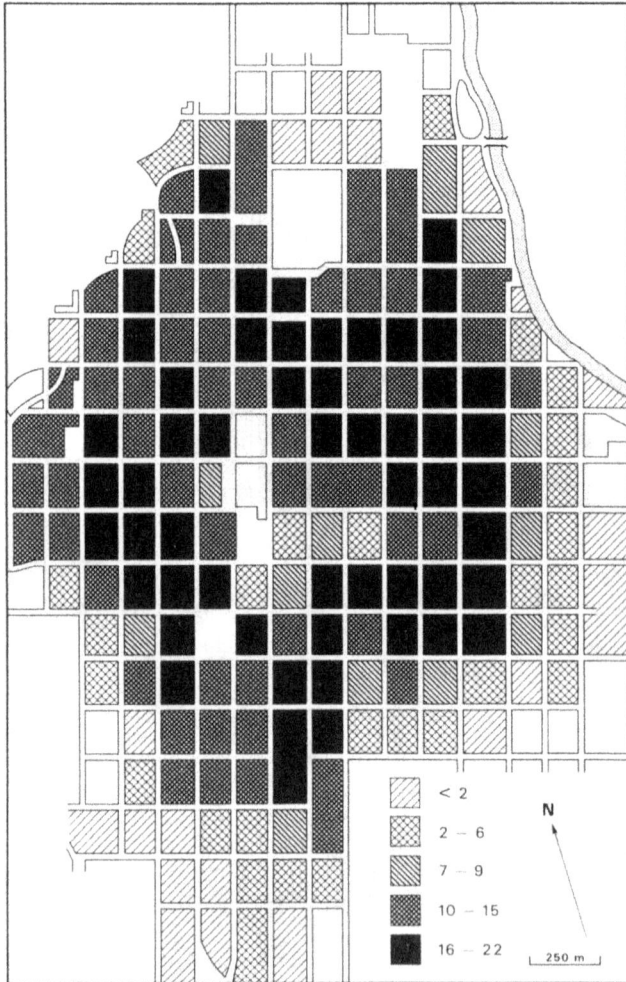

Figure 4.9 Preindustrial lower groups of Antequera by
manzana, 1792 (N = 2,112 adult males)

35.1 and the lower groups with an index of 40.9.

The indexes for the various occupational subgroupings are higher, reflecting in part the smaller size of these groups. Maps of these occupations (not included here) reveal some significant patterns, however. By far the most segregated segment of the elite was the merchant group, which clustered around the Plaza de Armas. High royal officials were somewhat more dispersed, and the large estate owners extremely (and surprisingly) so. Among the middle groups, the professionals showed a marked tendency to congregate on a few central streets, whereas the high-status artisans (including barber-surgeons, druggists, gilders, and silversmiths, among others) did not and were much more evenly distributed. Small landholders and traders (tratantes) were drawn more toward the periphery than the center. The low-status artisans were scattered throughout the city, though they were notably absent from the central core surrounding the Plaza de Armas. Some broad residential concentrations can be discerned for particular occupations: the majority of the blacksmiths lived on the east side of town; there was a concentration of carpenters in the southeast; hat-makers gravitated toward the periphery on the east, south, and west sides; shoemakers preferred the west and north-central locations; and weavers inhabited the northwest and southeast corners. The more numerous tailors were found in virtually all parts of town outside the central core. While a precise understanding of the factors responsible for these spatial clusterings of crafts remains elusive, surely considerations of kinship and compadrazgo, space needs, access to delivered raw materials, and proximity to labor in the Indian barrios were relevant variables.[18]

When particular occupations are combined into the broader class groups, however, much of the distinctiveness disappears. There was at least one representative of the middle groups in 77 percent of the city's facing blocks, and only 6 percent of the blocks did not contain at least one employed member of the lower groups. That the middle groups comprised the least spatially distinct category is not surprising in this preindustrial setting where class consciousness was only in its infancy. Table 4.6 shows that the dissimilarity between the middle and lower groups was correspondingly low.

A final comparison of the ecology of race and class can be made by contrasting Figures 4.10 and 4.11, which show the percentage of castas and lower groups residing in the city's 46 central manzanas. Despite the high prestige placed on center-city residence in colonial Latin American cities, we see that low-status people in both the racial and socioeconomic hierarchies had effectively penetrated the center of Antequera. While the Plaza de Armas was dominated by whites, who accounted for

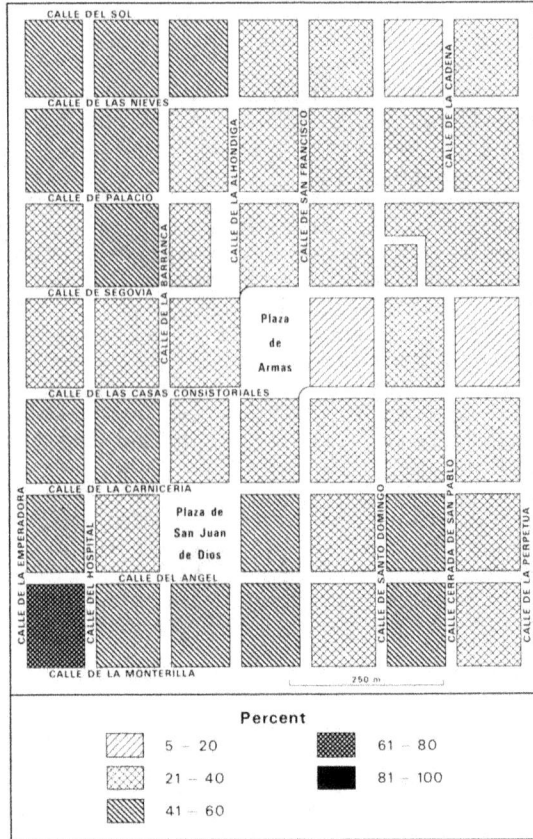

Figure 4.10 Percentage of castas in each of Antequera's
central manzanas, 1792 (household heads)

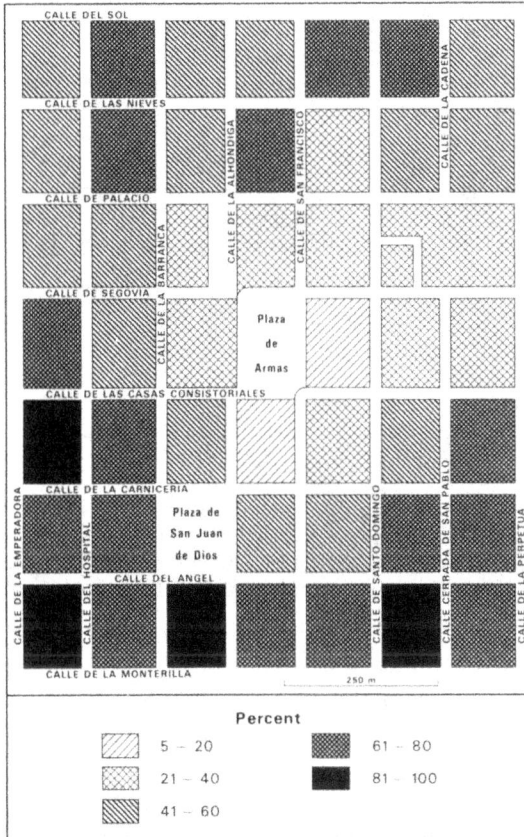

Figure 4.11 Percentage of preindustrial lower groups in each of Antequera's central manzanas, 1792 (adult males)

47 of its 52 household heads, the Plaza de San Juan de Dios—the city's principal market area—was home to 37 white and 38 casta households. Only two of the 39 adult males living in the Plaza de Armas belonged to the lower groups, but in the Plaza de San Juan de Dios, 36 were from the lower groups and 23 from the elite and middle groups. Taken as a whole, the area mapped in Figures 4.10 and 4.11 shows a slightly higher degree of segregation by class than by race. Although both the castas and the lower groups were underrepresented in the prestigious central city, the former were slightly <u>less</u> underrepresented than the latter. Compared to their average numbers per manzana in the city as a whole, adult males of the lower groups were underrepresented in the central area by 11 percent, whereas casta household heads were underrepresented by only 5 percent. The difference is small, but it suggests that segregation by class was at least as significant (if not more so) as segregation by race in Antequera in 1792.

IV

Further research on other colonial Latin American cities is needed in order to determine the broader significance of the case dealt with in this paper. Despite its importance in New Spain, Antequera was still a small, provincial city in the eighteenth century, and it may well be that patterns of segregation were significantly different in major capitals such as Mexico City or Lima. For the case at hand, however, the following conclusions may be drawn:

1. In 1792, Antequera had no "all white" or all Spanish areas apart from a few manzanas in the central core.
2. Except for the center and the outlying Indian barrios not included in this study, all neighborhoods and most blocks were racially mixed.
3. While the peninsular Spaniards and the elite (especially the merchants) were markedly segregated, the other racial groups and SEGs were not.
4. The socioeconomic diversity of the large creole group is underscored by its diversity of residence. Membership in the white, Spanish category was no guarantee of a high position in the socioeconomic hierarchy nor a prestigious, centrally-located residence.
5. Taken as a whole the residential analysis provides support for the proposition that in 1792, there was no longer a viable system of racially defined estates in Antequera. By this time, class had become just as important as race as a

determinant of social status in the stratification system.

NOTES

1. See David J. Robinson, "Córdoba en 1779: la Ciudad y la
Campaña," in Raul C. Rey Balmaceda (ed.), Homenaje a Federico A.
Daus (Buenos Aires, Sociedad Argentina de Estudios Geográficos,
1979), pp. 279-312; David J. Robinson and Michael M. Swann, "Geographical Interpretations of the Hispanic American Colonial City: A
Case Study of Caracas in the Late Eighteenth Century," in R. J. Tata
(ed.), Latin America: Search for Geographic Explanations (Boca Raton,
1975), pp. 1-15; Lyman L. Johnson and Susan Migden Socolow, "Population and Space in Eighteenth-Century Buenos Aires," in David J.
Robinson (ed.), Social Fabric and Spatial Structure in Colonial
Latin America (Ann Arbor, 1979), pp. 339-368. For a good discussion
of methodology and mapping techniques see David J. Robinson, "The
Analysis of Eighteenth Century Spanish American Cities: Some Problems and Alternative Solutions," Discussion Paper Series No. 4, Department of Geography, Syracuse University, 1975.
2. I want to thank William T. Markham for his criticisms of an
earlier draft of this paper and for his help with computer program-
ming. Thanks are also due to David M. Cook for assistance with the
computing. For the preparation and drawing of the maps I am deeply
indebted to Julia H. Chance, Lancha A. Chance, and especially David
J. Robinson and Valmor Philp. All interpretations in this paper are
my own, however, as are any shortcomings of the analysis.
3. See especially Otis Dudley Duncan and Beverly Duncan, "A
Methodological Analysis of Segregation Indexes," American Sociologi-
cal Review 20 (1955), pp. 210-217; Duncan and Duncan, "Residential
Distribution and Occupational Stratification," American Journal of
Sociology 60 (1955), pp. 493-503; Reynolds Farley, "Residential Seg-
regation in Urbanized Areas of the United States in 1970: An Analy-
sis of Social Class and Racial Differences," Demography 14 (1977),
pp. 497-518; Ceri Peach (ed.), Urban Social Segregation (London and
New York, 1975); Karl E. Taeuber and Alma F. Taeuber, Negroes in
Cities (Chicago, 1965). For comparative studies done outside the
United States see Peach, op. cit.; Kent P. Schwirian and Jesús Rico-
Velasco, "The Residential Distribution of Status Groups in Puerto
Rico's Metropolitan Areas," Demography 8 (1971), pp. 81-90; Surinder
K. Mehta, "Patterns of Residence in Poona, India, by Caste and Reli-
gion: 1822-1965," Demography 6 (1969), pp. 473-491.
4. For examples, see Kathleen Neils Conzen, "Patterns of Resi-
dence in Early Milwaukee," in Leo F. Schnore (ed.), The New Urban
History: Quantitative Explorations by American Historians (Princeton,
1975), pp. 145-183; Theodore Hershberg, et. al., "A Tale of Three
Cities: Blacks and Immigrants in Philadelphia: 1850-1900, 1930 and
1970," Annals of the American Academy of Politics and Social
Sciences 441 (1979), pp. 55-81; Nathan Kantrowitz, "Racial and Ethnic Residential Segregation: Boston, 1830-1970," Ibid., pp. 41-54;

Zane L. Miller, "Urban Blacks in the South, 1865-1920: An Analysis of Some Quantitative Data on Richmond, Savannah, New Orleans, Louisville, and Birmingham," in The New Urban History, pp. 184-204; Leo F. Schnore and Peter R. Knights, "Residence and Social Structure: Boston in the ante-Bellum Period," in Stephan Thernstrom and Richard Sennett (eds.), Nineteenth-Century Cities: Essays in the New Urban History (New Haven, 1969), pp. 247-257; Paul B. Worthman, "Working Class Mobility in Birmingham, Alabama, 1880-1914," in Tamara K. Hareven (ed.), Anonymous Americans: Explorations in Nineteenth-Century Social History (Englewood Cliffs, 1971), pp. 172-213.

5. The census is located in the Archivo General de la Nación (Mexico City), Ramo de Padrones, 13.

6. The map is included in an unpublished manuscript by José María Murguía y Galardi entitled Extracto general que abraza la estadística toda en su primera y segunda parte del estado de Guaxaca y ha reunido de orden del Supremo Gobierno y yntendente de provincia en clase de los cesantes José María Murguía y Galardi (1827). It is located in the Benson Latin American Collection of the University of Texas-Austin.

7. In addition to works cited in note 1 above, contributions to the study of Latin American urban ecology include S. D. Markman, "The Gridiron Town Plan and the Caste System in Colonial Central America," in Richard P. Schaedel, Jorge E. Hardoy, and Nora Scott Kinzer (eds.), Urbanization in the Americas from its Beginnings to the Present (The Hague, 1978), pp. 471-490; Theodore Caplow, "The Social Ecology of Guatemala City," Social Forces 28 (1949), pp. 113-133; F. Dotson and L. O. Dotson, "Ecological Trends in the City of Guadalajara, Mexico," Social Forces 32 (1954), pp. 367-374; A. T. Hansen, "The Ecology of a Latin American City," in E. B. Reuter (ed.), Race and Culture Contacts (New York, 1934), pp. 124-142; H. B. Hawthorn and A. B. Hawthorn, "The Shape of a City," Sociology and Social Research 33 (1948), pp. 87-91; N. S. Hayner, "Mexico City: Its Growth and Configuration," American Journal of Sociology 50 (1945), pp. 295-304; Leo F. Schnore, "On the Spatial Structure of Cities in the Two Americas," in Philip M. Hauser and Leo F. Schnore (eds.), The Study of Urbanization (New York, 1965), pp. 347-398.

8. A more extensive plan of Antequera and its environs which shows these places as well as the location of churches and government offices can be found in John K. Chance, Race and Class in Colonial Oaxaca (Stanford, 1978), p. 35.

9. For further details see John K. Chance and William B. Taylor, "Estate and Class in a Colonial City: Oaxaca in 1792," Comparative Studies in Society and History 19 (1977), pp. 454-487; or Chance, Race and Class, Chapter 6.

10. Chance, Race and Class, pp. 194, 181.

11. Our interpretation of Antequera's stratification system has recently been subjected to a detailed critique by Robert McCaa, Stuart B. Schwartz, and Arturo Grubessich in "Race and Class in Colonial Latin America: A Critique," Comparative Studies in Society and History 21 (1979), pp. 421-433. Taylor and I respond in detail to these criticisms in "Estate and Class: A Reply," Comparative Studies in Society and History 21 (1979), pp. 434-442. The findings in the present paper are germane to this debate and provide, I believe,

further support for our position that both racial _and_ class factors were at work.

12. For more on Antequera's urban Indians see John K. Chance, "The Urban Indian in Colonial Oaxaca," _American Ethnologist_ 3 (1976), pp. 603-632.

13. Duncan and Duncan, "Residential Distribution and Occupational Stratification."

14. Nathan Kantrowitz, _Ethnic and Racial Segregation in the New York Metropolis_ (New York, 1973), p. 15.

15. In their comprehensive study of non-white residential segregation in 207 U.S. cities in 1960, Taeuber and Taeuber (_op. cit._, pp. 34, 36) obtained a range of values from 60.4 to 98.1. Half the cities had values above 87.8; the mean value was 86.2. On the whole, they found no significant differences among them:

> In the urban United States, there is a very high degree of segregation of the residences of whites and Negroes. This is true for cities in all regions of the country and for all types of cities--large and small, industrial and commercial, metropolitan and suburban. It is true whether there are hundreds of thousands of Negro residents, or only a few thousand. Residential segregation prevails regardless of the relative economic status of the white and Negro residents. It occurs regardless of the character of local laws and policies, and regardless of the extent of other forms of segregation or discrimination (_ibid._, pp. 35-36).

16. Taeuber and Taeuber, _Negroes in Cities_, p. 215.

17. Chance, _Race and Class_.

18. I am indebted to J. Douglas Uzzell for this observation.

5
Marriage Patterns
and Regional Interaction
in Late Colonial Nueva Galicia

Linda L. Greenow

INTRODUCTION

Colonial Mexican marriage records provide a useful measure of social interaction between racial groups, and spatial interaction between a wide range of settlements.[1] Here, marriage registers of eight parishes in late colonial Nueva Galicia, an area which has attracted the attention of almost no historical demographers in the past, provided the data base for such an analysis.[2] All the records were legible, and complete for the periods chosen for study, and contained both racial and place of origin information for the great majority of the marriage partners. Three five-year sample periods were chosen for study representing developmental phases of the mid- and late-eighteenth century and early nineteenth-century. These periods were chosen on the basis of completeness and comparability of records for all eight parishes, and on the basis of other events which shed light on critical developments in the area, such as the "año de hambre" of 1786, the opening of the port of San Blas in 1772, and the population enumeration of 1791.

It is important to remember that, for the most part, the marriage registers studied here reveal only the places of "origin" and residence of marriage partners. A person who came to a parish center from some other <u>pueblo</u> or hacienda, either inside or outside the parish, was said to be an "<u>originario</u>" of that place. This term was undoubtedly used to distinguish a person's birthplace or previous place of residence from his residence within a parish at the time of marriage, and the priests usually wrote that a bride or groom was, for example, "originario de Agualulco y residente en este pueblo desde ocho años." But the term "originario" cannot be defined any more precisely than that. For some people it probably referred to birthplace, since they were described as having arrived in the parish center when they were infants. Others were "originarios" of a town they had once lived in,

but from which they had since moved (possibly several
times) and had only been a "residente" for a short time
in the parish where they were married. It is therefore
not clear whether a person's place of "origin" was his
birthplace, any previous place or residence, or his most
recent place of residence for some period.

It is also difficult to determine the limits of the
term "residente," which referred to both long-term residents and recent arrivals. (In several parishes, the
length of time of residence was not indicated at all.)
Two people in Tepic married outsiders who had been "residentes" for only one week, and in several other cases,
the priest identified "residentes" who had been in Tepic
"muy poco tiempo." Whether or not these recent arrivals
had established a permanent home and became a part of the
community before marriage is not at all clear.

Where the marriage partners took up residence after
marriage is simply not known. Out-migration cannot be
measured through the marriage documents unless an entire
region is considered a closed unit so that the individuals leaving a given parish and marrying in another together make up the out-migrating population from that location.[3]

One of several possible migration scenarios could
therefore have taken place in each marriage: first, both
partners could have been "originarios" of the parish center where they were married and either remained there or
moved away; second, one or both partners could have moved
to the parish during childhood, where they lived for a
long period of time, and either remained there permanently after marrying or moved away; and third, one partner
could have arrived in the parish and married a resident
there, planning either to return home after the ceremony
or remain there as a resident.

Not knowing which of these situations was the case
in a given marriage places temporal and geographic limitations on the use of marriage registers for measuring
migration flows within the general population. The registers capture a pattern of migration of individuals at
only one critical period in the life-cycle, which happened to be recorded by the Church, and the information
on previous places of residence is ambiguous. For this
reason, the populations referred to in marriage migration
analysis are better distinguished as "marrying populations," since the conclusions drawn about them should not
be assumed to be characteristic of the general population.
The term "migration" should be qualified as "marriage migration" since the population movements that can be studied through marriage registers of a given parish are
movements of people who married in that parish center
after their arrival there.

The interaction represented by marriage migrants had
both social and economic implications, since much of the

population movement of all kinds that occurred in colonial Mexico was a function of economic opportunity, and
since settlement patterns, miscegenation, population concentration and economic growth were all affected by population movement. These economic and social consequences,
however, were functions of casual, transitory population
movement as well as permanent residential changes, and
care must be taken not to assume that it is only the latter which is indicated in the marriage registers.

THE STUDY AREA

     A total of approximately 5200 marriages were ana-
lyzed from eight parishes in late colonial Nueva Galicia:
Tonalá, Tlaquepaque, Zapopan, Chapala, Tequila, Ameca,
Compostela and Tepic (Table 5.1 and Figure 5.1). The
parish boundaries were not determined, but since pueblos
and haciendas within the parishes' jurisdictions were indicated in the registers it was possible to interpolate
such boundaries and locate them on base maps.[4] These
parishes were not the largest in Nueva Galicia, but they
played important roles in the region's economic development at various points in time.[5]
     Zapopan, Tlaquepaque and Tonalá were Indian parishes
on the outskirts of the capital city of Guadalajara. Today, Zapopan and Tlaquepaque have been absorbed within
the city limits and both Tlaquepaque and Tonalá are regional artisan centers for the production of pottery and
glassware. The development of the relationship between
the capital city and Tlaquepaque is unclear before the
late nineteenth century, when city residents began con-
structing summer homes in the pueblo. The surrounding
agricultural lands of Zapopan and Tonalá were the source
of wealth of some of the city's powerful landowning families.
     Tequila, Chapala and Ameca were centers of a pros-
perous agricultural region based on the production of
maize, wheat and livestock. Many of the wealthiest and
most powerful hacendados of the audiencia derived their
wealth from family-based agglomerations of haciendas and
ranchos in this region. These landowners consolidated
commercial interests with city-based merchants, or owned
tanneries, mills and shops of their own. They also
served often in the municipal government of Guadalajara
and therefore held both financial and political power.
     Compostela and Tepic represent a commercial and
livestock sector of Nueva Galicia's economy which played
a critical role in late eighteenth-century economic
growth. When the port of San Blas opened in 1772, merchants in Tepic emerged not only as traders but as finan-
ciers for the development of western ranching and mining.
Whether Compostela accompanied Tepic's rise to power has

TABLE 5.1
Frequency of Marriages

Parish	1759-1763	1790-1794	1805-1810	Total	%
Tlaquepaque	111	93	124	328	6.2
Tonalá	219	212	187	618	11.7
Zapopan	225	429	300	954	18.1
Chapala	151	160	184	495	9.4
Ameca	147	436	453	1036	19.7
Tequila	153	157	170	480	9.1
Compostela	197	251	100	548	10.4
Tepic	248*	273	286	807	15.3
Total	1,451	2,011	1,804	5,266	100.0

*Figures for Tepic are for 1779-1783.

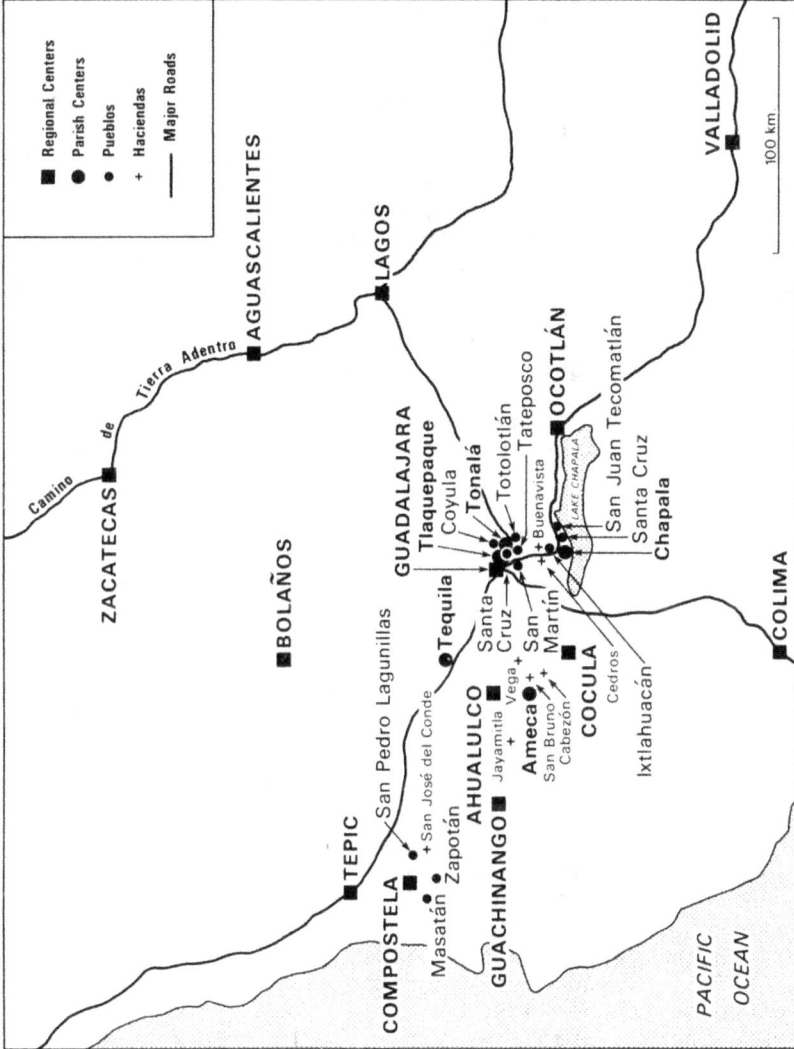

Figure 5.1 Settlements in Nueva Galicia

yet to be established.

PATTERNS OF INTERRACIAL MARRIAGE

Because marriage was a function of the availability
of appropriate partners, any variable affecting the prob-
ability of marriage for various segments of the population also affected the set of marriages which resulted,
which in turn forms the base of data for marriage migration analysis. Race in particular is a critical variable
to examine, since it is one of the few descriptors consistently indicated in the marriage registers. Age, occupation, and previous marital status of marriage partners are sometimes indicated, but only inconsistently
through time and for different places.

The eight parishes represent a cross-section of marrying populations of a variety of racial mixtures (Tables
5.2 and 5.3). Zapopan's, Tonalá's and Tlaquepaque's marrying populations were the most homogeneous, almost entirely Indian. Tequila's and Chapala's marrying populations were principally composed of Indians as well, with
large proportions of Spaniards, mulatos and mestizos.
Ameca's, Compostela's and Tepic's marrying populations
were fairly balanced mixtures of Indians, Spaniards and
mulatos.

The populations of Zapopan, Tonalá, and Tlaquepaque
seldom married outside their racial groups (Table 5.4).
Interracial marriages never accounted for more than
eleven percent of all parish marriages. This is not surprising since there were few non-Indians in the marrying
population. Interracial marriage is therefore best considered by studying Chapala, Tequila, Ameca, Compostela
and Tepic. The general trends for racial intermarriage
in these parishes are shown in Table 5.4, in which the
Cook and Borah method of describing racial marriage mixing is utilized.[6] The index is the ratio between the observed number of marriages taking place, and the number
of such marriages that would be expected to take place if
marriages between the races was a random process, dependent only on the relative proportions of partners of each
racial group. When the ratio is greater than one, more
marriages than expected have taken place between the two
races involved, and when the ratio falls below one, then
the converse is the case.

In general, Spaniards tended increasingly to marry
members of other socio-racial groups, a fact not noted
elsewhere in eighteenth-century Mexico; they became as a
group more exogamous as time passed. On the other hand,
Indians and mulatos became increasingly endogamous. It
is clear, as elsewhere, that the patterns of intermarriage between other racial groups changed inconsistently
throughout the period, but with two exceptions: marriages

TABLE 5.2
Race of marriage partners

Parish	Percent of marrying population						
	Spanish	Mulatos	Indians	Mestizos	Coyotes	Other	Not in- dicated
Tlaquepaque	1.8	0	97.6	0.3	--	--	0.3
Tonalá	4.2	0.6	92.7	1.3	--	--	0.1
Zapopan	5.5	1.1	90.5	1.8	0.8	0.2	--
Chapala	12.9	10.4	63.1	5.0	5.1	0.9	2.6
Ameca	29.9	28.4	23.1	11.0	4.7	1.2	1.6
Tequila	32.2	(7.9)**	44.1	11.5	2.5	0.5	1.3
Compostela	21.0	31.4	23.4	2.4	7.6	0.5	13.9
Tepic	23.2	29.6	19.7	9.5	5.1	0.8	12.1

**Mestizos

TABLE 5.3
Racial distribution of marrying populations

	Percent of marrying population		
	1759-1763	1790-1794	1805-1810
Chapala			
Spanish	8.3	12.6	15.5
Mulato	10.6	12.3	9.5
Indian	61.9	67.9	64.7
Ameca			
Spanish	46.3	24.9	29.5
Mulato	1.0	28.7	37.1
Indian	43.2	23.2	16.6
Tequila			
Spanish	22.2	30.9	42.7
Mestizo	16.3	11.1	7.3
Indian	42.5	46.8	43.0
Compostela			
Spanish	21.8	19.1	24.0
Mulato	31.9	30.3	33.0
Indian	22.6	24.7	22.5
Tepic			
Spanish	17.7*	21.6	29.4
Mulato	30.8	20.9	36.7
Indian	11.9	28.2	18.4

*Figures for Tepic are for 1779-1784.

TABLE 5.4
Mean ratios of observed to expected marriages in all parishes

1759-1763

| | | Males | | |
		Spanish	Indian	Mixed
	Spanish	4.33	0.01	0.91
Females	Indian	0.03	2.13	0.49
	Mixed	1.61	0.52	1.49

1790-1794

| | | Males | | |
		Spanish	Indian	Mixed
	Spanish	2.66	0.46	0.38
Females	Indian	0.30	2.17	0.60
	Mixed	0.90	0.46	1.96

1805-1810

| | | Males | | |
		Spanish	Indian	Mixed
	Spanish	2.75	0.22	0.54
Females	Indian	0.25	2.54	0.76
	Mixed	0.64	0.53	1.90

of <u>casta</u> women to Indian men became more common, while
the marriages between Spanish females and Indian men became quite common later, especially among non-Indians
(Table 5.5). The most noticeable feature of interracial
marriage in Chapala was that Indians, which formed a
large part of the population, never married into any
other single racial group at a significant rate.

In Ameca, racial barriers to marriage became less
important through time among Indians as their proportion
of the population decreased. By the turn of the century,
only 16.6 percent of marriage partners were Indian;
clearly they could not expect to marry other Indians, and
nearly two-thirds of them married exogamously (Tables 5.3
and 5.5). The large increase in marriages between Indians and non-Indians between 1759-1763 and 1790-1794 de-
serves further examination. The appearance in the second
period of a large mulato population with highly exogamous
tendencies suggests that it was the Indian-mulato marriage that increased the rate of exogamous marriage for
Indians. An examination of the rates of marriage between
Indians and each of the other races shows that it was the
collective increase in numbers of mulatos, mestizos,
coyotes and other racial groups which gave Indians opportunities to marry outside their race. The possibility of
marriage to a Spaniard remained minimal.

In Tequila, the general trend for increasing racial
exogamy was reversed (Table 5.5). Mestizos, which always
formed the smallest proportion of the marrying population,
consistently married into other races (Tables 5.3 and
5.6). However, by the end of the century, mestizos and
other mixed racial groups formed a relatively insignificant portion of the marrying population; over 85 percent
of the marriage partners were either Spaniards or Indians,
the two racial groups which were least likely to inter-
marry. This strengthening of racial boundaries in marriage can be seen in the pattern of specific interracial
pairings; the only significant interracial marriages by
the final period took place between mulato males and mes-
tiza females. Intermarriage between Indians and Spaniards, the largest part of the marrying population, was
almost nonexistent.

A similar pattern occurred in Compostela, where the
1790s witnessed an overall dip in interracial marriage
which was present in all three major racial groups (Tables 5.5 and 5.6). The mestizo and coyote groups were
always the most exogamous races. In the 1790s, they
formed a very low percentage of the marrying population
and the consequences were illustrated in lower exogamous
rates among Spaniards, Indians and mulatos, the racial
groups with whom they normally intermarried.

In Tepic, interracial marriage was a function of the
links between the mulato and Indian populations. In the
second period, the proportion of mulatos in the marrying

TABLE 5.5
Percent of racially exogamous marriages

	1759–1763	1790–1794	1805–1809
Tlaquepaque	0	3.2	3.2
Tonalá	5.5	3.8	1.1
Zapopan	1.8	8.2	10.7
Chapala	3.3	21.2	29.5
Ameca	14.9	31.2	32.2
Tequila	43.8	38.2	30.9
Compostela	24.1	9.2	26.0
Tepic	16.3*	37.7	26.1

*Figures for Tepic are for 1779–1783.

TABLE 5.6
Racial exogamy by racial group

	Percent of marriages in each period		
	1759–1763	1790–1794	1805–1809
Chapala			
Spanish	43.8	41.7	64.3
Mulatos	23.6	60.0	75.0
Indians	13.0	17.1	24.4
Ameca			
Spanish	31.6	22.1	26.2
Mulatos	**	52.9	41.0
Indians	1.6	50.4	59.8
Tequila			
Spanish	38.1	43.5	32.1
Mestizos	86.4	75.0	90.9
Indians	44.7	41.9	38.6
Compostela			
Spanish	40.7	25.5	45.2
Mulatos	47.6	21.2	50.0
Indians	43.9	22.9	56.7
Tepic			
Spanish	26.3*	24.6	27.4
Mulatos	33.8	71.6	33.3
Indians	16.3	37.7	26.1

*Figures for Tepic are for 1779–1783.
**Insufficient cases.

population was the lowest of the three periods (Table
5.3). With few of their own racial group to marry, mulatos married mestizos and Indians. The effect on the Indian marrying population was clear; at that same time,
the Indian proportion of the marrying population reached
a peak, along with its overall tendency to marry into
other racial groups.

What were the essential principles of interracial
marriage in eighteenth-century Nueva Galicia? First, a
significant change in exogamy rates of any one segment of
the population had widespread consequences. The set of
potential marriage partners at one point in time was the-
oretically a zero-sum population. If, as in Ameca, Spanish females tended to marry men of other races, then the
chances for other females to marry outside their racial
group were increased. If, as in the cases of Tequila and
Compostela, the only racial groups with exogamous tendencies formed a small part of the population, then everyone's chances to marry outside their race were reduced,
and Indians were the least likely to find partners of
other racial groups.

Second, in parishes with large Indian populations
such as Zapopan, Tonalá, Chapala and Tlaquepaque, relatively little interaction took place between Indians and
non-Indians. The non-Indian may have been highly exogamous with respect to marriage, but little of that interaction took place with Indians. This occurred even in
the pueblos of Tonalá, Tlaquepaque and Zapopan, which
were on the outskirts of the city of Guadalajara and its
large population of many racial types.[7] The city's population, however close to those parishes, apparently did
not send potential marriage partners to these parishes.
Whether or not Indians left these parishes to move into
Guadalajara and marry there cannot be determined from
these data. It is clear, however, that an Indian had a
better chance for upward social mobility by moving out of
these parishes to a small town where the Indian population was only part of a heterogeneous society.

Finally, in a racially mixed population such as
Tepic's, in which the Indian population did marry across
racial lines, demographic changes which shifted the balance of racial groups in the marrying population led to
variable rates of racial exogamy. In parishes with a
fluctuating mixture of racial groups, there was insufficient evidence of a direct correlation between the
changes in a racial group's proportion of the total marrying population and its rate of exogamy. Rather, racial
exogamy in marriage depended on the balance of all racial
groups and their tendency to interact. If Spaniards and
Indians composed the majority of the population, racial
exogamy was less likely than if the Spaniards had been
mestizos or mulatos. Brading and Wu demonstrate a long-
term trend in the integration of mulato and Indian

populations through intermarriage in León.[8]   This also
occurred in areas of Nueva Galicia where the distinctions
between Indians and non-Indians were not as strong as in
Tonalá and Tlaquepaque.   In those areas, when demographic
conditions raised the exogamous marriage rate of Indians,
the increase came from marriage to mulatos and, to a
lesser extent, mestizos and coyotes.   This seems to have
been a widespread phenomenon; preferences of Indians for
these racial groups have also been noted in Parral,
Guanajuato and San Luis Potosí.[9]   To compare rates of
exogamy for racial groups of different places and times
does not necessarily indicate cultural biases or similarities; the differences in rates may simply reflect variation in the population bases which generated the set of
marriage partners.

INTER-PARISH MARRIAGE

The same parishes with nearly homogeneous Indian
populations and low rates of racial exogamy also had relatively closed populations with respect to spatial exogamy (Table 5.7).   Few people from outside the parishes of
Tonalá and Tlaquepaque married into the local populations.
The case of Zapopan is somewhat more complex.   A higher
proportion of marriages involved spatial exogamy than in
Tonalá and Tlaquepaque; however, almost all the marriage
partners resided in the parish at the time of marriage
and had lived there all their lives.
Five of the parishes had significant levels of interaction with other parishes in western Mexico (Table
5.7).   Chapala's residents married outsiders the least
frequently of the five; Tequila's were the most exogamous.
However, frequency of exogamous marriage, while it indicates the level of interaction between a parish's population and those of other parishes, does not indicate the
degree of localization of that interaction.   Mean marriage migration distances for the five parishes show that
Compostela and Tepic, on the western fringes of colonial
settlements, drew marriage partners from a much wider
field than the parishes closer to the administrative,
agricultural and population center of Nueva Galicia (Table 5.8).   Disaggregating the mean distances by race
shows that it was principally Spaniards migrating from
the far north and the Bajío to Tepic and Compostela who
extended their marriage fields far beyond those of the
more central parishes (Table 5.9).   What is surprising,
however, is the distances covered by Indians coming into
these areas.   In every case except Chapala, Indians migrated further than the mixed racial groups.   In some
cases, Indians migrated as far as Spaniards.
Mapping the marriage fields illustrates some of the
complexities of marriage migration.   Except for an

TABLE 5.7
Proportion of inter-parish marriages

Parish	1759-1763	1790-1794	1805-1809
Tlaquepaque	1.8	9.7	8.9
Tonalá	9.8	7.2	6.9
Zapopan	10.4	14.6	18.1
Chapala	13.5	17.6	18.8
Ameca	22.5	25.5	16.0
Tequila	45.2	42.1	46.0
Compostela	21.8	4.4	18.0
Tepic	47.7*	27.9	39.7

*Figures for Tepic are for 1779-1783.

132

TABLE 5.8
Mean migration distances (kilometers)

Parish	1759-1763	1790-1794	1805-1809
Chapala	61.7	66.5	51.5
Ameca	75.9	69.2	58.9
Tequila	78.2	88.5	62.5
Compostela	115.9	86.7	91.9
Tepic	144.1*	134.1	113.0

*Figures for Tepic are for 1779-1783.

TABLE 5.9
Racial variation in mean migration distances (kilometers)

	1759-1763	1790-1794	1805-1809	Total
Chapala				
Spanish	60.5	52.8	64.3	60.0
Castas	66.5	78.8	42.3	63.9
Indians	47.0	65.9	37.3	50.3
Ameca				
Spanish	77.9	70.6	76.6	74.2
Castas	48.0	64.7	49.9	59.5
Indians	76.0	75.6	35.5	62.8
Tequila				
Spanish	93.1	103.1	63.0	79.7
Castas	69.7	53.5	32.8	60.9
Indians	75.5	100.2	62.5	77.7
Compostela				
Spanish	126.5	70.9	142.2	154.5
Castas	104.0	88.6	82.4	109.6
Indians	138.6	104.9	60.3	142.6
Tepic				
Spanish	154.1*	151.2	164.9	154.5
Castas	113.2	118.5	91.5	109.6
Indians	164.3	134.1	113.0	133.2

*Figures for Tepic are for 1779-1783.

occasional newcomer from the north or from Valladolid,
Chapala's marriage field was quite localized. Significant numbers of Chapala's residents married people from
Ocotlán, Guadalajara and the area immediately surrounding
Lake Chapala. The area's economy, based on the export of
fish to Guadalajara and an agricultural base of grain and
livestock, probably did not generate as much general population movement as mining towns or trade centers, and it
seems to have served to supply the populations of Ocotlán
and Guadalajara with foodstuffs (Figure 5.2).

Marriages between originarios of Ameca and individuals from places quite far away from their parish were
common (Figure 5.3). By the 1790s, interaction with
northern mining areas had been particularly heavy. Guadalajara, Cocula and Guachinango were always well-
represented among marriage migrants to Ameca. Except for
Guachinango, however, Ameca's marriage field extended
furthest to the east, north and south, over-reaching
Chapala's marriage field and including many of the towns
which were Chapala's major sources of extra-parish interaction. The economic base of Ameca was agricultural;
large, prosperous haciendas owned by wealthy families
dominated the local economy and probably gave this area
economic stability which was attractive to unlucky miners, prospective farmers and ranchers, and merchants interested in steady trade. A large proportion of marriage
partners from outside Ameca were Spaniards, who were typ-
ically active in these occupations.

Tequila's marriage field was remarkably stable
throughout all three periods. Its economic base was similar to Ameca's, but a larger proportion of its marriage
partners came from outside the parish, particularly from
small towns near Tequila, such as Cocula, Atemanica and
Hostotipaquillo. Many of the migrants were Indians and
probably worked as laborers in the maguey fields (Figure
5.4).

Compostela was another setting entirely. Isolated,
and far from the prosperity and sophistication of Guadalajara and the large towns of the Lagos area, Compostela
was originally founded as the administrative center of
western Mexico. The seat of government was quickly moved
to Guadalajara when it became clear that distance to
Mexico City was a major disadvantage. It was, however,
on the edge of the mining areas of Hostotipaquillo and
Bolaños, and had the advantage of proximity to the port
of San Blas without the uncomfortable coastal climate.
Many of the outsiders who married into Compostela's population were Spaniards or mulatos who came from mining
centers both nearby and farther to the northeast (Figure
5.5). A substantial number also came from towns between
Compostela and Ameca, apparently an area with stronger
functional links to Compostela than to Ameca or Tequila.
Certainly the highway linking Compostela to Guadalajara

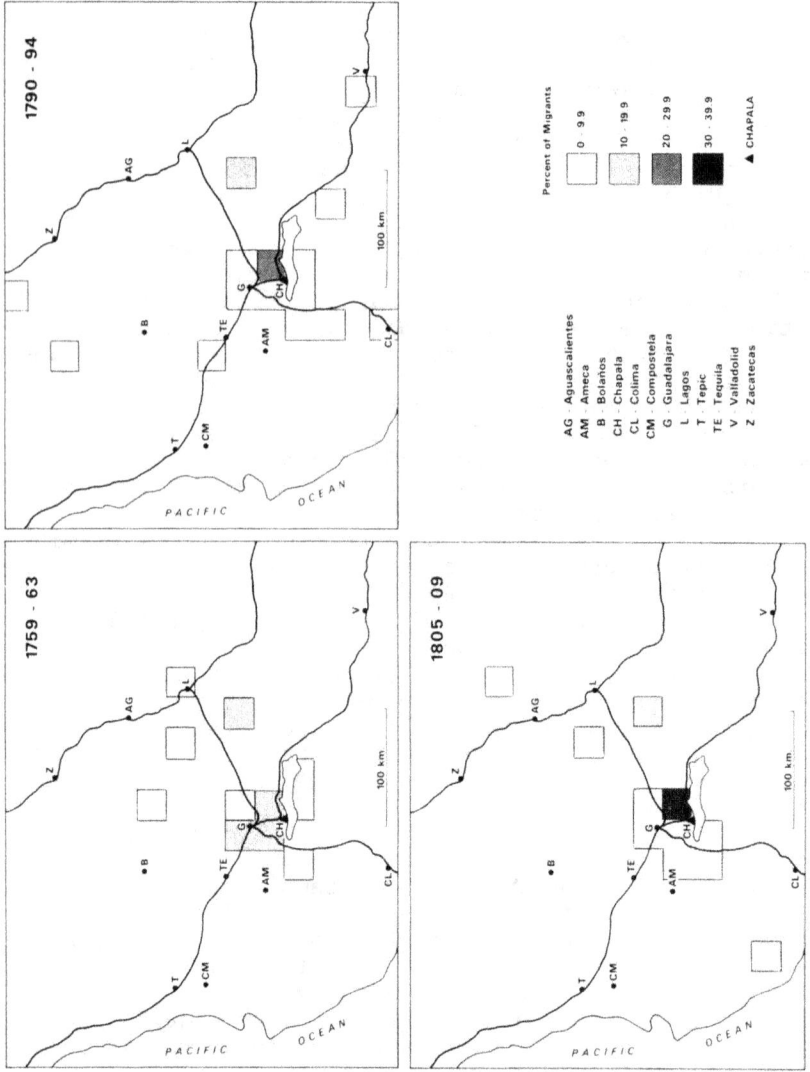

Figure 5.2 Origins of marriage migrants to Chapala

135

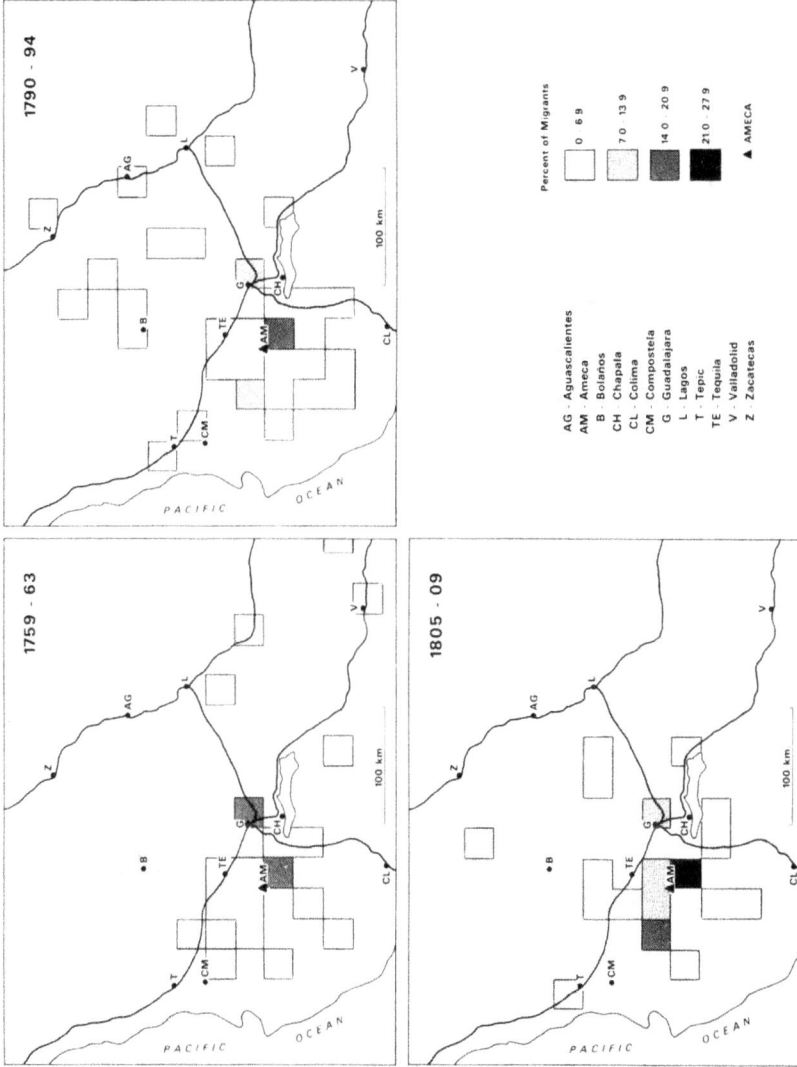

Figure 5.3 Origins of marriage migrants to Ameca

136

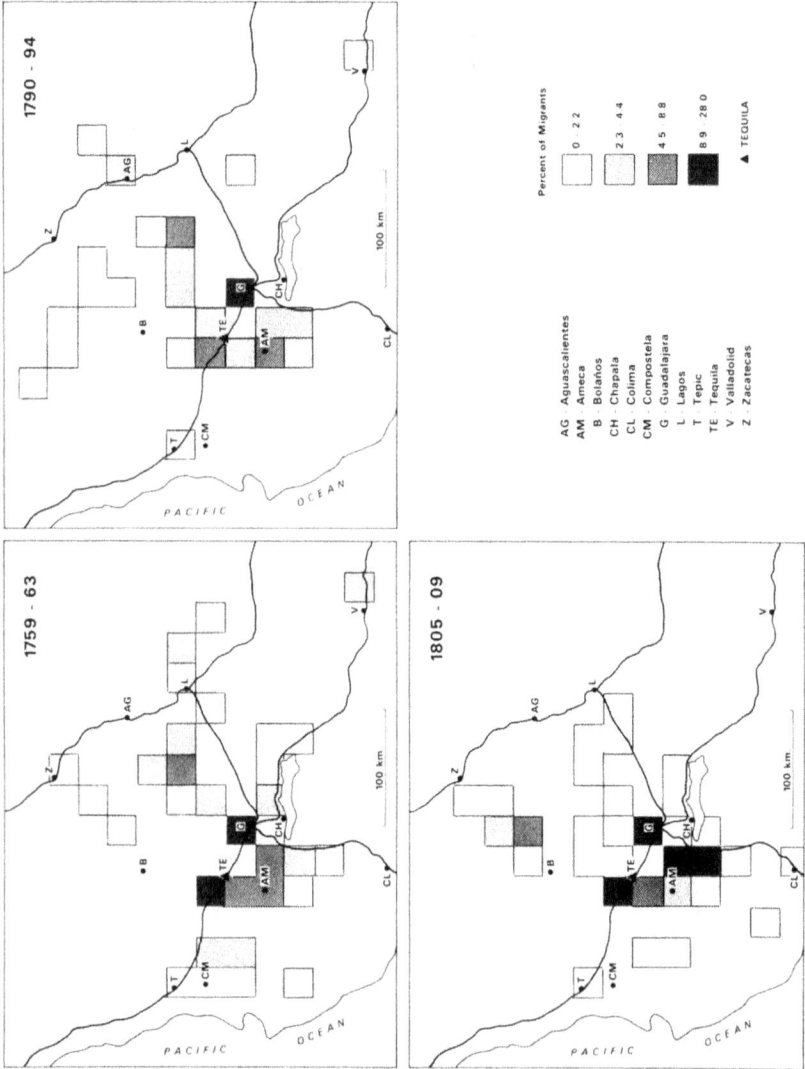

Figure 5.4 Origins of marriage migrants to Tequila

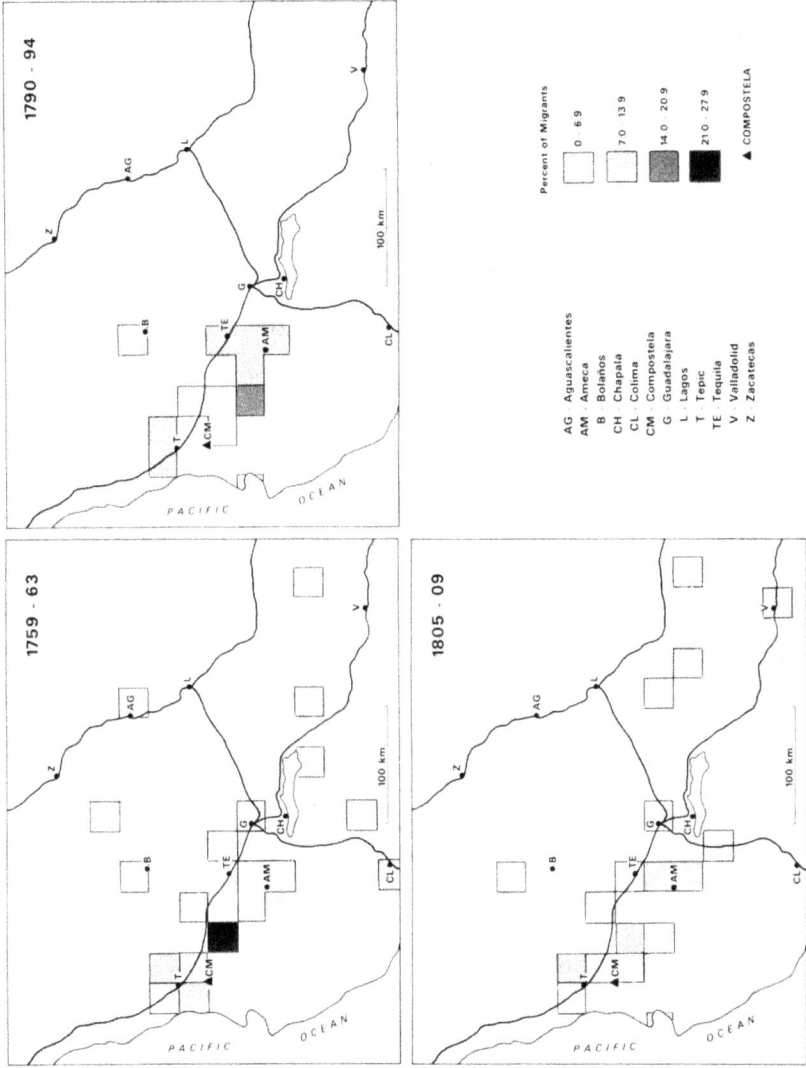

Figure 5.5 Origins of marriage migrants to Compostela

was a factor in the origins of newcomers; many of the
towns along that road were well-represented among
Compostela's marriage partners. In addition to transportation links, the races of migrants also clearly affected
the shape and size of marriage fields. In the 1790s,
Compostela's marriage field shrank when its racial exogamy rate declined dramatically. By that time, the proportion of Indians among migrants reached a peak; they
came primarily from pueblos and parishes near Compostela.

Of all the eight parishes, Tepic's population must
have been the most cosmopolitan. Its marriage field
overreached those of the other parishes and extended beyond, to Spain, Mexico City, Chihuahua, California and
Manila (Figure 5.6). Its dynamic economy and demographic
profile was based on its prominence as a major supplier
of livestock to many parts of Mexico, and the trading
community which grew as a result of that economic base as
well as activity generated by the port of San Blas. Many
naval officers stationed in San Blas had their permanent
residences or vacation homes in Tepic, and it probably
served as well to supply miners further north along the
coast and in the east around Hostotipaquillo and Magda-
lena, providing both equipment and capital from the accounts of wealthy merchants. In particular, however,
Tepic's residents married migrants from the area immediately around the parish (San Blas, Iscuintla, Sentispac
and Santa María del Oro), and from the region around
Ameca, including Cocula, San Martín de la Cal, Tala,
Ahualulco, Etzatlán and other towns within approximately
a 20-kilometer radius of Ameca. No single racial group
consistently dominated the incoming marrying population;
both the Spanish and Indian populations married across
racial lines at a significant rate when their racial
group dominated the incoming population (1790-1794 for
Indians and 1805-1809 for Spaniards).

The question of timing of the migrants' arrival at
the parish plays havoc with any attempt to fit marriage
migration patterns into a temporal context. Unless the
priest consistently recorded the length of time in years
that outsiders had spent in his parish, the marriage
field derived from his records can only represent cumulative population movement for an undefined period of time
for that segment of the population which eventually married in that parish. (Most disappointing of all is to
find that a priest meticulously recorded the arrival of
each migrant in terms such as "residente desde su infan-
cia" or "desde su tierna edad," without indicating the
migrant's age.) The marriage fields compiled here therefore represent the cumulative movements of potential marriage partners for a period of at least 25 years before
each study period.

This 25-year period can be examined in five-year intervals for the three parishes whose priests did

139

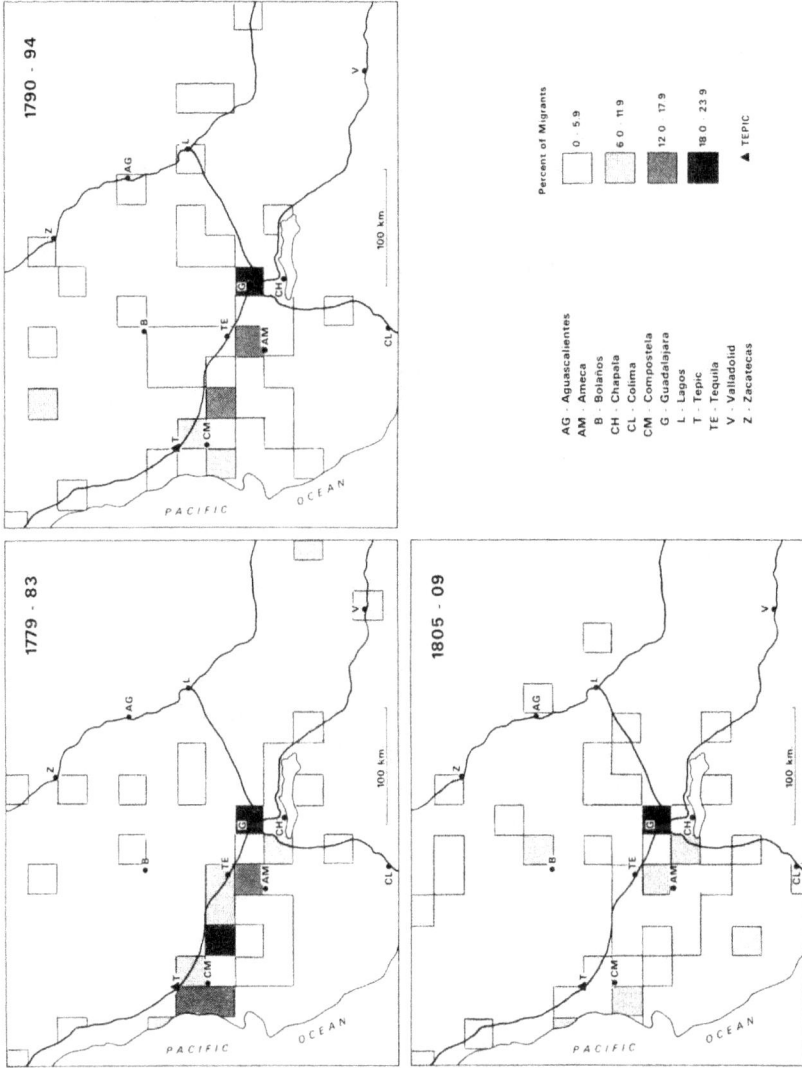

Figure 5.6 Origins of marriage migrants to Tepic

consistently record the length of residence of migrants
(Table 5.10). In the period 1759-1763, most marriage
partners who were born outside the parish had migrated
there within ten years of marriage. Those who had lived
in the parish for longer than that had either been
brought in as infants, or were older widows or single
people who had migrated when they were younger. This
pattern held throughout the century.

The one outstanding feature of this temporal dimension of migration is the great increase in movement following the epidemic of 1785. In every parish, no matter
how inconsistent the priests' records, more marriage
partners had migrated in 1786 than in any other year.
Furthermore, many of them married in the period 1790-
1794; by 1805, nearly all the migrants who would marry
had done so. The effect of this massive population movement was to expand marriage fields somewhat, although
mean marriage migration distances did not necessarily
increase. The region to the east of the line connecting
Zacatecas and Guadalajara seemed to be the origin of many
of the disaster migrants. For example, migrants who arrived in Tepic in 1784 and 1785 came primarily from its
immediate local area, from communities around Ameca--
Guachinango, Cocula and Ahualulco--and from the north
(Teul, Guejuquilla and Valparaiso). By 1786, migrants
arrived from Silao and Guanajuato. The effect in Compostela and Tequila was less dramatic; in 1786, migrants began arriving from Jalpa, Juchipila, Nochistlán, and
Teocaltiche, not traditional sources of marriage partners
for Tequila's and Compostela's residents.

This event clearly demonstrates the complexities of
race, regional economic development, demographic change
and the "openness" of communities. The differential im-
pacts of economic activity and demographic crises on
specific racial groups was reflected in their tendency to
migrate, their patterns of physical movement, and their
social mobility through interracial marriage. This is
evidenced not only in Nueva Galicia, but in northern New
Spain, where Swann has examined variation in spatial exogamy in mining and agricultural centers, and in urban
and rural settings, and in Michoacán, where Yacher has
noted the correlation between migration and racial endogamy.[10]

SPATIAL EXOGAMY WITHIN PARISHES

Because parish priests identified the pueblos and
haciendas of which their own parishioners were originarios, it is possible to examine regional interaction at
another scale: marriage between people from different
haciendas and pueblos of the same parish.

For this analysis, three parishes will be excluded.

TABLE 5.10
Date of arrival of marriage migrants to selected parishes

Date	Percent of migrants with known arrival dates		
	Ameca	Tequila	Tepic
1759-63	14.3	28.1	
1754-58	39.3	31.3	
1749-53	7.1	28.1	
1744-48	3.6	1.6	
Before 1744	35.7	10.9	
Total	100.0	100.0	
1779-83			21.5
1774-78			31.6
1769-73			26.5
1764-68			8.5
Before 1764			11.9
Total			100.0
1790-94	17.3	16.9	20.4
1785-89	39.7	52.5	28.7
1780-84	21.5	10.2	21.5
1775-79	6.6	9.9	6.8
Before 1775	14.9	19.3	13.6
Total	100.0	100.0	100.0
1805-09	29.2	21.8	19.8
1800-04	22.9	31.8	24.2
1795-99	2.1	24.5	28.6
1790-94	12.5	6.4	16.5
Before 1790	33.3	15.5	10.9
Total	100.0	100.0	100.0

Tlaquepaque, a vice-parish of San José de Analco, apparently consisted of only the pueblo itself; no other place is mentioned as being within its jurisdiction. In Tequila, only one pueblo in addition to the parish center appeared frequently enough in the marriage records to be appropriate for study.[11] In Tepic, marriage partners from within the parish came from a number of haciendas and ranchos in the parish, none of them alone supplying a significant proportion of marriage partners.[12]

Clearly the proportion of inter-pueblo and inter-hacienda marriages varied through time (Table 5.11). In most cases, only one or two pueblos within a parish tended to interact with other parish communities, and therefore affected the overall rate of spatial exogamy. In Zapopan, for example, it was principally residents of the parish center who married someone from outside their pueblo. The decline of this phenomenon over time was reflected in the overall level of spatial exogamy. Marriages between originarios of the parish center and other pueblos declined to almost negligible proportions by the turn of the century.

A similar situation existed in Compostela in the first period, when originarios of the Hacienda San José del Conde and the pueblo of Masatán were the only parishioners who married into other communities, both within and outside the parish. When they tended to interact less frequently with others outside their communities, as in the second period, the overall rate of inter-pueblo marriage declined until originarios of Compostela, San Pedro Lagunillas and Guichichila began marrying into other pueblos in the third period. In Tonalá, spatial exogamy at the sub-parish level was not only minimal, but was restricted primarily to the parish center and the haciendas and ranchos surrounding it. In Chapala, it was marriage partners from the Haciendas Cedros and Buenavista who were most likely to marry originarios from other places in the parish. In Ameca, where all the significant sub-parish units were haciendas, no single place was more "open" than the others; indeed, at one time or another, originarios of all of the haciendas married into other communities at a significant rate.

The general pattern of interaction that seems to have been characteristic among pueblos and haciendas in a given parish is fairly clear. First, the official parish center seemed to be more "open" than other pueblos; migrants from other parishes usually married natives of the parish center, perhaps because it was the most populated or most important place within the parish and therefore attracted newcomers on their arrival. Second, members of secondary parish settlements usually married within their own communities; if they did not, they were most likely to marry someone from the parish center, rather than a resident of another secondary pueblo. Third, the

TABLE 5.11
Spatially exogamous marriages within parishes

Parish	Percent of all marriages in parish in each period		
	1759-1763	1790-1794	1805-1809
Zapopan	12.4	8.9	8.0
Tonalá	6.8	6.6	11.8
Chapala	19.9	15.0	15.2
Ameca	9.5	27.8	22.7
Compostela	7.6	1.6	14.0

haciendas of Chapala, Tonalá and Ameca were more "open"
than the pueblos of any of the parishes, which suggests
that the economic and social life of the agricultural
unit led to more interaction and population movement than
life in a pueblo.

The spatial relationships that result from this pattern of interaction are similar to those of the hierarchy
of cities within Latin American countries today; a parish
center, like a national capital, had as its satellites
outlying pueblos and haciendas, with which it interacted
but which did not interact much among themselves. This
provides at least one clue to the nature of the parish as
a socio-economic unit: parish boundaries seem to have included communities with functional relationships to a
common parish center, but did not necessarily represent
the limits of a cohesive, well-integrated set of communities and agricultural units.

CONCLUSION

How does marriage migration analysis help to describe regional patterns of interaction among communities
in colonial western Mexico? How do these patterns compare
with those of other areas of colonial Mexico?

First, it is clear that there were fundamental differences between Indian parishes and those of mixed populations. Obviously, rates of interracial marriage would
be low in communities with relatively homogeneous populations. Less self-evident is the almost negligible level
of interaction between Indian parishes and a nearby regional center such as Guadalajara, or any other center
for that matter. There were, of course, administrative
ecclesiastical ties and probably functional economic
links through the tithe system. Essentially, however,
these Indian parishes were isolated from the mainstream
of social interaction, regardless of how closely it
passed by (Tonalá and Tlaquepaque were located along the
major highway connecting Guadalajara with the large population centers of the Lagos commercial and agricultural
district; Zapopan was on the road to the Pacific coast
and the port of San Blas). Even more surprising is the
isolation of pueblos within Indian parishes. It was not
the case that Indians as a racial group simply did not
move. In Tequila and Tepic they accounted for up to one-
third of all marriage partners who originated from outside the parish; in Ameca, Chapala, and Compostela they
accounted for roughly 30 percent less than that. It is
important to remember, however, that western Mexico did
not offer a large indigenous population even at the time
of Conquest. Cook and Borah have estimated general population growth throughout west-central Mexico in the colonial period and illustrate an early decline in indigenous

population.[13]   Total population figures for later periods
indicate a relatively well-balanced ethnic mixture which
was generally reflected at the pueblo level.   Patterns
and principles of interracial marriage in Nueva Galicia
may therefore not be comparable to areas with Negro populations or with high concentrations of any of the other
three racial groups, and the relative isolation of Indian
communities may not be typical of the Indian population
as a whole.
    Second, if a hierarchy of parishes were to be con-
ceptualized, with isolated Indian parishes on the first
level, the second level might be parishes of mixed populations with a localized field of economic and social relationships.   The absence of integrated pueblos and
haciendas within the parish is also characteristic.   Certainly Chapala is an excellent example of this configuration, with an economic base that tied it to the nearby
regional capital of Guadalajara, and social links primarily with Guadalajara, Ocotlán and local parishes.   In the
cases of Ameca, Tequila and Compostela, their marriage
fields complemented each other, and probably their economic hinterlands as well.   Ameca and Tequila seemed to
face eastward to their marriage fields; most of those
living further west, except for the parish of Guachaningo,
appeared in the marriage registers of Compostela and
Tepic.   In the 1790s, Ameca's marriage field expanded to
the north and northwest, and Compostela's contracted,
with nearby Indian pueblos forming the core of the marriage field.   A region of locally-oriented parishes can
be imagined whose patterns of social and economic development were interdependent.   In particular, recalling the
impact of racial variations in marriage migration on the
"openness" of racial groups, it is clear that economic
changes in one parish must have affected the shapes and
characteristics of social and economic regions of surrounding parishes.
    Third, in the case of an important regional center
such as Tepic, the field of social interaction overreached those of less significant parishes for quite a
distance, just as the field of economic links extended to
the trading communities of Spain.   In Tepic, local haciendas provided such a small number of marriage partners
that spatial endogamy below the parish level is impossible to measure.   It is unclear whether this was a function of a physical environment incapable of sustaining
densely-populated agricultural units or whether the parish priest simply did not always distinguish the various
haciendas by name.
    Given the economic bases of a set of communities,
then, and a general characterization of their demographic
bases, the measurement of marriage migration fields and
the analysis of the impact of change in the racial composition of the marrying population provide a set of

general regional boundaries within which those communities functioned. It is difficult to determine with certainty the temporal and spatial dimensions of general migration flows from marriage records, but regions of social and economic links can be determined and gross changes in their shapes and sizes can be identified.

NOTES

1. Carmagnani analyzes the effect of economic change on interracial marriage for San Luis Potosí and Charcas in Marcelo Carmagnani, "Demografía y sociedad: La estructura social de los centros mineros del norte de México, 1600-1720," Historia Mexicana, Vol. 2 (1972), pp. 419-459. The relationship between race, occupation and intermarriage is discussed in: David A. Brading, "Grupos étnicos, clases y estructura ocupacional en Guanajuato (1792)," Historia Mexicana, Vol. 21 (1972), pp. 460-480. A classic study of racial patterns of marriage is found in Sherburne F. Cook and Woodrow Borah, "Racial Groups in the Mexican Population since 1519," in Essays in Population History: Mexico and the Caribbean, 2 vols. (Berkeley, 1971 and 1974), Vol. 2, pp. 180-269. Brading and Wu analyze marriage preferences and social interaction in David A. Brading and Celia Wu, "Population Growth and Crisis: León, 1720-1860," Journal of Latin American Studies, Vol. 5 (1973), pp. 1-36. A geographical perspective on marriage is more difficult to come by. Both racial aspects of marriage and spatial dimensions of marriage migration are analyzed in: David J. Robinson, "Population Patterns in an Old Mining Region: Parral in the Late Eighteenth Century," Geoscience and Man, Vol. XXI (1979), pp. 83-96; Michael M. Swann, "The Spatial Dimensions of a Social Process: Marriage Migration in Late Eighteenth-Century Nueva Vizcaya," in David J. Robinson (ed.), Social Fabric and Spatial Structure (Ann Arbor, 1979), pp. 117-181; and Leon Yacher, Marriage, Migration and Racial Mixing in Colonial Tlazazalca (Michoacán), 1750-1810 (Syracuse University, Department of Geography, Discussion Paper No. 37, 1977).

2. The marriage registers were available through the kind assistance of the Genealogical Society of Utah.

3. For just such studies, see Robinson in this volume; and also D. J. Robinson, "Population Patterns," op. cit.; Swann, op. cit.; and Yacher, op. cit.

4. Because the relative locations of settlements within parishes did not affect the analysis, the base maps are not included here.

5. For further discussion of economic regions in late colonial Nueva Galicia and the importance of the places discussed here, see Linda L. Greenow, Spatial Dimensions of the Credit Market in Late Colonial Nueva Galicia, dissertation, Syracuse University, 1980; and Eric Van Young, "Urban Market and Hinterland: Guadalajara and Its Region in the Eighteenth Century," Hispanic American Historical Review, Vol. 59 (1979), pp. 593-635. According to the population

count of 1791 by subdelegación, the parishes studied here were of a moderate size: Etzatlán (including Ameca): 10,714; Tonalá (including Tlaquepaque): 5,447; Tepic (including Compostela): 5,015; Tlajomulco (including Chapala): 5,938; Tala (including Zapopan): 3,497. These figures are available in José María Serrera, Guadalajara Ganadera (Sevilla, 1976), p. 21.

6. Sherburne F. Cook and Woodrow Borah, "Racial Groups in the Mexican Population," op. cit.

7. The racial distribution of the capital of Guadalajara in 1791 was as follows: Europeos, 186; Españoles, 9,386; Indios, 4,241; Mulatos, 6,538; Otras castas, 3,898; Población total, 24,249. "Censo de la Intendencia de Guadalajara (años 1791-1793), elaborado por el visitador Dr. Menéndez Valdés durante la visita que practicó al territorio," Archivo General de las Indias (Sevilla), Guadalajara 250. Cited in Serrera, op. cit., p. 21.

8. Brading and Wu, op. cit.

9. Robinson, op. cit.; Brading, op. cit.; and Carmagnani, op. cit.

10. Swann, op. cit.; Yacher, op. cit.

11. The pueblo was Amatitlan, which accounted for by far the largest single share of marriage partners who were originarios or residentes of pueblos outside the town of Tequila but within its parish. In the period 1759-63, 45% of such marriage partners came from Amatitlan; from 1790-94, 43%; and from 1805-09, 51%. The remainder came from a number of haciendas and pueblos scattered throughout the parish.

12. Marriage partners in the parish of Tepic but outside the parish center were originarios or residentes of fourteen haciendas and ranchos. These units supplied the following percentages of marriage partners: 1779-83: 5.6%; 1790-94: 3.1%; 1805-09: 3.5%.

13. Sherburne F. Cook and Woodrow Borah, "The Population of West-Central Mexico (Nueva Galicia and Adjacent New Spain), 1548-1960," in Essays in Population History: Mexico and the Caribbean (Berkeley, 1971), Vol. 1, pp. 300-375.

6
Indian Migration in Eighteenth-Century Yucatán: The Open Nature of the Closed Corporate Community

David J. Robinson

INTRODUCTION

Colonial developments within the Yucatán peninsula have received increasing attention during recent years. Gerhard[1] has provided a superb guide to the changes in administrative structures and a mine of information on encomienda developments. Other authors have outlined the process of agricultural extension and diversification,[2] or the changing population structure of the region.[3] Such works can be added to a distinguished list of earlier studies that have stood the test of time.[4] Though few of the above studies relate specifically to Indian population change, it is clear that for each and every one of them, that topic is of vital significance. Whether it be the encroachment of Hispanic culture on native practices, the changing structure of the urban market, the evolution of the encomienda system, developments in kinship and compadrazgo relationships--all these and more require a detailed knowledge of the state of, and changes in, the Indian population. It may also be suggested that the many more modern analyses that probe the Yucatán process of modernization[5] also have relied to a considerable extent upon assumed patterns of socio-economic development during earlier periods.

One of the most significant features to have surfaced as a result of recent historical investigations is the extent of spatial movement within and between the Indian communities. Farriss[6] has identified three types of population redistribution: "flight," which is the escape of Indians from Spanish rule into the unpacified frontier margin; "drift," which is the movement to other towns within the Spanish colonial domain; and "dispersal," which represents the hiving-off of new settlements from parent townships. Such a migration typology is very similar to that outlined by Hunt,[7] who stresses that the actual migration pattern was structured in a hierarchical fashion, with Indians moving first to nearby larger

settlements, and then eventually onwards and upwards to
Mérida:

> Mérida was the largest beacon of them all, and Indians
> came from far and wide, though often the advance was a
> gradual one from a far-away district, to a closer one,
> until the barrios of the city were reached. The jump
> might be made by an individual, or it could take genera-
> tions.[8]

While the push and pull factors that may have operated
are outlined below, it is important to note that Farriss
and Hunt, as well as others who have noted Indian migration, see such patterns as reflecting the impact of Hispanic culture upon an acculturating native population.
Thus, when agricultural developments lead to pressure on
Indian lands, migration might be initiated. Similarly,
as Patch has argued, when population growth at the central place of the region, Mérida, reached certain levels,
this triggered a stimulation of agricultural development
that also had a dislocating effect upon the Indian population. Embedded in all of such arguments, of course,
lies the Indian community. To Wolf it possessed all the
hallmarks of his "closed corporate" model--with restricted membership, communal jurisdiction over land, a
religious system of notable endurance, and mechanisms
which ensured the redistribution of surplus wealth, and
maintained barriers against the entry of goods and ideas
from outside.[9] And for Redfield[10] the ethnographic present was used as a direct window on the Yucatecan past;
the most remote, and usually the smallest, communities of
the 1940s were said to reflect a past condition of much
of the peninsular Indian world, a realm of "closed" communities, in the words of Wolf[11] "socially and culturally
isolated from the larger society in which they exist."

   Yet such a view of the past condition of Indian
Yucatán hardly matches the mounting number of clues regarding mobile Indians. This paper thus addresses various aspects of the central question--what was the rate,
extent, and direction of Indian migration in the colonial
period. It confines itself to the eighteenth century
since that period provides both the best set of data, and
the changing economic circumstances that allow one to
monitor the relations between population change and the
development process in the widest sense. Some might ar-
gue that such a study is unnecessary given the work of
authors quoted above. However, it may be noted that in
none of those works is it possible to assess population
movement in any quantitative manner. With the census
data of Cook and Borah, and Gerhard, it is possible to
infer a shifting population base, if one could assume
that the distinctive regions each had a stable population,
but a study of one parish has shown that to be a most

unwise assumption.[12]
    Another feature of many of the studies quoted above
is their lack of precision regarding the spatial dimensions of population distribution and change. In spite of
the elegance of Farriss' typology, and the comprehensive-
ness with which Hunt examines the local records, there
still remains much that is unstated. Which were the
towns that served as way-stations en route to Mérida?
And where did the frontier lie at specific dates? Without such specific information it is more than a little
difficult to adequately test such notions as "dispersal"
and "drift." And the crude sketch maps of Hunt[13] may
suggest the expansion and crosscurrents of relationships
of settlements in the Mérida area, but they do little
more than that. Like many other regions in colonial
Mexico, we know remarkably little of the geography of the
eighteenth century.

THE DATA SOURCES

    Instead of attempting to utilize the fragmentary
data base provided by nominative censuses of the Yucatán,
here, use is made of data pertaining to individuals,
which can be gained from the parish registers. Two data
sets can be generated for the eighteenth century. First,
population migration can be ascertained from the origins
of both spouses given in the marriage certificates, and
recorded in the libros de matrimonios. Since such data
has now been used for the analysis of several other colonial Mexican communities[14] it is possible to compare patterns, rates, and types of migration concerned with marriage. Normally, outside of the Yucatán the phrase
"natural de" has been assumed to refer to "native of" in
the sense of place of birth or nurture. However, it is
clear from references in the Yucatán registers that here
we are dealing not with place of birth (known by the
stated place of baptism), but rather with their pueblo of
tribute and encomienda affiliation.[15] For bride, groom,
and often their parents and the testigos to the ceremony,
is given their place of origin in this manner. A pecu-
liarity in the data is the fact that many fathers were
recorded as natives of communities other than those of
their children, which might mean that affiliations were
altered by means of residential rules, or that in some
cases the tribute and baptism pueblos are intermingled?
There appears to be no easy solution to this problem,
other than a detailed tracing of sample individuals from
their baptismal registration, through their appearance on
tribute lists, to their marriage, and thence to the baptism of their children. Such work was not possible for
the present study.
    Since it might be argued that records that allow one

to only monitor the moves of those who got married in the legal sense could provide a biased sample, it is fortunate that in the Yucatán--and quite unlike any other area yet studied in Mexico--a second source permits one to monitor shifts in residence of a larger population. In the registers of Indian baptisms (and only Indian baptisms it should be noted) each parent is specified as "natural de," again allowing one to trace the movement of persons from one settlement to another. Many of the entries include phrases such as "Martín Pech, natural de Tixkokob, originario de Santiago . . . ," or ". . . tributario de Tekax, originario de Yaxa, y vecino de la estancia . . . ." As with marriage records, it appears that the phrase "natural de" refers to the pueblo of tribute, rather than the pueblo of birth. However, for the purposes of tracing population movements such data as exists is extremely valuable, for it permits one to calculate at the level of large numbers of individuals the relative proportions leaving certain pueblos and entering others. This paper utilizes data on some 2000 individuals getting married, and 10,000 parents of children being baptised.

Four settlements were selected for analysis, Umán, Tixkokob, Conkal, and Sotuta (Figure 6.1). They were chosen for the following reasons: Umán had been analyzed earlier with regard to its demographic evolution from the late seventeenth century, and it had extremely good marriage and baptismal records (it may be noted that "good" has to be construed within the relatively "poor" condition of most of the Yucatán parish records which have been very badly damaged by water, worms and neglect). Since it was located some ten miles southwest of Mérida, it was decided that a community to the east, at approximately the same distance would provide a comparable location to examine intra-regional movements. So that it would be possible to identify any southward, frontier movement, it was decided to select a community with good records in what had been designated the "borderlands" by Cline,[16] and which lay towards the frontier margin on the maps of Cook and Borah[17] and Gerhard.[18] Sotuta appeared to be the best documented settlement. Since the costa region appeared to be of great significance in patterns of population movement, a second settlement was chosen from that zone, Conkal, as a means of controlling for any variation between settlements in the same general proximity to Mérida. Mérida and Valladolid were not selected for this analysis, principally because of the much larger numbers of calculations that would have to be performed. They are, however, presently being studied in the hope of presenting a range of settlements from the largest to some of the smallest, and from close by the socio-economic core to the margins of Spanish control.

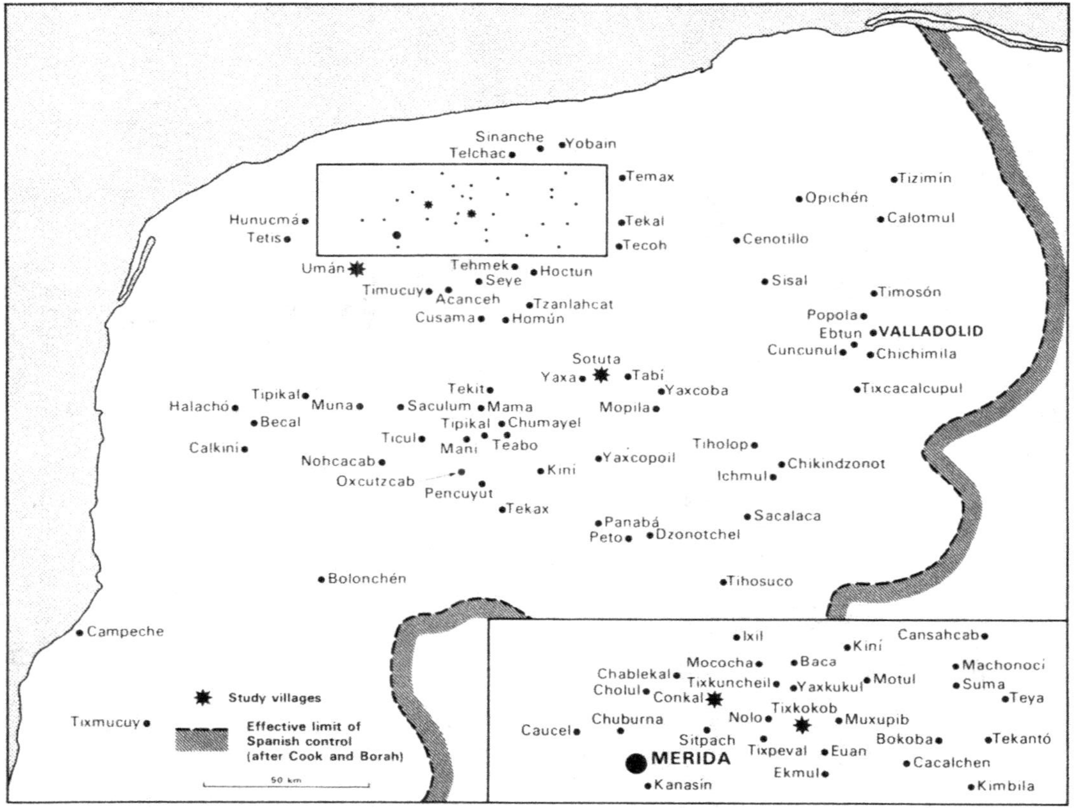

153

Figure 6.1 Location of Yucatecan study villages

ANALYSIS OF RESULTS

Longitudinal Profiles of Migration

One of the principal difficulties in presenting the
results of an analysis of migration in Yucatán, as elsewhere, is that of reducing the units of analysis to a
level that facilitates comprehension, but does not remove
the complexity of the patterns and processes which existed in reality. Here, most of the data is presented at
the partido level, rather than at the level of individual
pueblos.

The origins of marriage partners in Umán (Figure 6.2)
reflect a high and sustained level of exogamy throughout
the eighteenth century. While the usual figures for exogamous marriages in colonial Mexico range between 15-20
percent, the evidence from Umán is quite distinctive.
From 38.5 percent exogamous in the period 1689-1693, the
percentage steadily increases to climax at mid-century
and decrease slightly to 50 in the late 1760s. By the
end of the eighteenth century it had again increased to
over 65 percent. This meant that of those marrying in
Umán's church (or the dependent chapels at Samahil,
Bolonpoyche, and Dzibikal), over two thirds had previously been attached to other Indian settlements. One is
clearly dealing with a century-long process of regional
population movement. The costa region is the principal
source area for the migrants in all periods save that of
1808-1812, when the Mérida barrios of Santiago, Santa Ana,
and San Cristóbal combine to equal the stream of persons
from the east. Another notable feature is the fact that
although Umán is located west of the provincial capital,
its main source regions lie to the east. There is little
evidence in these maps to show that Mérida was the primary goal of migrants; indeed, many moved from their communities across the urban center to settle in Umán.
Again, with so many moving to a settlement without a
great deal of open land, one wonders just what the at-
traction of Umán was?

If one examines the data for origins of parents
whose children were baptised in Umán parish, a very similar pattern emerges. It is important to note that the
intervals between the sample five year periods have been
maintained at about 25 years to ensure that very few parents are included in subsequent sample periods. The data
demonstrate that from some 25 percent of non-local individuals at the close of the seventeenth century, the proportion increases to over seventy percent by the beginning of the nineteenth century (Table 6.1).

The location of the migrant origins is remarkably
similar to that of marriage partner origins (Figure 6.3).
More migrants enter Umán from the Campeche region in the
1720s, but the predominant trend is for migrants to have

155

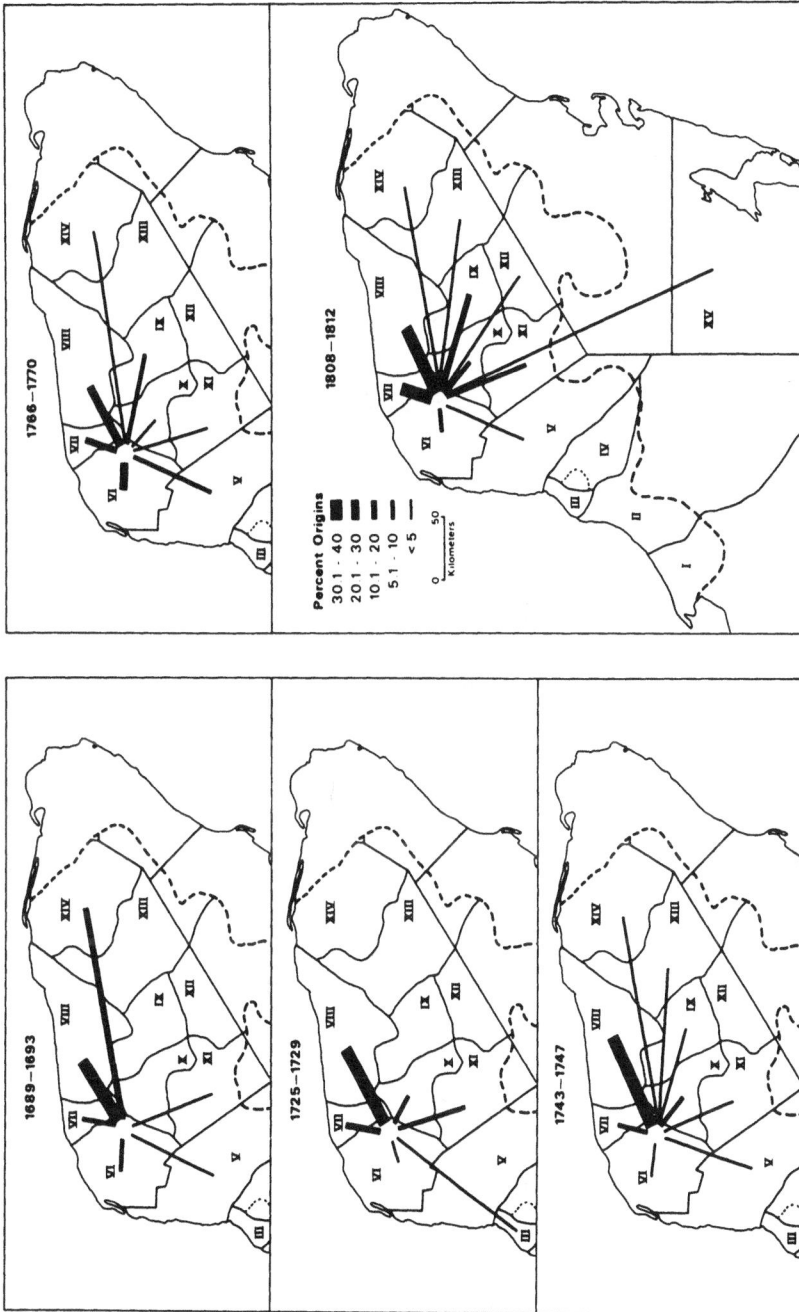

Figure 6.2 Origins of marriage migrants, San Francisco de Umán, 1689–1812

TABLE 6.1
Baptisms in Umán parish, Yucatán, 1689-1817

ORIGINS	1689-1694		1725-1729		1743-1747		1766-1770		1788-1792		1808-1812	
	N	%	N	%	N	%	N	%	N	%	N	%
Within parish												
Bolonpoyche	63	28.6	25	3.1	30	2.5	35	2.9	63	3.8	50	2.5
Umán	23	10.4	55	6.7	49	4.1	59	5.0	219	13.3	266	13.5
Samahil	60	27.2	56	6.8	94	7.9	2	0.2	34	2.0	32	1.6
Dzibikal	--	--	64	7.8	89	7.4	121	10.2	148	8.9	110	5.6
Unspecified	20	9.1	260	31.9	150	12.6	200	16.9	28	1.7	--	--
Total	166	75.4	460	56.5	412	34.6	417	35.3	492	29.8	458	23.3
Outside parish	54	24.5	355	43.5	778	65.3	762	64.6	1154	70.1	1500	76.6
Total Indios	220	100.0	815	100.0	1190	100.0	1179	100.0	1646	100.0	1958	100.0
Non-Indios	25		196		222		326		252		114	
Total baptisms	245		1011		1412		1505		1898		2072	

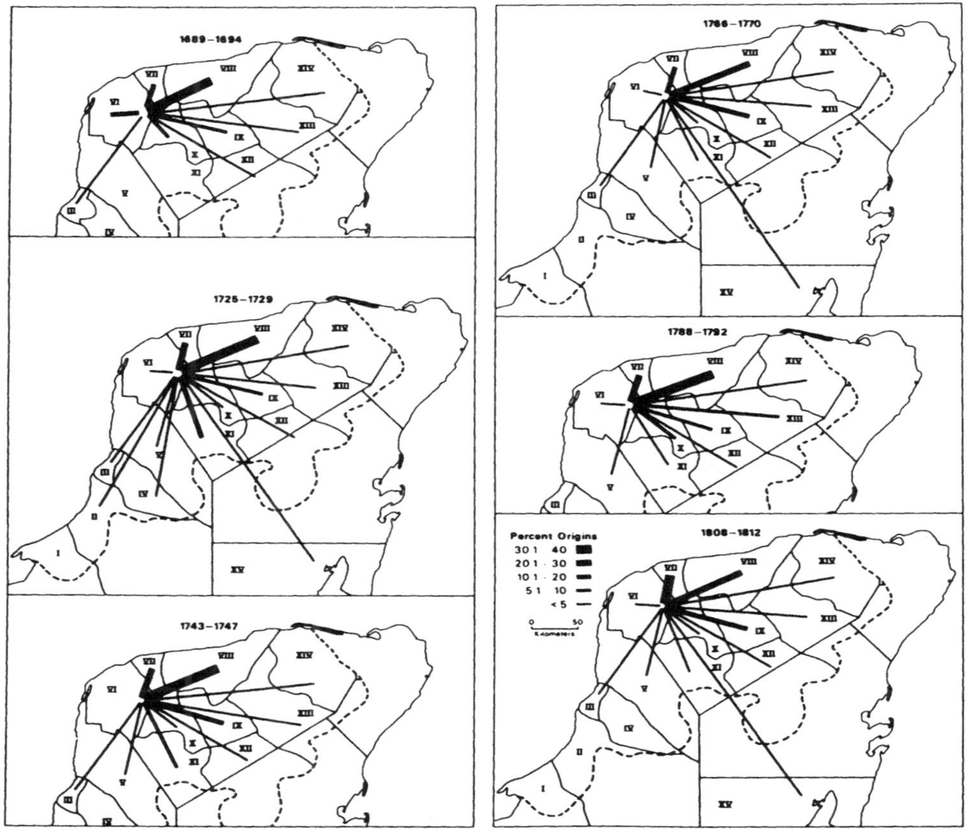

Figure 6.3 Origins of migrants (parents of baptised children), San Francisco de Umán, 1689-1812

originated in the east and north, from settlements in the densely populated coastal and Mérida zone, as well as from afar as Tizimín and Bacalar.

If one now examines the same series of data for Sotuta, a more peripheral settlement in the Beneficios Bajos district, it is evident that a lower rate of exogamy prevails (Table 6.2). Nevertheless, marked and non-random patterns are clear (Figure 6.4). In the early part of the century the Mérida barrios provided most of the migrants who moved to Sotuta, but by the middle of the century the costa region was increasing its share of the total flow, and in the 1770s exceeded that of Mérida. In the latter part of the century a three-pronged movement can be observed from Mérida, the costa, and also along the frontier line from the Sierra Alta district. Less than 30 percent of the total number of migrants ever originate from within the Beneficios Bajos region itself, a feature which is paralleled in the case of Umán. It appears that if one moved at all, then one moved usually to a destination outside one's own local region.

TABLE 6.2
Exogamy rates for selected Yucatán settlements

Period	Conkal %	Umán %	Tixkokob %	Sotuta %
1725-1729	33.3	43.5	69.1	22.1
1743-1747	34.9	65.3	43.9	34.7
1766-1770	50.2*	64.6	NA	52.5
1788-1792	62.0	70.1	56.2	67.2
1808-1812	NA	76.6	31.7	NA

NA = Not available due to records in illegible condition or missing.
*Figures for Conkal refer to years 1772-1776, since all others missing.

Cross-sectional Analysis of Migration

Since the diachronic mode of analysis makes it difficult to accurately compare the situations of different settlements, it is advantageous to examine the synchronic patterns at selected temporal cross-sections. If, for example, one changes the scale of analysis from the regional shifts of population to that at the individual

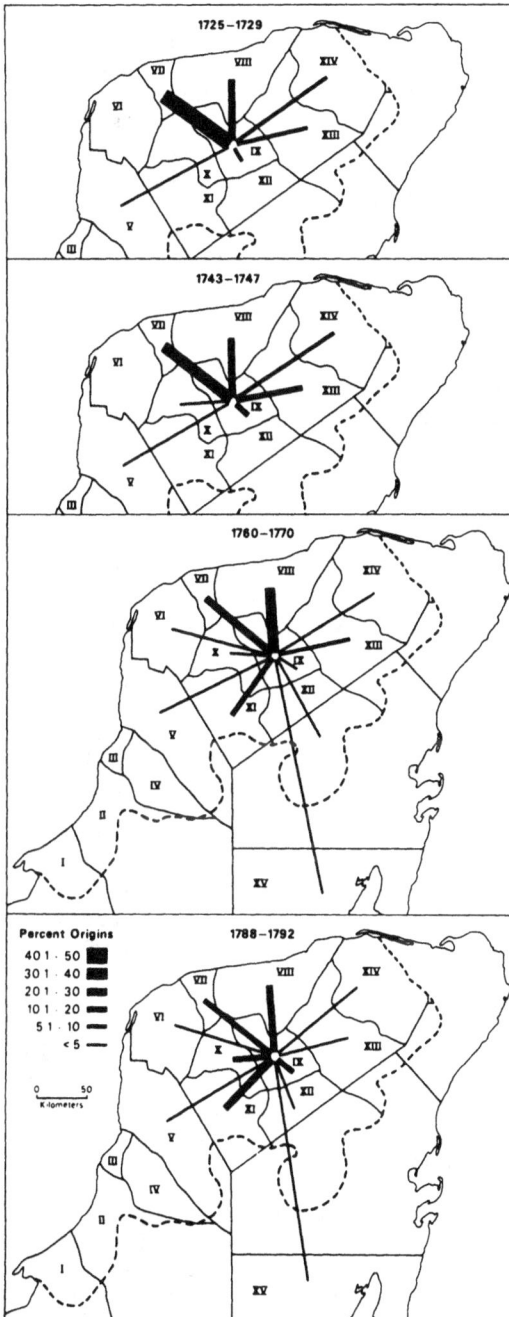

Figure 6.4 Origins of migrants (parents of children baptised),
Sotuta, 1725-1792

pueblo level, then the complexity of migrant origins becomes clear. The 1788-1792 origins for Sotuta now dis-
integrate from the three-pronged regional flows to a mass
(some might say mess) of distinctive sources. Only Maní
and Mérida account for more than ten percent of the total
migrant population, others coming from as far north as
Yobain, from the Valladolid region to the east, and a
scatter from the southern borderlands of Peto, Tihosuco,
Sacalaca and Tecax (Figure 6.5).

If, instead of plotting the origins of migrants one
examines the geometry of the several migration fields,
some quite interesting contrasts emerge (Figure 6.6).
First, it is clear that the total extent of the Tixkokob/
Umán/Sotuta fields are not significantly different, some
22,000 square kilometers for the total area of each.
However, the areas from which fifty percent of all migrants originate show considerable variation. Tixkokob's
smaller field includes only some 280 square kms., mostly
including the important settlements of the nearby Mérida
area, and a scatter in the Costa district. Umán, on the
other hand, though the same distance away from Mérida,
has a much more extensive fifty-percent field extending
into the Sierra Alta. Sotuta's smaller field, almost
circular in shape, accurately reflects the balanced distribution of settlements sending migrants to it.

A comparison of the patterns of migration to Conkal,
Tixkokob, Umán, and Sotuta in the period 1788-1792 shows
just how regionalized the flows were (Figure 6.7). Both
Tixkokob and Conkal reflect their location to the east of
Mérida, collecting most of their migrants from the Costa
(some 55%) and the Mérida district. It is of interest to
note that while 28 percent of Sotuta migrants originated
from the Costa, only 18 percent left the Beneficios Bajos
for Tixkokob. Clearly one of the next tasks will be to
calculate net migration rates for sets of regions.

Another aspect of migration within Yucatán which is
evident from the detailed records of the parish registers
is the extent to which individual pueblos within the same
parish have relatively distinctive migration fields.
Since in all cases the records of individual chapels and
churches have to be aggregated to the parish level before
they are tabulated and mapped, it is possible to isolate
the specific migration fields of pueblos. The results
for Tixkokob parish in the period 1788-1792 are seen in
Figure 6.8. While the cabecera of Tixkokob had a fairly
extensive field, with most migrants coming from a zone of
settlements in the southwest (including Halachó, Becal,
Calkiní, and Maní) and the southeast (from Sotuta,
Chikindzonot and Popola), if one examines the field of
the dependent pueblos of Ekmul and Euan it is clear that
they had distinctively restricted fields of migrants.
Euan attracted most of its migrants from the north, west
and east--mostly from within a radius of 20 kms.; only

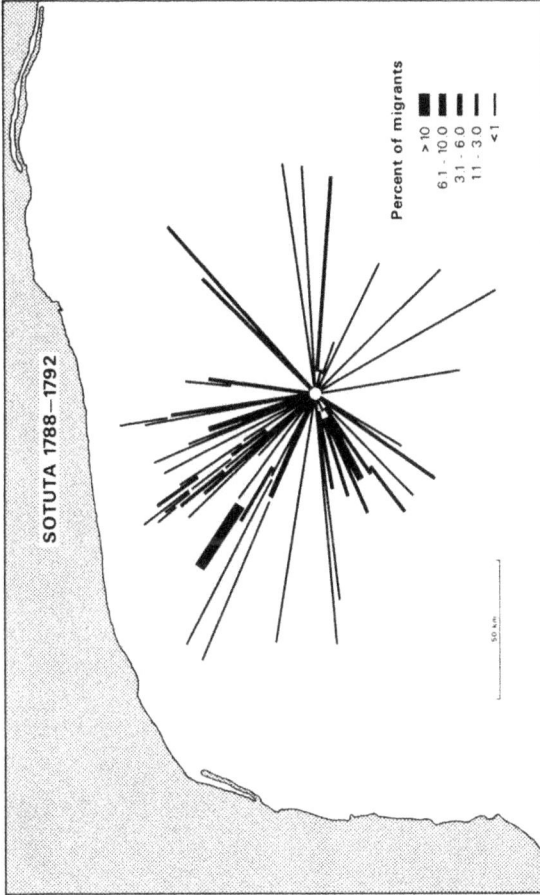

Figure 6.5 Origins of migrants to Sotuta, 1788-1792

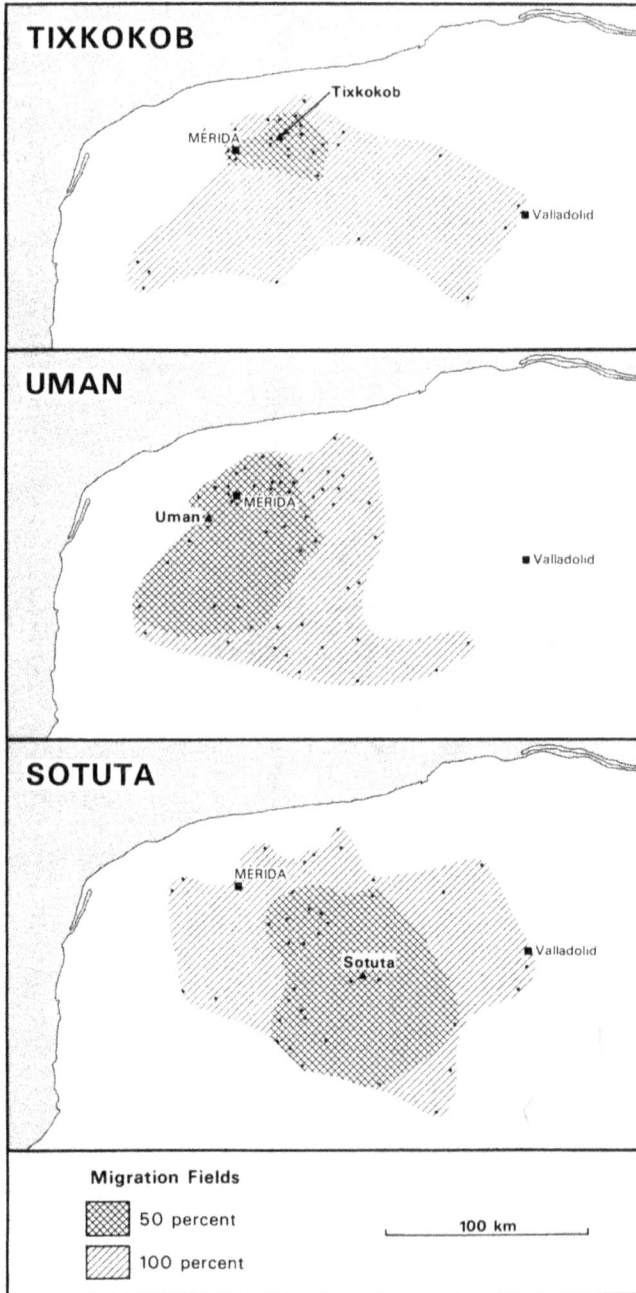

Figure 6.6 Selected migration fields, Yucatán, 1788-1792

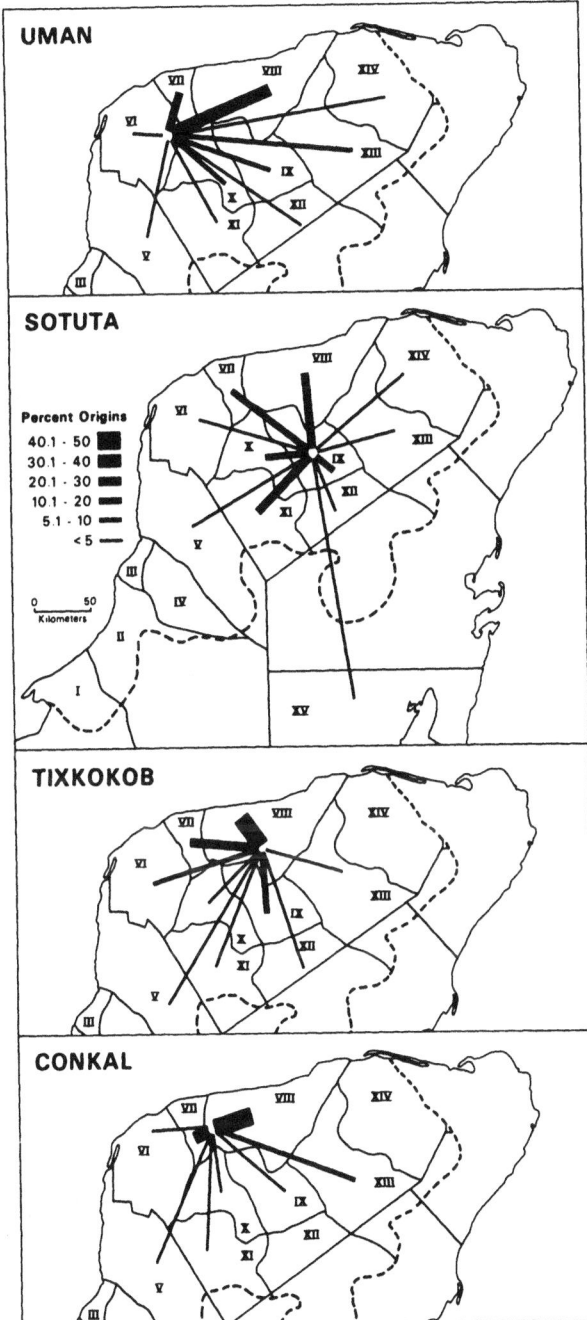

Figure 6.7 Origins of migrants (parents of children baptised), in selected Yucatecan settlements, 1788-1792

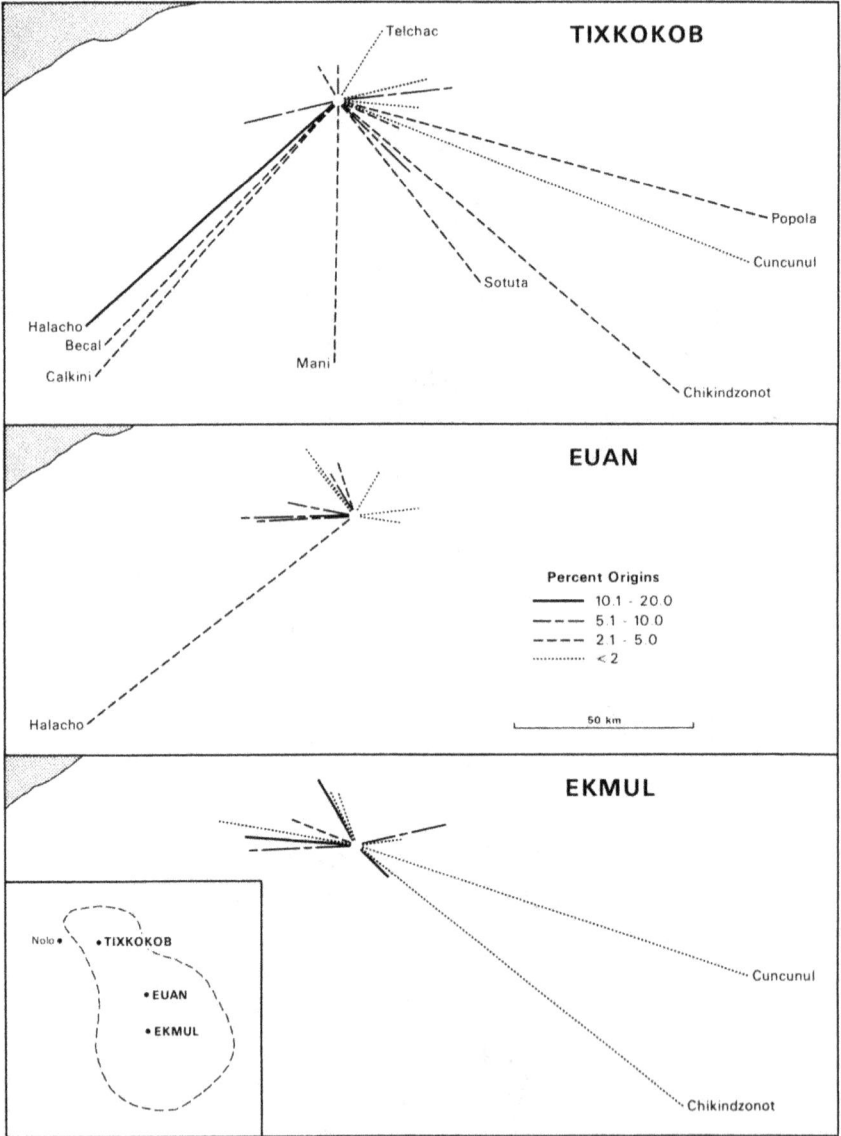

Figure 6.8 Origins of migrants to Tixkokob and its dependent
pueblos, 1788-1792

the stream from Halachó in the southwest disturbed this
general pattern. Similarly Ekmul's links out to Chikindzonot and Cuncunul were the only ones extending further
than a broad zone of origins within 35 kms. of that
pueblo. Other settlements demonstrate similar differentiation at the sub-parish level, which suggests that migration streams may not have been moving from cabecera to
cabecera, as is suggested by the hierarchical model of
Hunt, but rather in a much more complex pattern. Some
moved from pueblo to pueblo; others moved from pueblo to
cabecera; yet others moved from cabecera to pueblo. What
is certain is that the largest proportion of migrants
within each parish normally migrated to the central cabecera (e.g. Tixkokob in Figure 6.8). Depending upon the
total number of dependent sub-settlements, and these did
vary considerably within the Yucatán, then the cabecera's
percentage of the total migration might be relatively
high (e.g. 75% in Sotuta) or quite low (34.5% in Conkal).
      Another means of measuring migration flows is also
available. Since for each parent their place of origin
is identified, it is possible to calculate the range of
settlements involved in the marriage selection process
(Figure 6.9). Conkal is here used as an example. The
top diagram in Figure 6.9 identifies those places from
which spouses migrated to marry a partner from Conkal itself. It can be seen that some fifty percent of all such
partners came from the band of settlements including
Chicxulub, Cholul, Motul, and further afield Ebtún, and
Calkiní. The remaining diagrams identify for separate
settlements the origins of marriage partners who had arrived in Conkal and baptised a child there in the period
1788-1792. Thus the Mérida figures show how important
the urban barrios were as an origin for many later Conkal
residents; equally important is the fact that those marrying into the Mérida population came from a wide area--
from again Ebtún, Calkiní, and also Izamal, Ixil and
Sinanche. This demonstrates that stages in the migration
process may be identified. Before all of these persons
had arrived in Conkal they had passed through the Mérida
jurisdiction.
      The origins of marriage partners for Cholul, Motul,
and Ekmul are also well differentiated (Figure 6.9).
Cholul received most of its migrants from persons who had
come from Motul, Ebtún and Sitpach; Motul marriage partners came principally from Ixil, Ebtún, Temax, Kiní, and
Mama. Ekmul's field included Ixil, Yobain, and Acanseh.
Ebtún, on the other hand, was firmly linked to Santiago
barrio of Mérida, and to Tixkokob and Sitpach. Mococha
partners found most of their spouses in Santiago and
Yobain. Ixil too was linked to Santiago, Izamal, and
Tixkokob. These diagrams show that the patterns of movement between Yucatán settlements were complex and multi-
staged.

166

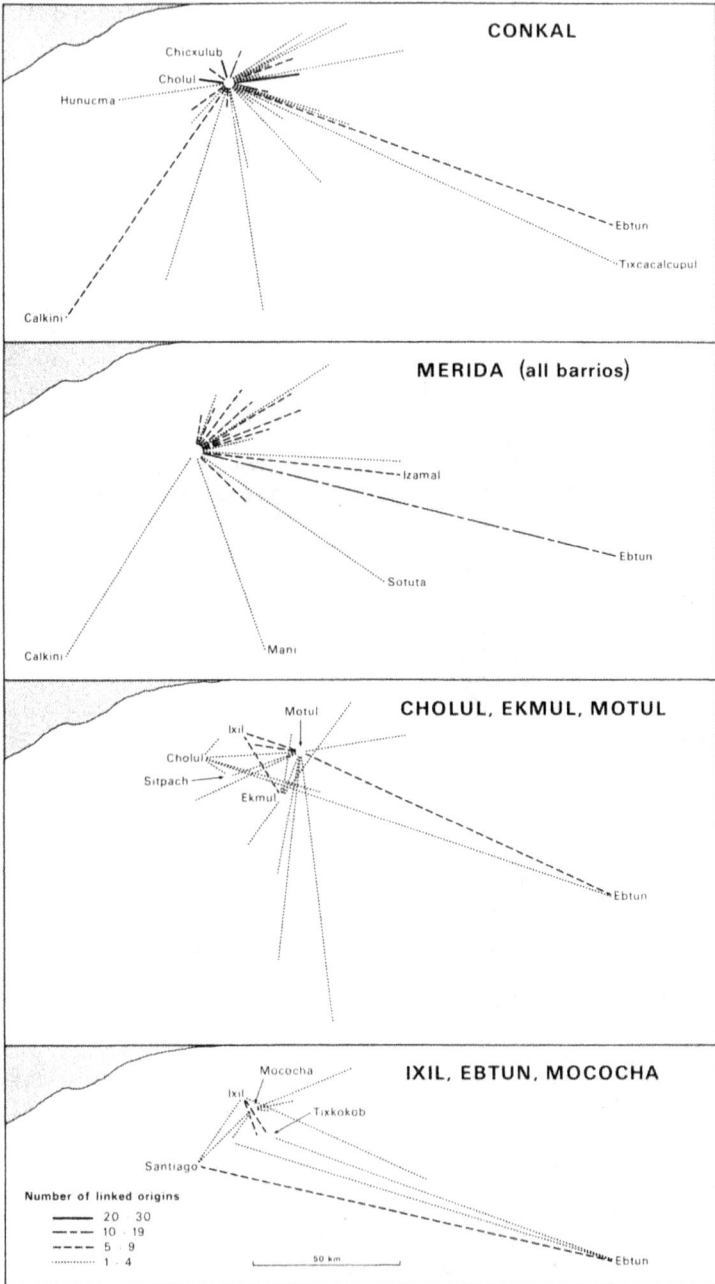

Figure 6.9 Origins of migrants to Conkal and other
intermediate points, 1788-1792

The complexity of the migration process is only fully revealed when sets of individuals are traced through time and space. As an example one may cite cases involving the settlement of Tixkokob. In almost all of the eighteenth century baptisms not only are the parents of the child given, but in many cases so too are the names of its maternal and paternal grandparents, together with their pueblos of origin (of tribute?). This means that it is possible to identify three generations of individuals, and in many cases to identify what was happening to an individual family as its members migrated from their original pueblo.

On 9 November 1796, in Tixkokob a son of Ignacio Chi and Francisca Yuit was baptised. Chi himself had come from Becal, and his father was Marcos Chi, his mother Antonia Chucab. They too were from Becal. The next year Mauricio Chi, Ignacio's brother, baptised his child. Mauricio's wife, Rosa Yuit came from Bokoba, the same pueblo as Ignacio's wife Francisca. Two brothers had married two sisters from the same pueblo. That same year Damaso Pat, from Maní baptised his child at Tixkokob. His wife was Estebana Chi from Becal, and her father was Marcos Chi. She was the sister of Ignacio and Mauricio, and had married a man from Maní before both of them had moved to Tixkokob.

Space precludes any further exemplification of the manner in which it is possible to trace the fortunes of the common Indian families of the Yucatán in the eighteenth century. It should be clear, however, that for a sample of cases it would be possible to recover the migration paths of individuals from a sample of settlements. In that way it might be possible to ascertain whether there were any persistent streams of migrants from settlement to settlement over several generations. That this was the case is suggested by the incidence of very distinctive name groupings in the parish registers. A Poot, a Pat, a Chi, or a Chan can readily be identified with specific settlement areas, a feature that appears to be of some antiquity in the peninsula.[19]

SOME ALTERNATIVE EXPLANATIONS FOR MIGRATION

That a relatively high rate of migration characterized the Yucatán peninsula in the eighteenth century can no longer be denied. More difficult is the task of identifying reasons for such a rate. Some of the migration may well be associated with the moves of Indians to and from the frontier of Spanish control and settlement. Certainly the data for Sotuta would tend to support such an idea. However, until we have Farriss' detailed monograph, which should identify with more precision the specific location of that frontier margin, it is

difficult to be certain of the amount of migration that
may be explained by such a changing set of circumstances.
Since such moves to the open lands of the frontier would
presumably have been in search of land, such a process of
migration should be in direct relationship to population
pressure on land resources in the northern portion of the
Yucatán. Patch's study of the changing density of Spanish estates and commercial agriculture also provides valuable data. It may be noted that the parishes selected
here for analysis fall neatly into Patch's range of categories of Indian involvement in Spanish estate agriculture,[20] but the differences in the rate of Indian migration does not appear to be related in any way to such
agricultural development. It is encouraging to note that
in the 1720s large numbers of forasteros are reported in
several communities outside those studied here,[21] suggesting that non-local population was a common feature
throughout the region.
 Another potential explanation is that most of the
migrants had to search out mates from outside their own
communities owing to the lack of suitable eligibles from
within the local marriage pool. While this can be seen
to have been an important cause of migration elsewhere in
colonial Mexico, there is little reason to believe that
exogamy rules, or shortages of potential partners was the
reason for such significant migration. Even if those who
shared the same patronym were excluded from marriage, it
seems unlikely that the relatively large settlements
could not have provided sufficient eligibles. However,
it will only be possible to estimate the field of eligibles when more work has been completed on baptismal and
marriage rates in selected regions of the area.
 A much more reasonable explanation of the high rate
of migration may be that most Indians who moved did so to
avoid the burdens of tribute, servicio personal, the repartimiento sales, and limosnas and obvenciones. Clearly,
as Gosner has pointed out,[22] it was in the interests of
the encomendero, the priest and the pueblo caciques to
ensure that the Indians did not withdraw from the taxation system, but from an Indian point of view the reverse
was the case. If by moving from one's village one could
escape the burden of Spanish authority then that would
have been a strong incentive indeed. Since those who remained in the villages had to pay more to make up for
those who left, the situation could only have got steadily worse. The chief complaint of the Juzgado de Indios
by the 1720s was the fact that so many Indians were
leaving their settlements.

> en razón de su poco afán por el trabajo, y de su deseo
> de verse libres de las presiones de que eran objeto por
> parte de sus caciques, justicias y fiscales, no solo
> para que trabajasen los tequios y milpas de su comunidad,

sino también para que participasen de los repartimientos
y servicios a españoles . . . Este era, pues, el motivo
de que prefirieran las estancias, ranchos y milperías--
estos dos últimos sobre todo, por su mayor aislamiento.[23]

By this means the estate owners procured labor, and
the Indians escaped all the pressures of social obligations. Of course, this escape cost the Indians much in
terms of breaking up family and community ties, but if,
as was suggested above, it turns out that whole families,
or indeed groups of families engaged in the practice,
then such costs may not have been so onerous. It is
clear that the Spanish could not halt the process of migration, for the lack of attention paid to cédulas of the
1740s which ordered the reduction of all forasteros, ne-
cessitated the creation of the position of cobrador de
indios dispersos.[24]

RESEARCH FOR THE FUTURE

The present study has done no more than expose the
rate and range of migration in the Yucatán during the
eighteenth century. Much more work will need to be done
to fill in the details of the complex process. First,
more communities will need to be examined to see whether
the migration patterns vary significantly by size of settlement, or by distance from the center of economic activity. Second, since the notion of "closed corporate
communities" is seriously eroded by the Yucatán colonial
data, the means of controlling access to land resources
by Indians, the rate of incorporation of non-locals into
the new settlements' compadrinazgo structure, and the
openness of communities all need to be studied in depth.
One may now hypothesize a long-term secular change in the
spatial "openness" of the Yucatecan Indian village (Figure 6.10) that may be more closely calibrated by empiri-
cal data. It is of interest to note that criticisms of
the "closed corporate community" model are now appearing
in widely dispersed contexts.[25]
Only when such questions as these have been addressed will it be possible to fully estimate the significance of the Indian migrations within colonial Yucatán.
For the moment, however, such migration appears to be yet
another characteristic quite unique to the Yucatán, setting it off from other Indian regions of colonial Mexico.

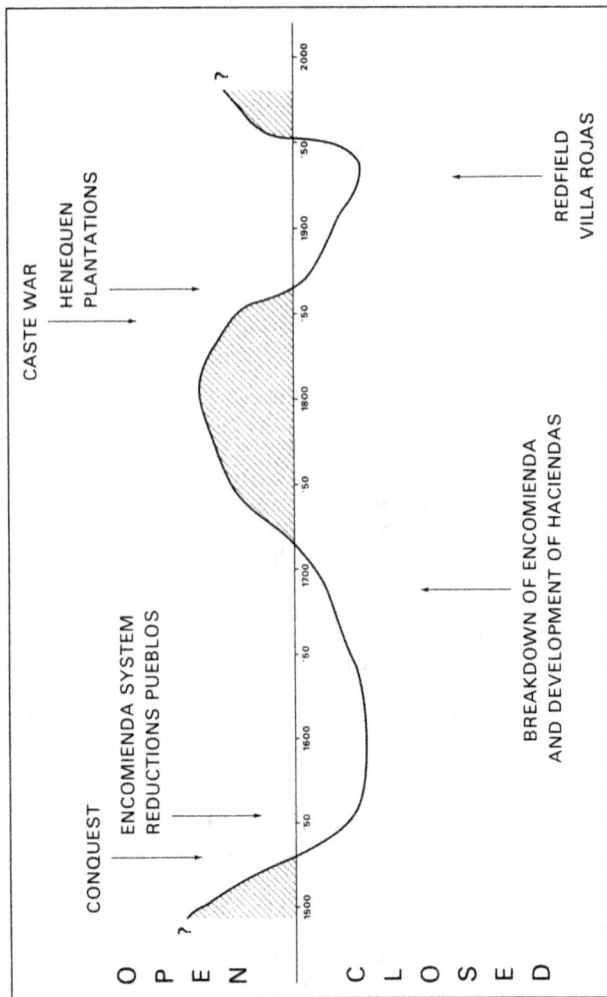

Figure 6.10 Hypothesized changes in "open/closed" nature of Yucatecan settlements

NOTES

1. P. Gerhard, The Southeastern Frontier of New Spain (Princeton: Princeton University Press, 1979).
2. M. Espejo-Ponce Hunt, Colonial Yucatán: Town and Region in the Seventeenth Century, Ph.D. dissertation, University of California, Los Angeles, 1974; M. Espejo-Ponce Hunt, "The Process of Development of Yucatán, 1600-1700," in I. Altman and J. Lockhart (eds.), Provinces of Early Mexico (Los Angeles: University of California Press, 1976); R. Patch, "La formación de estancias y haciendas en Yucatán durante la colonia," Revista de la Universidad de Yucatán, Vol. 18, No. 106 (1976), pp. 95-132; R. Patch, "El mercado urbano y la economía compesina en Yucatán durante el siglo XVIII," Revista de la Universidad de Yucatán, Vol. 20, Nos. 117-118 (1978), pp. 83-96; A. Strickon, "Hacienda and Plantation in Yucatán: An Historical-Ecological Consideration of the Folk Urban Continuum in Yucatán," América Indígena, Vol. XXV (1965), pp. 35-63.
3. S. F. Cook and W. Borah, Essays in Population History (Berkeley: University of California Press, 1971-1974), "The Population of Yucatán, 1517-1960," Vol. II, pp. 1-179; N. M. Farriss, "Nucleation versus Dispersal: The Dynamics of Population Movement in Colonial Yucatán," The Hispanic American Historical Review, Vol. 58 (1978), pp. 187-216; M. C. García Bernal, La Sociedad de Yucatán, 1700-1750 (Sevilla: Estudios Hispano-Americanos de Sevilla, CCVII, 1972); K. Gosner, "Umán Parish: Open, Corporate Communities in Eighteenth Century Yucatán," Paper presented at 75th Annual Meeting of Association of American Geographers, Philadelphia, 1979; D. J. Robinson and C. McGovern, "Population Change in the Yucatán, 1700-1820: Umán Parish in its Regional Context," Paper presented at 75th Annual Meeting of Association of American Geographers, Philadelphia, 1979; J. Ryder, "Internal Migration in Yucatán: Interpretation of Historical Demography and Current Patterns," in Grant Jones (ed.), Anthropology and History of Yucatán (1977), pp. 191-231; F. de Solano y Pérez-Lila, "La población indígena de Yucatán durante la primera mitad del siglo xvii," Anuario de Estudios Americanos, Vol. 28 (1971), pp. 165-200; F. de Solano y Pérez-Lila, "Estudio socio-antropológico de la población rural no indígena de Yucatán, 1700," Revista de la Universidad de Yucatán, Vol. 17, No. 98 (1975), pp. 73-149; P. Thompson, Tekanto in the Eighteenth Century, unpublished Ph.D. dissertation, Tulane University, 1978.
4. H. F. Cline, Regionalism and Society in Yucatán, 1825-1847: A Study of Progressivism and the Origins of the Caste War, Ph.D. dissertation, Harvard University, 1947, available in "Related Studies in Early 19th Century Yucatán Social History," Microfilm Collection of Manuscripts on Middle American Cultural Anthropology, 6th Series, University of Chicago, 1950; J. F. Molina Solis, Historia de Yucatán durante la época española (Mérida, 1921-1927); R. L. Roys, Personal Names of the Maya of Yucatán, (Washington: Carnegie Institution of Washington, Publication 523, 1940); R. L. Roys, The Indian Background of Colonial Yucatán (Washington: Carnegie Institution of Washington, Publication 548, 1943); R. L. Roys, Political Geography of the Yucatán Maya (Washington: Carnegie Institution of Washington, Publication 613, 1957); J. I. Rubio Mañé, Archivo de la Historia de

172

Yucatán, Campeche, y Tabasco (1539-1795) (México: Imprenta Aldina, 3 vols., 1935); F. V. Scholes, C. R. Menendez, J. I. Rubio Mañé and E. B. Adams (eds.), Documentos para la historia de Yucatán (Mérida, 1938).

5. V. Inge Buisson, "Gewalt und Gegengewalt im 'Guerra de Castas' in Yukatan, 1847-1853," Jahrbuch für Geschichte, Vol. 15 (1978), pp. 17-27; R. Redfield and A. Villa Rojas, Chan Kom: A Maya Village (Stanford: Stanford University Press, 1962); N. Reed, The Caste War of Yucatán (Stanford: Stanford University Press, 1964); B. Riese, "Kulturelle Aspekte Indianischer Gewalt im Kastenkrieg in Yukatan," Jahrbuch für Geschichte, Vol. 15 (1978), pp. 29-40; R. A. Thompson, "Structural Statistics and Structural Mechanics: The Analysis of Compadrazgo," Southwestern Journal of Anthropology, Vol. 27 (1971), pp. 381-403; E. Wolf, "Closed, Corporate Peasant Communities in Meso-America and Central Java," Southwestern Journal of Anthropology, Vol. 13 (1957), pp. 1-18.

6. N. M. Farriss, "Nucleation versus Dispersal," p. 204.

7. M. Espejo-Ponce Hunt, Colonial Yucatán, pp. 226-230.

8. M. Espejo-Ponce Hunt, Colonial Yucatán, p. 227.

9. E. Wolf, "Closed, Corporate Peasant Communities," p. 6.

10. R. Redfield, Folk Culture of Yucatán (Chicago: University of Chicago Press, 1941), p. 341.

11. E. Wolf, "Closed, Corporate Peasant Communities," p. 5.

12. D. J. Robinson and C. McGovern, "La migración regional Yucateca en la época colonial--el caso de San Francisco de Umán," Historia Mexicana, Vol. 30 (1980), pp. 99-125.

13. M. Espejo-Ponce Hunt, Colonial Yucatán, p. 243.

14. L. L. Greenow, in this volume; and D. J. Robinson, "Population Patterns in a Northern Mexican Mining Region: Parral in the Late Eighteenth Century," in J. J. Parsons (ed.), Geoscience and Man, Essays in Honor of Robert C. West (Louisiana State University, 1979), Vol. XXI, pp. 83-96; M. M. Swann, "The Spatial Dimensions of a Social Process: Marriage and Mobility in Late Colonial Northern Mexico," in D. J. Robinson (ed.), Social Fabric and Spatial Structure in Colonial Latin America (Ann Arbor: University Microfilms International, 1979), pp. 117-180; L. Yacher, Marriage Migration and Racial Mixing in Colonial Tlazazalca (Michoacán), 1750-1800, Syracuse University Department of Geography Discussion Paper Series, No. 32, 1977.

15. K. Gosner, "Umán Parish," p. 4.

16. H. F. Cline, Regionalism and Society in Yucatán, p. 165.

17. S. F. Cook and W. Borah, Essays in Population History, pp. 140-141.

18. P. Gerhard, The Southeastern Frontier, p. 19.

19. R. L. Roys, Personal Names of the Maya, p. 35.

20. R. Patch, "La formación de estancias," map 2.

21. M. C. García Bernal, La Sociedad de Yucatán, pp. 14-15.

22. K. Gosner, "Umán Parish," p. 12.

23. M. C. García Bernal, La Sociedad de Yucatán, p. 95.

24. K. Gosner, "Umán Parish," p. 13.

25. E. B. Keatinge, "Latin American Peasant Corporate Communities: Potentials for Mobilization and Political Integration," Journal of Anthropological Research, Vol. 29 (1973), pp. 37-58;

A. T. Rambo, "Closed Corporate and Open Peasant Communities: Re-opening a Hastily Shut Case," <u>Comparative Studies in Society and History</u>, Vol. 19 (1977), pp. 179-188.

7
Population Change in the Quinizilapa Valley, Guatemala, 1530–1770

Christopher Lutz

The parish of San Miguel Dueñas is situated in a valley southwest of Antigua Guatemala and Ciudad Vieja (Figure 7.1) in the Department of Sacatepequez. Today this parish comprises the municipios of San Miguel Dueñas, Santa Catarina Barahona and San Antonio Aguas Calientes with its aldeas of San Andrés Ceballos and Santiago Zamora. From around the mid-sixteenth century until about 1750 these five pueblos (i.e. the three municipio cabeceras and the two aldeas mentioned) plus the contiguous pueblo of San Lorenzo el Cubo (today part of the municipio of Ciudad Vieja), known as San Lorenzo Monroy in the colonial period, were administered by the Franciscan convent in Almolonga or Ciudad Vieja. With the secularization of the jurisdictions of the religious orders in the mid-eighteenth century came the creation of the separate parish of San Miguel Dueñas. Today this parish is slightly reduced in size as San Lorenzo forms a part of both the parish and the municipio of Ciudad Vieja.[1]

The valley in which these six pueblos are located undoubtedly displayed a greater natural beauty and geographical unity prior to the draining of Lake Quinizilapa in the late 1920s than it does today.[2] Up until that time all of the Quinizilapa Valley's pueblos, with the exception of the more elevated San Lorenzo, sat near or on the shores of the lake. Due to the lower altitude of this valley than that of Antigua (Panchoy) and its more coastal climate (a transitional climate between the tierra templada and the tierra caliente zones) Lake Quinizilapa appears to have been a long-term health hazard for the surrounding pueblos. The lake was partially drained in the 1920s out of concern for the apparently high incidence of yellow fever and malaria in the region.

Even without the lake the towns which make up the parish of Dueñas (plus San Lorenzo) have a geographical unity forming a micro-region apart from the surrounding area. The Quinizilapa Valley lies between the volcanos of Agua to the east and Acatenango and Fuego to the west.

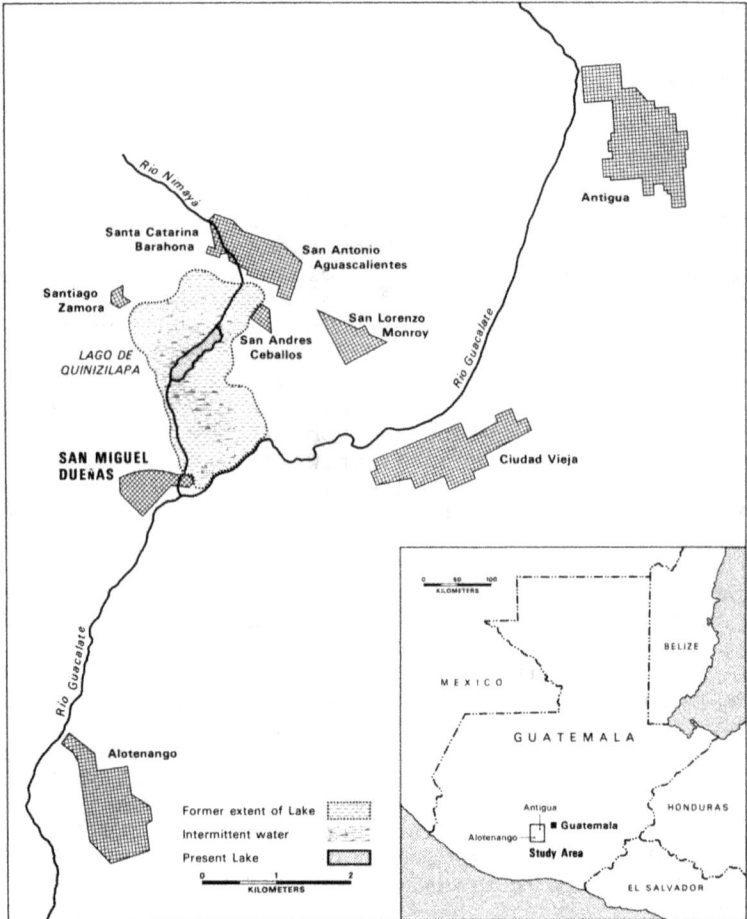

Figure 7.1   Settlements of the Quinizilapa Valley

The explosions and smoking of Fuego have been a constant part of the lives of the inhabitants of these pueblos since their founding over 450 years ago.

These pueblos, and almost all the towns in the immediate hinterland of the two early, permanent capitals of Spanish Central America, Santiago en Almolonga (1527-1541) and Santiago de Guatemala (1541-1773--today La Antigua Guatemala), were established around 1530 (probably in the late 1520s) by Spanish conquistadores-vecinos of the earlier of the two cities. Most Guatemalan Indian pueblos originated in preconquest settlements or were formed by the forced aggregation of a number of scattered settlements in close proximity to their present sites by Spanish civil and ecclesiastical authorities in the first decades after the conquest.[3] But this was not the case in this region. When the Spanish under Pedro de Alvarado founded Santiago en Almolonga (approximately three kilometers east of Lake Quinizilapa) in 1527 the Cakchiqueles had already been in revolt for three years. Cakchiquel resistance was not crushed until 1530.[4] The unrest of the times, however, did not reduce the Spanish vecinos' desires and needs for lands to provide for their families, servants and slaves.

Little is known about the late post-classic and Spanish contact period settlement patterns of the region where the Spanish established their early capitals. Archaeological surveys up to now reveal little or no evidence of late Mayan occupations with the exception of the Cakchiquel encampment Bulbuxyá (gushing water), established to protect nearby milpas. Under Spanish rule this settlement came to be called in corrupted Nahuatl Almolonga and, later, Ciudad Vieja.[5]

Whatever the indigenous settlement patterns which existed at Spanish contact by the late 1520s the Cakchiqueles were in revolt and had withdrawn from the valleys to more inaccessible refuges. The Spanish vecinos were obliged to acquire by capture or purchase Indian slaves and settle them on their lands, including those which the Quinizilapa pueblos occupy today.[6]

The lands on which the valley's Indian settlements were established dated from the distribution of lands made to the first generation of Spanish conquistadores soon after the foundation of Santiago en Almolonga in 1527. It appears that most Spaniards received lands on the same day that they were accepted as vecinos of the city and were formally ceded already designated urban lots (solares) by the Cabildo. Each Spaniard who sought citizenship in the city presented a written petition to the Cabildo formally requesting that he be accepted as a vecino and that he be ceded the solar he had been designated sometime earlier. On the reverse side of these written petitions each prospective vecino described the agricultural lands that he wished to be granted. It

appears that the requests were usually acceded to, providing that a particular grant did not prejudice the
rights of vecinos who had already received lands nearby.
The distribution of agricultural lands in the valleys and
surrounding mountains was especially heavy in 1528 and
1529.[7]

The settlement of these slaves created a series of
milpas or pueblos in the region representing diverse lin-
guistic groups from widespread regions of present-day
Guatemala and beyond. Santa Catarina Barahona, one of
the pueblos under study, according to the vecinos' own
testimony, was founded with Indian slaves from Chamelco
(probably San Juan Chamelco in Alta Verapaz), Utlatecas
(Utatlán, capital of the Quiché state), Atitlán (Santiago
Atitlán, capital of the Tzutujil state), Chontales
(Tabasco or Oaxca in modern, southern Mexico) and Pipiles
(Pacific coast of Guatemala, possibly Esquintepeque or
today, Escuintla). The precise origins of the slaves
settled on the other lands or milpas in the Quinizilapa
Valley are unknown but the pattern found in Santa Catarina Barahona appears to have been typical of both that
valley and the rest of the immediate hinterland of the
Spanish capital.[8] While a large number, probably a majority, of the slaves were settled on the milpas as agricultural laborers, some Spanish vecinos used their slaves
in the mining of precious metals nearby, as in the case
of the inhabitants of Santiago Zamora, and probably more
distant regions (Honduras?) in the case of the slaves of
Diego de Monroy, the señor of the milpa of San Lorenzo
Monroy. In 1575 the vecinos and, by then, former slaves
and descendents of slaves of the milpa of San Lorenzo
Monroy stated:

> . . . and then they sent us to the mines with bateas
> [for gold panning] to work and then came President
> Alonso Cerrato [Alonso López de Cerrato], may he be in
> Heaven, who in the name of His Majesty ended our work
> in the mines . . .[9]

Our knowledge of the daily lives of the slave inhabitants of the milpas of the Quinizilapa Valley in the
second quarter of the sixteenth century is vague at best.
In 1549-50, a landmark date for the inhabitants of the
valley, the slaves of this valley and of the entire ad-
joining valley of the Spanish capital (Panchoy) were
emancipated when Licenciado Alonso López de Cerrato, the
President of the Audiencia of the Cofines, arrived and
sought to enforce the New Laws. The Indian inhabitants
of Santa Catarina Barahona claimed López de Cerrato had
ordered that they be liberated and return to their homelands but that God decided to ". . . settle us [here]
with woman and children and grandchildren . . . ."[10]
López de Cerrato's attempts to enforce the New Laws on

behalf of the Indians of the city's hinterland did not, however, change their lives for the better to the degree that the term "emancipation" suggests.[11] For all too soon the former slaves were burdened with the payment of land rents (terrazgos; see Table 7.1) on the lands where they lived as they still belonged to their former Spanish masters or their heirs. San Antonio was an exception to this pattern; the former slaves of Juan de Chavez said that they were ceded the lands on which they were settled and that when other Spaniards sought to take away their lands President López de Cerrato defended their rights.[12]

While the terrazgos came almost simultaneously with emancipation more onerous forced labor obligations soon followed along with the imposition of tribute payment to the Crown beginning in the early 1560s. Forced labor or mandamiento labor and tribute were burdens which the former slaves suffered in common with many highland Guatemalan Indian pueblos which could be conveniently ex- ploited by the Spanish authorities and individual vecinos. The close proximity of the former slave settlements to the center of Spanish power and population in the city of Santiago de Guatemala served to increase the pressures placed on them.

The male inhabitants of the Quinizilapa pueblos and other Indian pueblos and barrios surrounding the Spanish capital were regularly called upon to supply the city with products not available elsewhere and labor services. Due to their lacustrine setting most of the Quinizilapa pueblos were obliged to supply the Spaniards of the city with fodder (sacate) for their horses at a fixed price of one real per load (carga). The cutting, bundling and hauling on their backs with the aid of a tumpline to the assigned location in the city and the return trip must have cost one Indian vecino from the Quinizilapa towns the better part of an entire day's labor.[13] In addition to these obligations, at least in the late sixteenth cen- tury, the tributaries of the Quinizilapa pueblos were ob- liged to send large numbers of men (apparently a number in proportion to their total populations) to plant, weed and harvest Spanish wheat fields near the capital. On other occasions the vecinos of these towns and others surrounding the Spanish city complained of having to sweep the city's streets and the Casas Reales without any compensation. Another unpleasant task that regularly be- fell the male vecinos of these pueblos was the cleaning of drainage canals and the river bed of the Río Pensativo just prior to the rainy season so as to reduce the chances of flooding in the Spanish city.[14]

An accurate estimate of the number of slaves settled in the six milpas of the Quinizilapa Valley around 1530 is difficult to derive. We do know the number of slaves owned by certain vecinos of the Spanish capital at vari- ous times during the 1530s and 1540s, but the use made of

180

TABLE 7.1
Terrazgos paid by the milpas of the Quinizilapa Valley, c. 1580

Name of Milpa	Name of Founder c. 1530	Recipient of Terrazgo c. 1580	Annual Payment
San Andrés Ceballos	Pedro de Ceballos	heirs of Ceballos	20 fanegas maize 20 chickens 20 tostones
San Lorenzo Monroy	Diego de Monroy	María de Monroy (1576)	20 fanegas maize
Juan de Chaves llamada San Antonio de Padua (Aguas Calientes)	Juan de Chaves	no terrazgo paid; lands ceded c. 1550 by Chaves to the vecinos of the milpa	
Santa Catarina Barahona	Sancho de Barahona	Sancho de Barahona "El Mozo"	60 fanegas maize 40 chickens
Santiago de Zamora	Alonso de Zamora	Juan de León (1575) "señor de las tierras"	20 fanegas maize 15 tostones
San Miguel Dueñas	Miguel de Dueñas	"Dueñas, señor de las tierras"	40 fanegas maize 20 chickens

Source: Lutz, Santiago de Guatemala, Tables 6 and 9, pp. 130 and 159-161, respectively.

these slaves, whether they worked on agricultural lands near the Spanish capital or were mostly used in mining operations in distant Honduras, is usually unclear. It is also possible that slaves settled on the milpas around the Spanish capital were used seasonally or for a few years at a time panning or mining precious metals in say, Honduras, and then returned. The hardships of long marches combined with mine-related labor (especially at lower altitudes where the risk of death from epidemic diseases increased) must have taken a heavier toll on their numbers.[15] But then we cannot be certain that mine labor necessarily took a heavier toll than the demands placed on the slaves who resided in or near the capital. Aside from agricultural labor the 1530s and 1540s were decades of intense construction activity. One has only to remember that one city, Santiago en Almolonga, was founded in 1527 only to be destroyed by massive mud slides in September, 1541; and another, Santiago de Guatemala, was laid out and under construction a few months later.[16] Building construction must have been continuous throughout the period.

Another unknown concerns the frequency with which the Spanish vecinos acquired new slaves to replace those who died. Without the information (which is the equivalent of data on inward migration) it is nearly impossible to reconstruct the early population history of the milpas settled by slaves surrounding the early Spanish capital and its successor, Santiago de Guatemala. While slaves might have spent seasons or years engaged in mining in Honduras and periodically returned to Guatemala, there is also some evidence that other slaves, upon their emancipation by President López de Cerrato in 1548-1549, were settled on their former masters' milpas near Santiago de Guatemala. The precedent for settling former Indian mine slaves near the city was established by Bishop Francisco Marroquín in 1543 when the recently deceased Pedro de Alvarado's mining slaves (men, women and children) were freed and settled in the parcialidad of Jocotenango, known as Santiago Utatleca, located on the northern periphery of the then newly-established capital of Santiago de Guatemala.[17] As has already been mentioned, under López de Cerrato the former mine slaves of Diego de Monroy, the señor of the milpa of San Lorenzo Monroy, were returned and settled on that milpa around 1549; and this may not have been the only settlement among the Quinizilapa milpas to have experienced this process. It can be safely assumed, however, that while former mine slaves were added to one or more of these six milpas during emancipation (1548-49), after that period Spanish-directed immigration halted.

The coincidence of emancipation from slavery with the mid-sixteenth century would serve as a useful bench mark from which to begin an analysis of population

changes in the six milpas of the Quinizilapa Valley. Unfortunately, however, anything resembling reliable population data does not begin until around 1575. One explanation for the lack of specific population data for
the Quinizilapa pueblos until the mid-1570s is that none
of the former slave settlements even began to pay tribute
to the Crown until the mid-1560s.

Population estimates for the valley of the city of
Guatemala, which includes the Quinizilapa milpas, exist
from 1548-1550 through 1582. One estimate (Table 7.2)
refers to freed slaves, another to married Indians who
were not paying any tribute and the remaining figures are
contradictory and probably incomplete tributary counts.

By removing the most inconsistent data from consideration it is possible to demonstrate that the valley's
Indian population was in sharp decline between 1550 and
1581. The decline in population totals is corroborated
by reports of flight and high Indian mortality resulting
from hunger, sickness and epidemics.[18] It would be close
to pure speculation to even attempt an estimate of the
Quinizilapa milpas' population around 1550, but it would
be surprising if they all did not lose a large percentage
of their inhabitants in the course of the quarter century
that followed.

The impact of the great pandemics of the late 1540s
and 1570s upon the native populations of New Spain and
Spanish Guatemala is by now well established. But aside
from these two destructive waves of pestilence there are
documented reports of serious outbreaks of disease of
epidemic proportions during every decade (except the
1580s) between 1560 and 1770 in the immediate hinterland
of the Spanish urban center which includes the Quinizilapa micro-region.[19] The direct impact of these epidemics on the Quinizilapa pueblos is unknown in almost all
cases until the mid-eighteenth century when parish burial
registers provide direct information on epidemics and the
resulting mortality.[20]

RECONSTRUCTION OF THE POPULATION OF THE QUINIZILAPA
PUEBLOS

Reconstruction of population movements in the six
Quinizilapa pueblos will be based on a reduced series of
tribute and tributary totals. Unfortunately, there are
only four dates between 1575 and 1754-55 for which we
have population data for all six pueblos. These data are
expressed in every instance as numbers of tributaries.

Padrones would be useful to determine the ratio of
tributaries to population for these towns but they are
only extant from the mid-eighteenth century for the
Quinizilapa towns. While padrones are extant for a number of highland Indian towns from the sixteenth and

TABLE 7.2
Estimated Indian population of the valley of Santiago de Guatemala,
1548-1581

Date	Population size (Males)	Remarks	Source
1548-50	Est. 3000-5000 freed slaves	Number of slaves freed in the city and surrounding valley; naboríos apparently not included	William L. Sherman, personal communication, 7 January 1972
1560	Est. 5000-6000 married Indians	Number of married Indians in and around Spanish capital who did not pay tribute to anyone	Audiencia to the King, AGI, Guatemala 9 (Santiago: 30 June 1560)
1567	1669-1654 tributaries	Tributaries in the jurisdiction of the Corregidor of the valley; lower figure due to correction for 15 reserved, deceased or absent	Accounts of 1567 and 1572, AGI, Contaduría 967
1571-72	4025 tributaries	Many persons reported counted who were lawfully exempt from tributary status	Accounts of 1567 and 1572, AGI, Contaduría 967
1574	2663 tributaries	Probably an accurate count	Audiencia to the King, AGI, Guatemala 10 (Santiago: 13 September 1574)
1581	2271 tributaries	Married Indian tributaries	AGI, Patronato 183, Ramo 1°.

184

seventeenth centuries it would be unwise to apply their
tributary to total population (T/P) ratios to the Quinizilapa towns because of the differences in their origins.[21] Towns with preconquest roots often survived the
conquest period and the sixteenth century population decline with at least remnants of their prehispanic socio-
economic structures intact. Hereditary rulers and their
families often continued to rule their towns and maintained a degree of special status and privilege vis-à-vis
their subject populations. All of this resulted in a
more complex social structure in the sixteenth century
prehispanic towns than in the settlements populated by
slaves and, after 1550, their descendents. These basic
differences would appear to have resulted in two different pueblo types with distinctive population structures.
Given these differences it seems unlikely that a T/P ratio for a preconquest town could be safely applied to the
towns of slave origins without seriously distorting upward the population size of the latter towns. For this
reason population changes will be discussed here only in
terms of tributaries until census-type data becomes
available beginning in the mid-eighteenth century.

The tributary data for the Quinizilapa towns begins
for all six pueblos around 1575, or just prior to the
devastating pandemic of the late 1570s. For three of the
pueblos (Santiago Zamora, San Andrés Ceballos and San
Lorenzo Monroy) tributary totals also exist for 1581.
While Santiago Zamora actually grew between 1575 and 1581,
San Andrés Ceballos and San Lorenzo Monroy sharply declined (Table 7.3) during the same short period. In order to make comparisons of population change between individual towns or between different periods we have
adopted the coefficient of population movement (ω) developed by Cook and Borah.[22] When the tributary totals for
the three towns for each year (1575 and 1581) are combined and the coefficient of population movement value is
compared with that for the valley of the city of Guatemala (for the period 1574-1581) we see that the values
are very similar.[23] Table 7.4 shows in more detail the
extent of population decline (as measured by tributaries)
for the entire valley of the city of Santiago de Guatemala between 1570 and 1581.

For the period 1575-1638 comparative data exist for
all six Quinizilapa pueblos. The ω values for four of
the towns demonstrate a small population decline between
1575 and 1638. The data in Tables 7.5 and 7.6 and other
less comparative and more scattered data for intermediate
dates suggest that the nadirs of population decline for
three of these pueblos (San Lorenzo Monroy, San Miguel
Dueñas and Santa Catarina Barahona) probably occurred
sometime between 1600 and 1630.[24] The same pattern also
appears to apply to San Antonio Aguas Calientes except
that this town recovered more vigorously and slightly

TABLE 7.3
Comparison of population movements in three Quinizilapa milpas and
the valley of the city between 1575 and 1581

Jurisdiction	Tributaries circa 1575	Tributaries circa 1581	Coefficient of Population Movement (ω)
Santiago Zamora	37	44	+2.89
San Andrés Ceballos	30	20	-6.80
San Lorenzo Monroy	64	49	-4.46
Total of the three milpas	131	113	-2.46
Valley of the city	2,663*	2,271	-2.27

Sources: Audiencia to the King (Santiago: 13 September 1574), AGI,
Guatemala 10; "Los indios que eran esclavos . . . [1576]," AGI,
Guatemala 54; Accounts of 1576, AGI, Contaduría 968; "Razón de las
tasaciones . . . [1582]," AGI, Guatemala 966; and AGI, Patronato
183, Ramo 1°.

*Tributary total for 1574.

TABLE 7.4
Estimated Crown tributary figures, valley of the city of Santiago de
Guatemala, 1570 to 1581

Year	Number of Tributaries	Total tributary decline from previous count
1570	3,093	--
1571	3,022	-71
1574	2,663	-359
1579	2,531	-132
1581	2,271	-260

Sources: AGI, Contaduría 967 and 968; and Audiencia to the King
(Santiago: 13 September 1574), AGI, Guatemala 10.

TABLE 7.5
Coefficients of population change (ω) for the Quinizilapa towns

Period	Santiago Zamora	S. Andrés Ceballos	S. Lorenzo Monroy	S. Antonio A. C.	S. Miguel Dueñas	Sta. Catarina
1575-1581	+2.89%	-6.80%	-4.46%	--	--	--
1575-1638	+0.51%	-0.50%	-0.71%	+0.02%	-0.27%	-0.62%
1581-1638	+0.26%	+0.17%	-0.31%	--	--	--
1638-1684	+2.12%	+0.32%	+2.18%	+0.75%	+2.84%	+2.25%
1684-1755	+0.71%	+0.41%	+0.42%	+0.22%	-0.29%	+0.62%

TABLE 7.6
Tributary totals (tributarios enteros): Quinizilapa towns, 1575-1755

Year	Santiago Zamora	S. Andrés Ceballos	S. Lorenzo Monroy	S. Antonio A. C.	S. Miguel Dueñas	Sta. Catarina
1575	37	30	64	~102	~45	~57
1581	44	20	49	--	--	--
1638	51	22	41	103	38	39
1684	131	25½	108	145	130	105½
1755*	216	34	145	169	106	162

Sources: "Los indios que eran esclavos . . . [1576]," AGI, Guatemala 54; "Razón de las tasaciónes . . . [1582]," AGI, Guatemala 966; "Relación del Proceso . . . [1638]," AGI, Guatemala 70; AGCA, A3 824 15.207 ("Liquidación . . . [1684]"); AGCA, A3 1616 26.578 ("Razón de los Tributarios . . . [1754]"); AGCA, A3 948 17.706 (1755).

*Tributary counts for San Antonio Aguas Calientes, San Miguel Dueñas and Santa Catarina Barahona are from 1754 not 1755. All of the 1754-55 tributary totals are adjusted upward to compensate for the elimination of women from the tributary rolls so that these totals are comparable to those for the earlier dates, all of which include women in the tributary counts.

earlier than the four which showed negative ω values for the period 1575-1638. As in the period 1575-1581 of the six Quinizilapa towns only Santiago Zamora demonstrated sustained growth during this period of transition. Nevertheless, it appears as though a majority of the Quinizilapa pueblos began their demographic recovery during the 1620s and 1630s. As has been pointed out previously by other researchers, population studies based on tributary counts must always take into account the lapse that occurs between the time when a given population begins to increase (more annual births than deaths) and the time when that growth results (when the new born have reached their majorities) in increased numbers of tributaries.

In the period 1638-1684 all six pueblos (Figure 7.2) of the Quinizilapa Valley experienced population growth. The towns of Santiago Zamora, San Lorenzo Monroy, San Miguel Dueñas and Santa Catarina Barahona grew at faster rates than either San Antonio Aguas Calientes or San Andrés Ceballos, the smallest of the towns. Explanations as to the reason why San Antonio, the largest of the pueblos in 1638, should have grown more slowly than all the other Quinizilapa towns, with the exception of San Andrés, are not apparent. The slower population growth of San Andrés Ceballos could have been the result of near stagnation due to the small size of that pueblo, at least from the late sixteenth century. A reduced pool from which to select prospective spouses might have pushed younger vecinos, especially men, outside the village in search of marriage partners. In 1755 out of a total married male population of twenty-five, thirteen men from San Andrés Ceballos were married to Indian women from other pueblos. This total was higher than that for Santa Catarina (9) and slightly lower than that for Santiago Zamora (16) even though both these latter pueblos were five to six times more populous than San Andrés.[25]

The pattern of population increase which began in the mid-seventeenth century (1638-1684) in the Quinizilapa towns continued during the period 1684-1755. The only exception to this pattern was the pueblo of San Miguel Dueñas which, from the early sixteenth century, had experienced an historical development quite distinctive from the other five pueblos. The divergent history of Dueñas derived from the introduction of sugar cultivation combined with the settlement of an unknown but apparently reduced number of African slaves on Spanish-owned lands which lay near the shores of Lake Quinizilapa and the pueblo of Dueñas in the early post-conquest decades. At present little is known about the success or failure of sugar cultivation in this region during the colonial period. But in the late 1760s only Dueñas of the region's pueblos contained an agricultural estate deserving of mention by Archbishop Cortés y Larraz—the Hacienda de Batres with nine resident mozos and a

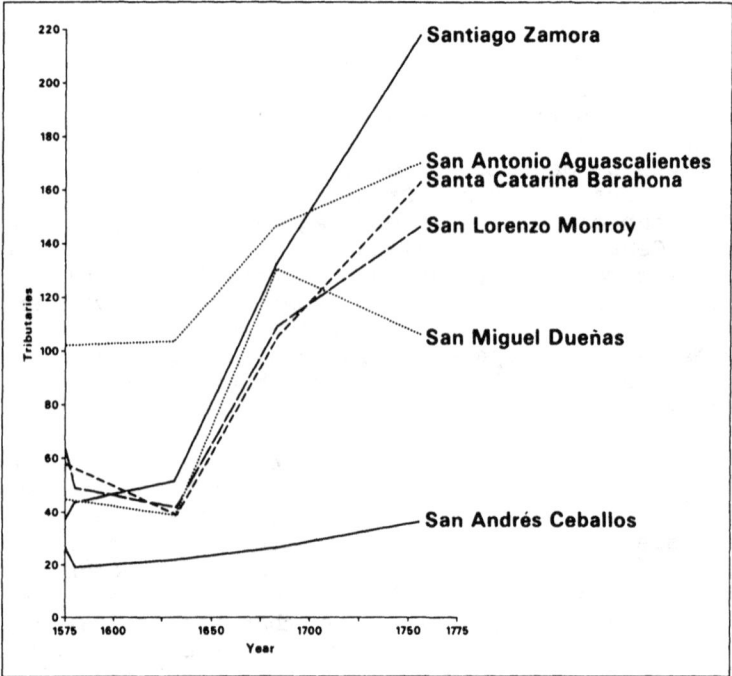

Figure 7.2 Population change in the Quinizilapa towns, 1575-1755

mayordomo.[26] The earliest parish registers from Dueñas
reveal the impact of the African slaves introduced more
than two centuries earlier. Free mulattoes and ladinos
are frequently mentioned as vecinos of Dueñas. By the
mid-eighteenth century San Miguel Dueñas was well along
in the process of ladinization. Ladinization in Santiago
de Guatemala and, by extension, in certain towns which
for reasons of commerce and/or sugar cultivation had concentrations of persons, both slave and free, of African
descent was strongly influenced by this element and not
just by mestizos as has so often been claimed in the traditional historical and anthropological literature on
Guatemala.[27]

Tributary counts for the Quinizilapa pueblos for the
late eighteenth and early nineteenth centuries have yet
to be located. However, for the late 1760s the first apparently reliable population counts or censuses by categories of civil status are available. This information
consists of the responses to questionnaires sent out under the direction of Archbishop Pedro Cortés y Larraz.
These responses are not uniformly complete but the one by
the parish priest of the six pueblos provides the total
numbers by pueblo (Table 7.7) of the following: number of
families; married males and couples; widows and widowers;
adults (unmarried); and children (párvulos, probably including everyone from 0 to 12 years of age). Later research will have to determine the accuracy of these data
by checking them against parish register totals and new
tributary lists. Likewise, the relative accuracy of the
modern, published Guatemalan national censuses (beginning
with that of 1880) in terms of completeness of data and
the changing ratios of Indian and ladino populations
needs to be considered.[28] Taking into account the possible problems with the data, Table 7.8 demonstrates the
magnitude of the growth of the Quinizilapa pueblos over
the last two centuries (1768-1973) by comparing census
totals from 1768, 1880 and 1973. All of the pueblos have
consistently grown over this period with the exception of
Santiago Zamora which, curiously, was by far the most
populous of the six towns in 1768. The low percentage of
children (10%) in Santiago Zamora's 1768 population compared with a total of 35 percent children in the five
other towns (combined) suggests that perhaps it had suffered from some localized epidemic(s) which struck infants and children.[29] The combined Indian and ladino
populations for the six towns shows almost a four-fold
increase in the course of 200 years which is a far
smaller increase than that experienced for the Republic
of Guatemala as a whole.[30]

Subsequent population studies on the Quinizilapa
towns must come to terms with the possible impact of the
formerly more extensive lake on the health conditions of
the pueblos. The introduction of coffee culture and

TABLE 7.7
Population data for the Quinizilapa towns, 1768

	S. Miguel Dueñas (N)	(%)	S. Antonio A. C. (N)	(%)	S. Andres Ceballos (N)	(%)	Sta. Catarina Barahona (N)	(%)	Santiago Zamora (N)	(%)	S. Lorenzo Monroy (N)	(%)	Total (N)	(%)	Total less Zamora (N)	(%)
Indians:																
Families	98		81		20		83		131		57		470		339	
Married persons	124	(42)	260	(47)	62	(53)	254	(43)	504	(62)	176	(59)	1380	(52)	876	(47)
Widows/Widowers	22	(8)	25	(4.5)	8	(7)	17	(3)	36	(4)	13	(4)	121	(4.5)	85	(4.6)
Adults (unmarried)	63	(21)	75	(13.5)	14	(12)	81	(14)	193	(24)	14	(5)	440	(16.5)	247	(13.4)
Sub-total	209		360		84		352		733		203		1941		1208	
Children (párvulos)	86	(29)	194	(35)	32	(28)	232	(40)	79	(10)	97	(32)	720	(27)	641	(35)
Total	295		554		116		584		812		300		2661		1849	
Persons per family	3.0		6.8		5.8		7.0		6.3		5.3		5.7		5.5	
Persons per married man (casado)	4.7		4.3		3.7		4.6		3.3		3.4		3.9		4.2	
Children per married couple	1.4		1.5		1.0		1.8		0.3		1.1		1.0		1.5	
Children per family	0.9		2.4		1.6		2.8		1.7		1.7		1.5		1.9	
Ladinos:																
Families	36															
Married persons	56	(36)														
Widows/Widowers	8	(5)														
Adults (unmarried)	50	(33)														
Sub-total	114															
Children (párvulos)	40	(26)														
Total: Indian & Ladino	449															
Men*	224		196		62		308		423		146					
Women*	225		258		54		276		389		154					

Source: AGI, Guatemala, 948, Vol. 30, "Testimonio de las respuestas . . . [1768]."

*Sum of Men and Women for all towns except Dueñas to be found above as total of Indian population.

TABLE 7.8
Comparison of population size of the Quinizilapa towns: 1768, 1880 and 1973

Town	1768			1880			1973		
	Indian	Ladino	Total	Indian	Ladino	Total	Indian	Ladino	Total
San Miguel Dueñas	295	154	449	383	2734	3117	1425	2790	4215
San Lorenzo Monroy	300	--	300	375	--	375	464	790	1254
Sta. Catarina Barahona	584	--	584	926	9	935	1064	82	1146
San Antonio A. C.	554	--	554	1508	12	1520	3024	150	3174
San Andrés Ceballos	116	--	116	200	--	200	377	5	382
Santiago Zamora	812	--	812	392	6	398	307	3	310
Total--6 towns	2661	154	2815	3784	2761	6545	6661	3820	10,481

Sources: "Testimonio de las respuestas . . . [1768]," AGI, Guatemala 948, Vol. 30; Guatemala, Censo General de 1880; Guatemala, Dirección General de Estadística, VIII Censo de la Población, 1973. Data from the 1880 and 1973 censuses were kindly provided by Sheldon Annis, (University of Chicago).

other forms of commercial agriculture since the middle of
the last century and the resulting loss of lands due to
these intrusions also have to be studied and considered
in terms of their impact on population change, especially
seasonal and permanent migration patterns. As in so many
other fields of study in Guatemala, the changing land
tenure patterns may be the key variable in the study of
the Quinizilapa Valley's population history.

NOTES

   1. Mateo Morales Urrutía, La división política y administrativa
de la República de Guatemala con sus datos históricos y de legisla-
ción (Guatemala: Editorial Iberia-Gutenburg, 1961), Tomo II, pp.
341-346, 357-359, 363-365, and 377-379.
   2. Quinizilapa is often spelled Quilizinapa but the first
spelling appears to make more sense linguistically, meaning in
Nahuatl "place of intermittent waters." See Alonso de Molina, Vo-
cabulario en Lengua Castellana y Mexicana y Mexicana y Castellana,
Edición Facsimilie (México: Editorial Porrua, 1970), p. 90.
   3. See, for example, mention of the founding of Sololá in 1547
in the Cakchiquel chronicle, The Annals of the Cakchiquels. Title of
the Lords of Totonicapán, Adrian Recinos, Delia Goetz and Dionisio
José Chonay, editors and translators (Norman: University of Oklahoma
Press, 1974), p. 136; and the establishment of Alotenango, at its
first site, about 1540 with Indians collected from Pacific coastal
towns. Francisco Vázquez, Crónica de la provincia del Santísimo
Nombre de Jesús de Guatemala (Guatemala: Sociedad de Geografía e
Historia de Guatemala, 1937-44, Biblioteca "Goathemala," Vols. XIV-
XVII) I, p. 87.
   4. One recent study that covers this period is Francis Polo
Sifontes, Los Cakchiqueles en la conquista de Guatemala (Guatemala:
Editorial "José de Pineda Ibarra," 1977), pp. 79-88.
   5. For a more complete discussion see Christopher H. Lutz,
Santiago de Guatemala, 1541-1773: The Sociodemographic History of a
Spanish American Colonial City (Ph.D. Dissertation, University of
Wisconsin-Madison, 1976). Also see: Stephen F. de Borhegyi, "Estudio arqueológico en la falda norte del volcán de Agua," Revista de
Antropología e Historia de Guatemala, Vol. II, No. 1 (January, 1950),
pp. 3-22; and Edwin M. Shook, "Lugares arqueológicos del altiplano
meridional central de Guatemala," Revista de Antropología e Historia
de Guatemala, Vol. IV, No. 2 (June, 1952), pp. 3-40.
   6. See William L. Sherman, Forced Native Labor in Sixteenth-
Century Central America (Lincoln: University of Nebraska Press, 1979),
esp. pp. 20-82, for a detailed discussion of Spanish slaving practices; and Lutz, Santiago de Guatemala, pp. 122-127.
   7. This paragraph is taken from Lutz, Santiago de Guatemala,
pp. 123-124. The primary source is the Libro viejo de la fundación
de Guatemala y papeles relativos a Don Pedro de Alvarado (Guatemala:
Sociedad de Geografía e Historia de Guatemala, 1934, Biblioteca

"Goathemala," Vol. XII), pp. 33-34 and <u>passim</u>.

8. See Lutz, <u>Santiago de Guatemala</u>, pp. 125-127 and William L. Sherman, <u>Indian Slavery in Spanish Guatemala, 1524-1550</u> (Ph.D. Dissertation, University of New Mexico, 1967), pp. 120-121 for list of the names and places of origin of Cristobal Lobo's slaves in 1549. Lobo was a vecino of Santiago de Guatemala.

9. See: "Los indios que eran esclavos . . . [1576]", Archivo General de Indias [hereafter cited as AGI], Guatemala 54; Lutz, <u>Santiago de Guatemala</u>, pp. 139-143 for a discussion of mining labor provided by Indian slaves who were later settled in and around Santiago de Guatemala; and Sherman, <u>Forced Native Labor</u>, <u>passim</u>.

10. "Los indios que eran esclavos . . . [1576]", AGI, Guatemala 54, f. 29.

11. See William L. Sherman, "Indian Slavery and the Cerrato Reforms," <u>Hispanic American Historical Review</u>, Vol. 51 (1971), pp. 25-50 and the contrasting view of Murdo J. MacLeod, <u>Spanish Central America: A Socioeconomic History, 1520-1720</u> (Berkeley, University of California Press, 1973), pp. 109-119.

12. "Los indios que eran esclavos . . . [1576]", AGI, Guatemala 54, f. 28. This would have occurred in the early 1550s.

13. Without exception all of the Quinizilapa towns complained of this burden. "Los indios que eran esclavos . . . [1576]", AGI, Guatemala 54, ff. 28 v. -32.

14. "Los indios que eran esclavos . . . [1576]", AGI, Guatemala 54; and Archivo General de Centroamerica [hereafter cited as AGCA], A1 2824 25.071 (1706). In the seventeenth and eighteenth centuries these towns are rarely mentioned in the repartimiento de indios to the wheat farms (<u>labores</u>) as wheat came to be cultivated more intensely in the valleys north, northeast and east of the immediate valley of the capital city, the valley of Panchoy. See, for example, Lutz, <u>Santiago de Guatemala</u>, pp. 555-556 and 585, n. 12.

15. Sherburne F. Cook and Woodrow Borah, <u>Essays in Population History</u>, 2 vols. (Berkeley: University of California Press, 1971-1974), I, pp. 79-82 discuss differential population decline in coastal and highland ecological zones in sixteenth-century Mexico.

16. For Santiago en Almolonga see: Janos de Szecsy, <u>Santiago de los Caballeros de Guatemala en Almolonga</u> (Guatemala: IAHG, 1953); and for Santiago de Guatemala see: Sidney David Markman, <u>The Colonial Architecture of Antigua Guatemala</u> (Philadelphia: American Philosophical Society, 1966); and Verle L. Annis, <u>The Architecture of Antigua Guatemala, 1543-1773</u> (Guatemala: Universidad de San Carlos de Guatemala, 1968, Bilingual edition).

17. See Lutz, <u>Santiago de Guatemala</u>, pp. 139 and 171, n. 32. Alvarado, who had many more slaves than other vecinos, had 330 gold-mining slaves from Totonicapán, Tecpanatitlán and Atitlán in 1538. See William L. Sherman, "A Conqueror's Wealth: Notes on the Estate of Don Pedro de Alvarado," <u>The Americas</u>, Vol. XXVI, No. 2 (October, 1969), p. 209.

18. See Lutz, <u>Santiago de Guatemala</u>, pp. 251-253 and 286.

19. The dates of documented epidemics are: 1560-61; 1563-65; 1592-93; 1600-01; 1607-08; 1614; 1623; 1631-32; 1647; 1650; 1665-66; 1669; 1676; 1686-87; 1693-94; 1696; 1699; 1704-05; 1707; 1708; 1709; 1716; 1723; 1724; 1725; 1728; 1733; 1741; 1746 (food shortage too);

1748; 1749; 1752; 1761 and 1769. See Lutz, Santiago de Guatemala, Appendix VI, pp. 743-752 and MacLeod, Spanish Central America, pp. 98-100.

20. The parish archive of San Miguel Dueñas has recently been microfilmed by the Genealogical Society of Utah.

21. Excellent padrones and tasaciones exist for the Cakchiquel speaking pueblos of Chimaltenango, Comalapa, Sumpango, San Juan Sacatepéquez, and San Pedro Sacatepéquez, in the AGI, Guatemala 45, for the late 1560s. For a detailed discussion of the T/P ratio see Cook and Borah, Essays in Population History, I, pp. 280-286.

22. Cook and Borah, Essays in Population History, I, pp. 89-91.

23. We must keep in mind that the decline in tributary numbers between 1578 and 1581 is not totally due to Indian deaths caused by hunger and epidemics but was also caused by flight. See, for example, the complaints of the Cabildo members and principales of San Antonio Aguas Calientes (called the Milpa de Juan de Cháves) and other Quinizilapa towns in "Los indios que eran esclavos . . . [1576]", AGI, Guatemala 54, f. 28 and ff.

24. See Accounts of 1622 and 1623, in AGI, Guatemala 15. But data on San Andrés Ceballos suggests that that pueblo might have reached a peak ca. 1600 and then gradually declined until some point in the mid to late 1660s. See AGCA, A3 258 5763 (1603); AGCA, A3 477 9960; and the Bishop to His Majesty (Santiago, 18 September 1661), AGI, Guatemala 157.

25. While San Andrés had a disproportionate number of its males married to women from other pueblos for its size Santiago Zamora (with 12) and Santa Catarina (with 13) each had a number of women married with men from other pueblos and with absent men (ausentes). On the other hand San Andrés had a total of only three women married to men from other pueblos or absent. See AGCA, A3 948 17.706.

26. See Pedro Cortés y Larraz, Descripción geográfico-moral de la diócesis de Goathemala, 2 vols. (Guatemala: Sociedad de Geografía e Historia de Guatemala, 1958, Biblioteca "Goathemala," Vol. XX), I, p. 37. The Luis Diez de Navarro map of the valley of the city of Santiago de Guatemala drawn soon after the earthquake of July 29, 1773 includes the Hacienda de Urias in Dueñas but apparently not that of Batres. See this map in the AGI map collection or in that of the AGCA Mapoteca.

27. For more detailed discussion of this point see: Lutz, Santiago de Guatemala, pp. 28-29 and 411-418.

28. John D. Early has demonstrated the problems in ethnic reporting resulting in inflated ladino totals and lower Maya Indian totals in the Guatemalan censuses of 1950 and 1964. See John D. Early, "Revision of Ladino and Maya Census Populations of Guatemala, 1950 and 1964," Demography, Vol. 11, 1974, pp. 105-116.

29. Santiago Zamora did suffer a "Peste de fríos calenturas" during 1764 and 1765 but not one párvulo is listed among the 46 deaths recorded in those two years. Archivo de la Parroquia de San Miguel Dueñas, "Libro no. 1°.--Defunciones del pueblo de Santiago Zamora desde el año 1764 hasta el de 1790," ff. 2v.-3.

30. See Nicolás Sánchez-Albornoz, The Population of Latin America: A History (Berkeley: University of California Press, 1974), Tables 5.11 and 6.1, pp. 169 and 184, respectively.

8
The Historical Demography of the Cuchumatán Highlands of Guatemala, 1500–1821

W. George Lovell

INTRODUCTION

In many colonial societies there exists a close relationship between population size and economic well-being. Spanish Central America illustrates this relationship clearly. The economic prospects of the colony were intimately linked to its historical demography. Thus with a large population from which to draw labor, the initial economic outlook seemed promising. As population declined during the sixteenth and seventeenth centuries, a severe economic depression set in. When population began to increase towards the end of the seventeenth and throughout the eighteenth century, the economy revived.[1]

The operation of this crude, causal connection between population size and economic well-being permeates a number of developments in Spanish Central America. Indian depopulation was a major factor behind the demise of the encomienda system. It also contributed towards the formation of the great estate, or hacienda, and the emergence of debt peonage.[2] Such important developments can therefore be fully understood only when viewed in relation to population trends and fluctuations. It is to the establishment of a demographic profile for the Cuchumatán highlands of Guatemala during the three centuries of Spanish domination in Central America that this paper is directed.

THE REGIONAL SETTING

The Cuchumatán highlands of Guatemala are the most

The author wishes to thank the Izaak Walton Killam Memorial Fund for Advanced Studies for the financial support during the years in which the archival investigations central to this paper were conducted.

massive and spectacular non-volcanic region of all Central America. Lying to the north of the Río Cuilco, and
to the north and west of the Río Negro or Chixoy, the
Cuchumatanes form a fairly well-defined physical unit
bordered on the north by the sparsely settled tropical
lowlands of the Usumacinta basin and to the west by the
Mexican state of Chiapas. The Cuchumatanes, with elevations ranging from 500 to more than 3600 meters, are contained within the Guatemalan departments of Huehuetenango
and Quiché, and comprise some 15 percent (approximately
16,350 square kilometers) of the national territory of
the Central American republic (Figure 8.1).

During the first two centuries of Spanish rule in
Guatemala the Cuchumatán country was part of the administrative division known as the corregimiento or alcaldía
mayor of Totonicapán and Huehuetenango. This unit included all of the present day department of Totonicapán,
most of Huehuetenango, the northern half of Quiché, the
easternmost portion of Quezaltenango, and the Motozintla
area of the Mexican state of Chiapas. Towards the end of
the colonial period the corregimiento or alcaldía mayor
of Totonicapán and Huehuetenango was made a provincia
composed of two jurisdictions: the partido of Totonicapán
and the partido of Huehuetenango. The jurisdiction referred to as the partido of Huehuetenango corresponds in
approximate territorial extent to the area here designated the Cuchumatán highlands. Today about one-half
million people inhabit the region, of whom roughly three
out of four are Indian. The native peoples of the Cuchumatanes are of Mayan descent and speak several closely
related languages belonging to Mayan stock, the most important of which are Aguacateca, Chuj, Ixil, Jacalteca,
Kanjobal, Mam, Quiché, and Uspanteca.

DEMOGRAPHIC PROFILE OF THE CUCHUMATAN HIGHLANDS
(1520-1821)

Any attempt to reconstruct the population history of
the Cuchumatán highlands is beset by a lack of consistent, representative data. The paucity of source materials containing demographic information is particularly
notable for the sixteenth and early seventeenth centuries. The late seventeenth and eighteenth centuries, by
comparison, are reasonably well-documented. Perhaps the
safest procedure is to regard early estimates of population size as necessarily tentative and to scrutinize with
caution later calculations before reaching any final conclusions.

The earliest surviving record known to contain population data for every significant settlement in the Cuchumatán highlands is a list of tributarios (Indian tribute payers) for the years 1664 to 1678.[3] Prior to this

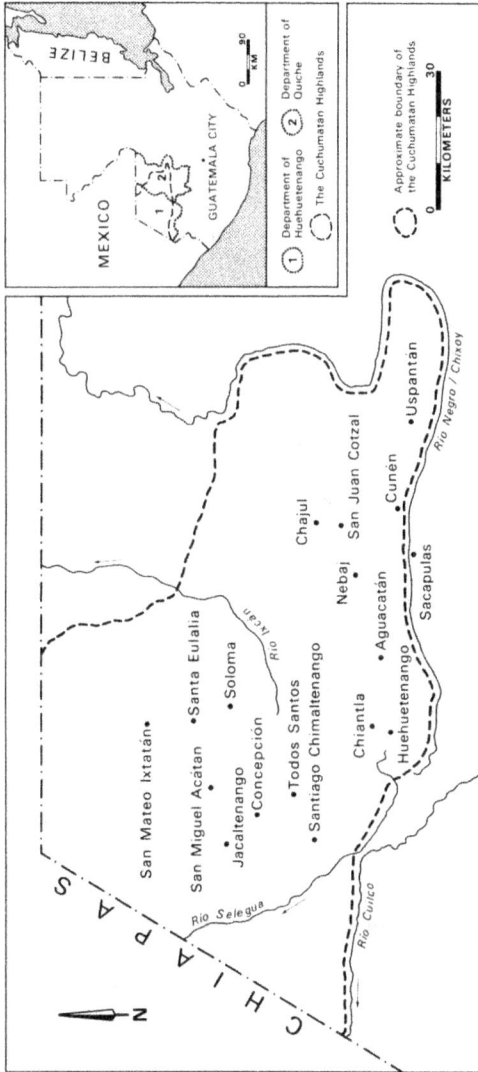

Figure 8.1 Location of the Cuchumatán highlands
and selected settlements

late seventeenth century tribute count few reliable figures exist. The data upon which estimates of the magnitude of the sixteenth century population can be made are
appallingly scarce. Among these data are reports of the
size of Indian armies encountered during the battles of
conquest, as recorded by the seventeenth-century chronicler Francisco Antonio de Fuentes y Gúzman in his monumental Recordación Florida;[4] the number of tributarios in
certain Cuchumatán towns assessed by the President of the
Audiencia of Guatemala, Alonso López de Cerrato, between
1548 and 1551;[5] and the number of tributarios in the town
of Huehuetenango, assessed by President García de
Valverde between 1578 and 1582.[6]

Employing as a demographic source estimates of the
size of the Indian armies which confronted the Spaniards
in the course of conquest is obviously not undertaken
without considerable risk. It has been alleged, for example, that Spanish conquistadores, in order to glorify
their military feats, were guilty of grossly exaggerating
the size of the Indian forces defeated in battle. This
argument, however, fails to take into account the fact
that successful conquerors often later became influential
administrators and would therefore frequently be charged
with tribute assessment for both the Spanish Crown and
Spanish colonists. Since population size directly determined the levy of tribute, any conquistador with prospects of one day being responsible for assessing Indian
tribute capacity would tend to count with at least some
measure of discretion.

Consistent with a view which favors taking contemporary testimony and subjecting it to scholarly scrutiny, a
study by Thomas Veblen has shown that Spanish estimates
of Indian army sizes recorded for the Totonicapán area
correspond reasonably well with data derived from other
historical sources.[7] Perhaps most significantly, Veblen
claims that the work of Fuentes y Gúzman, long considered
an unreliable source for pre-Hispanic population data, in
fact contains highly plausible figures for Indian army
sizes. Veblen explicitly states that "the data available
on the size of the pre-Hispanic population of Totonicapán
provide no basis for rejecting the demographic information contained in Fuentes y Gúzman."[8] This appraisal is
of crucial importance because reports of Indian army
sizes are among the few extant historical data which can
be used to derive an estimate of the population of the
Cuchumatán highlands on the eve of Spanish conquest.

Spanish estimates of the size of Indian armies encountered during the conquest of the Cuchumatanes have
been recorded by Fuentes y Gúzman in the Recordación
Florida. Fuentes y Gúzman's source for the conquest of
the Mam was a document, now unfortunately lost, written
by the conquistador Gonzalo de Alvarado after the successful subjugation of the Mam in 1525. In his account

the chronicler gives no indication of the size of the Indian army which defended Mazatenango (San Lorenzo), but
does state that the town "in those days was well-
populated."[9]   Fuentes y Gúzman's chief sources for the
conquest of the Ixil and the Quichean people of Uspantán
included the first Libro de Cabildo, records of the municipal council of Guatemala, and a collection of documents
entitled the Manuscrito Quiché. Estimates of the size of
the Indian armies which confronted the Spaniards during
the entradas into the Cuchumatanes, along with the names
of towns supplying warriors, are shown in Table 8.1.
     The total number of Indian warriors the Spaniards
faced in battle in the Cuchumatanes between 1525 and 1530
was recorded by Fuentes y Gúzman as 34,000. For Totonicapán, Veblen uses a one to four ratio in correlating
army size to total population; for the Tlaxcala region of
central Mexico, Gibson uses a warriors to total population ratio of one to five.[10]   A ratio of one to four,
which Veblen considers "conservative," indicates a population of 136,000; a ratio of one to five gives a total
of 170,000. An average of these two figures produces a
rough estimate of the population of the Cuchumatán highlands between 1525 and 1530 of around 150,000.
     In the years immediately prior to the Spanish con-
quest, however, it is likely that Cuchumatán communities
were struck by the same lethal epidemic which, in 1520,
swept over much of highland Guatemala. This epidemic,
possibly a combination of smallpox and pulmonary plague,
entered the highlands of Guatemala from Mexico and had a
devastating impact on the Indian peoples of the region.
Old World in origin and consequently unknown in the Americas until the arrival of the Spaniards, the epidemic
decimated the immunologically defenseless native population and thus reduced both Indian numbers and resistance
to military conquest.[11]   The ravage of the disease is
described in a poignant passage from the Annals of the
Cakchiquels:

> It happened that during the twenty-fifth year [1520] the
> plague began, oh, my sons! First they became ill of a
> cough, they suffered from nosebleeds and illness of the
> bladder. It was truly terrible, the number of dead there
> were in that period . . . . Little by little heavy shad-
> ows and black night enveloped our fathers and grandfath-
> ers and us also, oh, my sons! When the plague raged . . . ,
> when the plague began to spread . . . . It was in truth
> terrible, the number of dead among the people. The peo-
> ple could not in any way control the sickness . . . .
> Great was the stench of the dead. After our fathers and
> grandfathers succumbed, half of the people fled to the
> fields. The dogs and the vultures devoured the bodies.
> The mortality was terrible. Your grandfathers died, and
> with them died the son of the king and his brothers and

TABLE 8.1
Indian army sizes recorded during the battles of conquest

Date and Place of Battle	Estimated Indian Army Size	Towns Supplying Warriors
1525: Mazatenango (San Lorenzo)	--	Mazatenango
1525: near Mazatenango	5,000	Malacatán
1525: Zaculeu	6,000	Huehuetenango, Zaculeu, Ixtahuacan and Cuilco
1525: Zaculeu	8,000	Various Cuchumatán communities affiliated with the Mam of Zaculeu
1530: Nebaj	5,000	Nebaj and other towns
1530: Uspantán	10,000	Uspantán, Verapaz towns, Cunén, Cotzal, Sacapulas

Source: F. A. Fuentes y Gúzman, Recordación Florida.

> kinsmen. So it was that we became orphans, oh, my sons!
> So we became when we were young. All of us were thus.
> We were born to die![12]

In terms of numerical decline, MacLeod claims that
one-third to one-half of the Indian population of highland Guatemala must have perished as a consequence of the
epidemic:

> Given present day knowledge of the impact of smallpox or
> plague on people without previous immunities, it is safe,
> indeed conservative, to say that a third of the Guatemalan
> highland populations died during this holocaust.[13]

A Cuchumatán population which between 1525 and 1530
numbered around 150,000 could, therefore, some five to
ten years earlier have numbered as much as 225,000 to
300,000. An average of these two figures produces a population estimate for 1520 of around 260,000. In order to
place this estimate into some kind of perspective, it is
worth noting that the population of the Cuchumatanes in
1950 was around 265,000.[14] This means that the population of the Cuchumatán highlands on the eve of Spanish
conquest may have been approximately the same size as the
mid-twentieth century population of the region. Although
this calculation is no more than a tentative estimate
based on meager historical documentation, its credibility
is supported by Veblen's estimate of the contact population of Totonicapán as being of roughly the same magnitude as that region's mid-twentieth century population.[15]

Of the two other sources which contain demographic
information relating to Cuchumatán towns in the sixteenth
century, the tribute count made by President Valverde between 1578 and 1582 is somewhat more reliable than the
one compiled 30 years earlier by President Cerrato because the latter relied partly on reports submitted by
local Indian leaders (caciques) rather than on personal
town inspections conducted by officials of the Crown. In
order to reduce the amount of tribute demanded by the
Spaniards, and thus perhaps secure more for themselves,
it is possible that caciques under-reported the number of
eligible tributarios each town supported.[16] The Valverde
count, undertaken personally by the President and his
designated officials, is particularly useful because it
contains two figures; the first is apparently a revised
version of the Cerrato assessment dating back to the mid-
sixteenth century while the second is the new Valverde
assessment.[17]

The town of Huehuetenango, formerly assessed at 570
tributarios, was adjusted downwards by Valverde to 367
tributarios.[18] A tributario at this time was a married
male Indian between the ages of 18 and 50; roughly one
out of every five persons would have fallen into this

category.[19] The Valverde statistics therefore suggest a total population for Huehuetenango in the middle years of the sixteenth century of around 2800, a figure which by 1580 had fallen to around 1800. In the tribute list for 1664-1678, the earliest extant document with comprehensive tributary data for every significant Indian community in the Cuchumatán highlands, Huehuetenango accounts for 3.9 percent of the total number of tributarios.[20] Assuming that Huehuetenango represented this same proportion in the sixteenth century, then the total number of Cuchumatán tributarios in 1550 was around 14,600 and in 1580 was around 9400. Using a population to tributario ratio of five to one, these figures indicate that the population of the Cuchumatán highlands in 1550 may have numbered about 73,000 and in 1580 may have numbered about 47,000.

These estimates alone are highly tentative, but it is possible to provide some independent frame of reference by which they can assume greater credibility. According to both MacLeod and Veblen, the mid-sixteenth century population of highland Guatemala probably numbered approximately half the size of the contact population owing to the devastating impact of the gucumatz plague of 1545-1548. Similarly, the number of Indians alive in the year 1580 was about half that of the mid-sixteenth century because of the equally devastating impact of the matlazahuatl pandemic of 1576-1581.[21] Acceptance of this thesis means that a contact population of 150,000, the estimate for the Cuchumatanes obtained from the size of Indian armies confronting the Spaniards during the battles of conquest, would by 1550 have fallen to about 75,000. This figure compares exceptionally well with the estimate of 73,000 derived from the Valverde count. A mid-sixteenth century population of 73,000 would by 1580 have numbered around 37,000. This figure compares reasonably well with the estimate of 47,000 also derived from the Valverde assessment.

For close to 100 years after the Valverde count there is almost no documentation which contains demographic information relating to Cuchumatán communities.[22] The one exception is an ecclesiastical census for the year 1604 which lists the number of towns and vecinos (householders) under the charge of the Dominican monastery at Sacapulas. Unfortunately, this census includes only those settlements under the jurisdiction of the Dominican and Franciscan orders. Since the majority of Indian towns in the Cuchumatanes were under the administration of the Mercedarian order, and consequently were not recorded, the utility of this otherwise important source is minimal.[23]

The tribute count of 1664-1678 is the next document after the Valverde assessment which contains detailed demographic data on the Cuchumatán highlands. This

extremely valuable document gives a complete breakdown,
by town and occasionally by small social components
(parcialidades) comprising certain towns, of the entire
tribute paying population of the region. The total number of tributarios at this time was 4040.[24] Fuentes y
Gúzman, during the second half of the seventeenth century, reckoned on a population to tributario ratio of
four to one.[25] Using this same ratio, 4040 tribute payers would be indicative of a total Cuchumatán population
of 16,162 between the years 1664 and 1678.

For the remainder of the colonial period there is no
shortage of reliable and comprehensive sources, chiefly
in the form of unpublished documents in the Archivo General de Centroamérica, upon which to reconstruct the population history of the Cuchumatán highlands. The abundant eighteenth- and early nineteenth-century documents
from which demographic data can be gleaned include tribute lists, reports of officials of the Crown, ecclesiastical records, and meticulous censuses which enumerate
the Cuchumatán population in great detail by age, sex,
class, and race. This information is synthesized in Table 8.2 and is represented graphically in Figure 8.2.

The overwhelming feature of the historical demography of the Cuchumatán highlands is the catastrophic decline in population following the Spanish conquest. Massive demographic collapse probably began in the years immediately preceding the battles of conquest and continued
throughout the sixteenth and for most of the seventeenth
century. Reaching its nadir about 1670, population began
to recover and grow throughout the eighteenth century,
although there were still occasional fluctuations. By
the end of the colonial period population was on a
steady, if slight, upward trend. Some explanations of
this overall pattern of decline, recovery, and growth may
be offered.

CAUSES OF DEMOGRAPHIC COLLAPSE AND READJUSTMENT

Amidst an almost perennial controversy, recent research by a number of scholars has convincingly demonstrated that several parts of the New World were densely
populated on the eve of its "discovery" by the Old World
and that native American populations declined drastically
in size following contact with the European invaders.[26]
The traditional interpretation of the catastrophic decline of the indigenous population in Spanish America,
between 80 and 90 percent in some regions, is the infa-
mous Leyenda Negra. The Black Legend attributes the
post-contact decrease in Indian numbers to the unmiti-
gated slaughter, ruthless enslavement, and harsh exploi-
tation of the native population by Spanish conquerors and
colonists.[27] It is not difficult to find references in

TABLE 8.2
The population of the Cuchumatán highlands, 1520-1825

Year	Population	Source
1520	260,000	Extrapolation of size of Indian armies recorded by Fuentes y Gúzman
1525-1530	150,000	Estimate based on size of Indian armies recorded by Fuentes y Gúzman
1550	73,000	AGI:AG 966. P/T ratio of 5:1. Huehuetenango as 3.9% of Cuchumatán tributarios
1580	47,000	AGI:AG 966. P/T ratio of 5:1. Huehuetenango as 3.9% of Cuchumatán tributarios
1664-1678	16,162	AGCA:A3.16, leg. 1601, exp. 26391. P/T ratio of 4:1
1690	19,824	Fuentes y Gúzman, Recordación Florida. P/T ratio 4:1
1760	21,176	AGCA:A3.16, leg. 950, exp. 17715. P/T ratio of 4:1
1768-1770	23,418	Cortés y Larraz, Descripción Geográfico-Moral de la Diocesis de Goathemala
1778	27,505	AGCA:A1.44, leg. 6097, exp. 55507
1779	28,047	AGCA:A1.44, leg. 6097, exp. 55507
1782	23,021	AGCA:A1.44, leg. 6097, exp. 55507
1783	25,027	AGCA:A1.44, leg. 6097, exp. 55507
1784	24,828	AGCA:A1.44, leg. 6097, exp. 55507
1788	24,678	AGCA:A3.16, leg. 246, exp. 4912. P/T ratio of 4.82:1
1790	23,623	AGCA:A3.16, leg. 237, exp. 4706. P/T ratio of 4.82:1
1797-1798	24,129	Hidalgo, Gaceta de Guatemala
1801	27,477	AGCA:A3.16, leg. 243, exp. 4853. P/T ratio of 4.82:1
1811	29,571	AGCA:A3.16, leg. 953, exp. 17773. P/T ratio of 4.82:1
1825	34,691	AGCA:B.84.3, leg. 1135, exp. 26030-26034

P/T = Population to Tributario ratio.

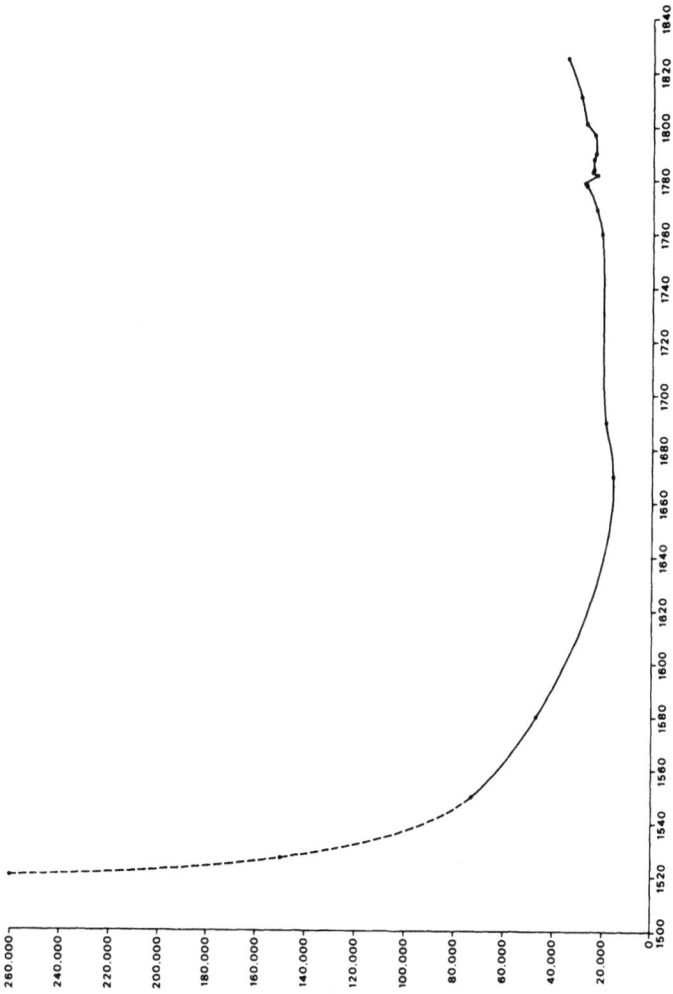

Figure 8.2 The population of the Cuchumatán highlands, 1520–1821

the literature which support the thesis of the Black Legend. According to Bartolomé de las Casas, for example, five million Indian lives were lost in Guatemala alone because of the excesses of the conquistador Pedro de Alvarado and his henchmen. In las Casas' own words:

> And this I dare affirm, that the enormities committed by . . . him especially that was sent to Guatemala . . . are enough to fill a particular volume, so many were the slaughters, violences, injuries, butcheries, and beastly desolations [committed by that abominable] tyrant [Pedro de Alvarado]; how many tears, how many sighs did he provoke, upon how many did he bring desolation in his worldly pilgrimage and endanger their damnation in the world to come?[28]

It is now quite certain, however, that the principal cause of aboriginal depopulation was not massacre and mistreatment at the hands of the conquering Spaniards but the introduction by the invaders of Old World diseases to which the Indians of the New World had no natural, physiological immunity.[29]

Until the arrival of the Europeans, the inhabitants of the New World lived in virtual isolation from those of the Old World. This long period of isolation weakened considerably the resistance of American Indians to most of the major diseases of mankind. Possibly because of the harsh climate characteristic of the Bering region, many diseases were never carried over from the Old World to the New World by the first migrants; the Arctic cold simply killed off both the disease organisms and those humans suffering from chronic sickness or contamination.[30] Alternative explanations may be that the migrations across the Bering Strait occurred so long ago that many diseases had not yet evolved in the Old World before the departure of the Amerindian ancestors; or the original group of migrants was so small that the loss of immunity factors was due to genetic drift.[31] Whatever the reason, the inhabitants of the New World developed tolerances only for a limited number of indigenous American diseases. During pre-Columbian times, the Indians of America appear to have been subjected primarily to gastro-intestinal disturbances and respiratory disorders.[32] Prior to the arrival of the Spaniards, therefore, the Indians enjoyed an existence relatively free of infectious diseases. Maladies such as smallpox, measles, mumps, typhus, influenza, and diptheria--all of which were endemic to the Old World--were completely unknown. When these diseases were inadvertently brought to America by Spanish conquerors and colonists, their devastating impact on hitherto isolated human communities may well have caused, in the words of one scholar, "the greatest destruction of lives in history."[33]

The first Old World disease to arrive in America was smallpox.[34] The impact of smallpox on the native population of the New World was at least as cataclysmic as the impact of the Black Death of 1346 to 1350 on European society; that is, one-third to one-half of the Indians who came in contact with the disease must have perished.[35]

Soon after sweeping through Central Mexico, smallpox spread southwards to the highlands of Guatemala, accompanied perhaps by pulmonary plague or typhus.[36] By the end of 1520, four years before the entrada of Pedro de Alvarado, the Indians of highland Guatemala were reeling from their initial encounter with what MacLeod has appropriately called "the shock troops of the conquest."[37] The chroniclers of the Cakchiquel lament that it "was in truth terrible, the number of dead among the people . . . in that period . . . when the plague raged."[38] This first bout of pestilence was followed about 12 years later by a pandemic of measles. Thereafter, major outbreaks of Old World diseases were a common feature of Indian life in colonial Guatemala and consistently resulted in high mortality among the immunologically defenseless native population.

It is unlikely that the Indian peoples of the Cuchumatán highlands escaped these deadly visitations. The testimony of Thomas Gage, in connection with an outbreak of typhus in 1631, indicates that the impact of disease tended to be widespread:

> The year following [1631], all that country [highland Guatemala] was generally infected with a kind of contagious sickness, almost as infectious as the plague, which they call tabardillo [typhus]. This fever in the very inward parts and bowels scarce continued to the seventh day but commonly took its victims away from the world to a grave the third or fifth day. The filthy smell and stench which came from those who lay sick of this disease was enough to infect the rest of the house, and all that came to see them. It rotted their very mouths and tongues, and made them as black as coal before they died. Very few Spaniards were infected with this contagion, but the Indians generally were taken with it.[39]

In addition to being affected by diseases of pandemic proportion, such as the one described above, the Indian people of the Cuchumatán highlands were also exposed throughout the colonial period to more localized outbreaks of disease (Table 8.3).

The recurrent outbreak of diseases to which the native population was immunologically defenseless is the chief factor behind the demographic collapse of the Indian peoples of the Cuchumatanes following the Spanish conquest. From 1520 until the end of Spanish colonial

TABLE 8.3
Local outbreaks of disease in the Cuchumatán highlands, 1548-1819

Year	Disease	Towns Affected	Source	Comments
c1548-c1615	"Pestes" (unspecified)	Towns of the "sierras de Cuchumatlán"	Remesal, Vol. II, p. 259	"Ahora con las pestes han venido los pueblos en diminución."
1666-1670	Tabardillo (typhus)	Huehuetenango	A3.16, leg. 1600, exp. 26390	Indian tribute lowered after epidemic carried off 45 adults.
1733-1773	Viruela (smallpox)	Sacapulas and Cunén	A3.16, leg. 2819, exp. 40918	Many tribute-payers perished. Indians unable to pay tribute and ask for exemption.
1774	"Peste" (unspecified)	Various towns	A3.16, leg. 943, exp. 17608	Alcalde mayor informs treasury that certain towns will not be able to pay tribute.
1780-1781	Viruela (smallpox)	All forty towns of the Partido de Huehuetenango	A1.44, leg. 6097, exp. 55507	Over 4000 deaths. Alcalde mayor authorized to use community funds to help fight the disease.
1786	Tabardillo	Concepción and Petatán	A1.4, leg. 6101, exp. 55666	
1795-1799	Tabardillo and viruela, tabardillo was particularly	Numerous towns, including Nebaj, Chajul, Todos Santos and San Martín	A1.24, leg. 6101, exp. 55666-669; A1.47, leg. 80121; A3.16, exp. 255, exp. 5719; A3.16, leg. 244, exp. 4869; A1.47, leg. 385	Over 500 deaths in Jacaltenango alone and an equal number in Concepción; visit to stricken towns by the alcalde mayor and a doctor, the former to adjust

widespread	Cuchumatán, Jacaltenango, Concepción	A1.49, leg. 192, exp. 3911; A3.1, leg. 2894, exp. 42846	tribute payment, the latter to fight the spread of disease.
1802-1807 Tabardillo, viruela, and sarampión (measles)	Numerous towns including San Juan Ixcoy, Santa Eulalia, Nebaj, San Pedro Soloma, San Mateo Ixtatán	A1.1, leg. 6105, exp. 55795; A1.24, leg. 6091, exp. 55306; A3.16, leg. 245, exp. 4909; A1.4, leg. 6107, exp. 55836; A1.4, leg. 6091, exp. 55307; A1.47, leg. 2162, exp. 1558; A3.16, leg. 2899, exp. 43063	Alcalde mayor requests that tribute should not be collected from certain towns. Locust invasion exacerbates situation. Food shortages and much human suffering.
1809-1812 Tabardillo, viruela, and fiebre putrida (type of fever)	San Miguel Acatán, San Mateo Ixtatán, San Juan Cotzal	A1.1, leg. 6093, exp. 55337; A1.49 leg. 386, exp. 8055; A1.4, leg. 6113, exp. 56214; A1, leg. 394, exp. 8238	Indians in stricken communities given a reprieve in the payment of tribute.
1814-1819 Tabardillo	Chiantla and Jacaltenango	A1.49, leg. 387, exp. 8072; A1.49, leg. 388, exp. 8099	Measures taken to halt spread of disease.

All archival citations refer to unpublished documents housed in the Archivo General de Centroamérica, Guatemala City.

rule in 1821, the Indians were subjected to unrelenting
waves of pestilence. Mortality was high. Between 1520
and 1670 population declined by more than 90 percent,
falling from perhaps 260,000 to a little over 16,000. By
the end of the seventeenth century the collapse had
abated and there were signs of a slight but significant
demographic recovery. Several fluctuations towards the
end of the eighteenth century, however, suggest that the
Indians had still not built up effective immunities to
diseases such as smallpox and typhus. Only at the very
end of the colonial period are there positive indications
of a general increase in Indian numbers (see Table 8.2
and Figure 8.2).

The impact of disease on Indian life in the Cuchumatán highlands was profound. Guatemalan archives contain thousands of documents which describe, in lugubrious
detail, the disruptions wrought by outbreaks of disease
on scores of Indian communities. These dislocations included: substantial loss of life; the inability of certain towns to meet the semi-annual tribute requirement
demanded by the Crown; the abandonment of disease-ridden
towns for the safety of uninfected or less infected rural
areas; and the failure on the part of Indians to work
their land, resulting in widespread hardship and depriva-
tion. The plight of the Indians under such desperate
circumstances is nowhere more tragically conveyed than in
a letter addressed to the alcalde mayor of Huehuetenango
by the ladino comisionado of the parish of Soloma, Marcos
Casteñeda. His observations may be considered representative of a substantive body of archival documentation
and have an applicability far beyond the time and place
of which he writes:

> For four years now [1803-1807] in the towns of [the par-
> ish of] Soloma there has been great distress owing to
> the high mortality caused by the epidemic of typhus
> which kills [the Indians] without relief or remedy,
> leaving them only in dire hardship. Through fear of
> death we [the ladino residents Marcos and Santiago
> Casteñeda] fled with our families to the solitude of
> the mountains and barren wastes of Chemal, suffering
> there the extremity of its climate, abandoning our
> houses and possessions in Soloma. But God having saw
> fit to end this terrible affliction, we are returning
> once again to our homes. To our horror we find that
> the majority of the Indians of Santa Eulalia have per-
> ished, and are lying unburied all over the place, their
> decaying corpses eaten by the animals which roam the
> countryside . . . . It is even more painful, however,
> to see the great number of orphaned children crying
> for the laps of their parents, asking for bread with-
> out having anyone to receive it from . . . . After so
> much hard work, these unfortunate Indians have been

reduced to a life of misery. Having returned to their
town [the Indians who survived] are without homes,
without resources to pay their expenses and tribute,
and without corn to feed themselves and their families.
If no measures are taken to assist these wretched people, they will without doubt starve to death, because
they did not plant corn in the places where they sought
refuge [from the epidemic], and so they have nothing to
live on, both for this year and for the next, since it
is now too late to plant their crops. It is very common in this parish to find large numbers of Indians,
old and young alike, walking from town to town, from
house to house, begging and searching for food . . . .
Señor Alcalde Mayor, inform the President that help
should be extended to the towns of this parish of
Soloma; at the very least [the Indians] of Santa Eulalia
and San Miguel Acatán could be exempted from paying
tribute for the years during which they have suffered
great misfortunes.[40]

Casteñeda, in another communication, reckoned that
the outbreak of typhus had killed "three-quarters of the
Indian population of San Miguel Acatán and Santa Eulalia"
and stated that most of the survivors of the epidemic
were rendered "destitute and homeless because their
houses were burned to rid them of the contagion."[41]
In response to a plea by the Indian alcaldes and
principales of Santa Eulalia to exempt the town from paying tribute during the disruptive years of the typhus
epidemic, the alcalde mayor was able only to obtain a
royal order granting a temporary respite from the obligation.[42] The refusal of the Spanish authorities to grant
the Indians a total tribute exemption prompted the parish
priest of Soloma, Fray Juan José Juarez, to write the
following rebuke to the alcalde mayor:

It strikes me that what is most important to you is
that the Indians pay their tribute so that you receive
your salary, but I think the Indians will be unable to
pay, either this year or later, [because] they have
lost their crops and consequently have nothing to pay
with.[43]

The tone of this address imparts some sense of the
numbed resignation with which servants of the Crown in
outlying rural districts would respond, during times of
crisis, to the apathy, ineptitude, and lack of responsibility of men in distant seats of authority. Apparently
even during an epidemic involving considerable loss of
life and appalling human suffering, an appropriate course
of remedial action was beyond the workings of government
bureaucracy.

CONCLUSION

By introducing Old World diseases to an immunologically defenseless native population, the Spanish conquest
of America precipitated a demographic collapse that was
probably the most catastrophic in the history of mankind.
The magnitude and rapidity of Indian depopulation in the
Cuchumatán highlands following conquest by Spain conforms
to a pattern already well-established for a number of
other long settled parts of Latin America.[44] A population of perhaps 260,000 on the eve of conquest, roughly
the same size as the mid-twentieth century population of
the Cuchumatanes, had by 1670 declined to around 16,000,
a fall of slightly more than 90 percent over a period of
150 years. The demographic recovery which began in the
last quarter of the seventeenth century continued
throughout the eighteenth and nineteenth centuries. For
most of this time population increase was slow and spo-
ratic because of the persistent outbreak of diseases to
which the Indians only gradually acquired immunities. It
was not until the third decade of the present century
that population began to increase sharply, due chiefly to
the impact of modern medical technology in substantially
reducing rates of human mortality. By 1950, after a process of decline, recovery, and growth lasting over 400
years, the population of the Cuchumatán highlands reached
a level equivalent to that which it may have numbered
prior to the arrival of the Spaniards and their pestilen-
tial allies.

NOTES

1. M. J. MacLeod, Spanish Central America: A Socioeconomic History, 1520-1720, (Berkeley and Los Angeles: University of California
Press, 1973), p. 374.
2. MacLeod, op. cit., pp. 130 and 224.
3. Archivo General de Centroamérica (hereafter AGCA), A3.16,
leg. 1601, exp. 26391.
4. F. A. de Fuentes y Gúzman, Recordación Florida: Historia
Natural, Material, Militar y Política del Reino de Goathemala, (Madrid: Biblioteca de Autores Españoles, Tomo CCLIX, 1972), pp. 18-22
and 51-71.
5. Archivo General de Indias: Audiencia de Guatemala (hereafter
AGI:AG), 128. Although at least 11 Cuchumatán towns may be identified in the Cerrato census, only nine have a record of how many
tributarios they contained. The breakdown is as follows:

Name of Town	No. of Tributarios	Name of Encomendero
Ixtatán	65	Diego Sánchez Santiago
Jacaltenango	500	"Menor hijo de Gonzalo de

Name of Town	No. of Tributarios	Name of Encomendero
		Covalle"
Aguacatán	100	Juan de Celada
Chalchitán	60	Hernán Pérez Penale and Alvaro de Pulgar
Soloma	40	Diego de Alvarado and Juan de Castrogui
Uspantán	--	Ignatio de Bobadilla and Santos Figueroa
Huehuetenango	500	Juan de Espinar
Sacapulas	160	Juan Paez and Cristobal Salvatierra
Malacatán	80	Ignatio de Bobadilla
Motozintla	138	Hernán Gutierrez de Cibaji and Hernán Mendez de Sotomayor
Cuchumatán (Todos Santos)	--	"Menores hijos de Marcos Ruíz" and García de Aguilar

A partial version of the Cerrato census may be found in published form in F. de Solano, Los Mayas del Siglo XVIII: Pervivencia y Transformación de la Sociedad Indígena Guatemalteca durante la Administración Borbónica, (Madrid: Ediciones Cultura Hispanica, 1974), pp. 80-82.

6. AGI:AG, 966. A brief analysis of the Valverde census may be found in R. M. Carmack, Quichean Civilization: The Ethnohistoric, Ethnographic, and Archaeological Sources, (Berkeley and Los Angeles: University of California Press, 1973), p. 143.

7. T. T. Veblen, "Native Population Decline in Totonicapán, Guatemala," Annals of the Association of American Geographers, Vol. 67, No. 4, December 1977, pp. 496-497.

8. Ibid., p. 497.

9. Fuentes y Gúzman, op. cit., p. 57.

10. Veblen, op. cit., p. 487; and C. Gibson, Tlaxcala in the Sixteenth Century, (New Haven: Yale University Press, 1952), p. 139.

11. MacLeod, op. cit., pp. 39-40.

12. A Recinos and D. Goetz (translators), The Annals of the Cakchiquels, (Norman: University of Oklahoma Press, 1953), pp. 115-116.

13. MacLeod, op. cit., p. 41.

14. M. M. Urrutia, La División Política y Administrativa de Guatemala, (Guatemala: Editorial Iberia, 1961), Tomo I, pp. 432 and 644.

15. Veblen, op. cit., p. 499.

16. Carmack, op. cit., pp. 138-140; and Veblen, op. cit., p. 495. Cerrato was strongly criticized by Bishop Marroquín for relying on tribute counts provided by caciques. This practice, together with the freeing of Indian slaves and the lowering of the amount of tribute required of each Indian tributario, made Cerrato extremely unpopular among the Spanish residents of Quatemala.

17. Carmack, op. cit., p. 143.

18. AGI:AG 966.

19. Veblen, op. cit., p. 495.

20. AGCA, A3.16, leg. 1601, exp. 26391. The total number of tributarios in the Cuchumatanes was 4040½. Huehuetenango was assessed at 156½.

21. MacLeod, op. cit., p. 19; and Veblen, op. cit., p. 496. Gucumatz, cocoliztli, is an undetermined type of plague; MacLeod believes the descriptions of the disease resemble the symptoms of pulmonary plague. Matlazáhuatl is a disease of disputed origin which some scholars believe to be typhus; cf. S. S. Cook, "The Incidence and Significance of Disease Among the Aztecs and Related Tribes," Hispanic American Historical Review 26 (1946), p. 321, and P. Gerhard, A Guide to the Historical Geography of New Spain (Cambridge: Cambridge University Press, 1972), p. 23.

22. The fact that almost no documentation exists for the period 1580-1664 may be due to any number of survival hazards, such as flood, fire, earthquake, theft or negligence. The lack of documentation, however, may also be simply a reflection of how relatively neglected were the Indian peoples of the Cuchumatanes during the seventeenth century.

23. The 1604 ecclesiastical census, entitled Memoria de los frailes menores que hay en la provincia de Guatemala, is housed in the Biblioteca del Real Palacio, Madrid. It appears in published form in Solano, op. cit., pp. 106-108.

24. AGCA, A3.16, leg. 1601, exp. 26391.

25. Fuentes y Gúzman, op. cit., pp. 15-18 and 22-44.

26. W. M. Denevan (ed.), The Native Population of the Americas in 1492 (Madison: University of Wisconsin Press, 1976), pp. 1-12. S. F. Cook and W. Borah, Essays in Population History: Mexico and California, Vol. 3, (Berkeley and Los Angeles: University of California Press, 1979), p. 102, summarize their decades of collaborative research on the historical demography of central Mexico in one succinct sentence: "We conclude, then, that the Indian population of central Mexico, under the impact of factors unleashed by the coming of the Europeans, fell by 1620-1625 to a low of approximately 3% of its size at the time that the Europeans first landed on the shore of Veracruz."

27. Gibson, Spain in America (New York: Harper and Row, 1966), pp. 43-47 and 136-137.

28. B. de las Casas (trans. J. Phillips), The Tears of the Indians: Being an Historical and True Account of the Cruel Massacres and Slaughters of Above Twenty Millions of Innocent People; Committed by the Spaniards in the Islands of Hispaniola, Cuba, Jamaica, etc. As also in the Continent of Mexico, Peru, and Other Places to the West Indies, to the Total Destruction of These Countries (London, 1656), pp. 43-53.

29. A. W. Crosby, Jr., The Columbian Exchange: Biological and Cultural Consequences of 1492 (Connecticut: Greenwood Press, 1972), pp. 35-58 and "Virgin Soil Epidemics as a Factor in the Aboriginal Depopulation in America," William and Mary Quarterly, Third Series, Vol. 33, 1976, pp. 289-299; Gerhard, op. cit., p. 23; MacLeod, op. cit., pp. 19-20 and 38-40; and W. H. McNeill, Plagues and Peoples (New York: Anchor and Doubleday Press, 1976), pp. 176-207.

30. Crosby, op. cit., pp. 30-31.

31. R. Gruhn (personal communication).

32. Cook, op. cit., p. 324. Some scholars think that syphilis is a New World disease introduced to Europe after the Spanish conquest. For a review of the early history of the disease, see Crosby, Columbian Exchange, op. cit., pp. 122-164.

33. MacLeod, op. cit., p. 20.

34. Crosby, Columbian Exchange, op. cit., pp. 42-58, examines the impact that the first pandemic of smallpox had on the native peoples of America.

35. MacLeod, op. cit., pp. 6-19. For a review of the effect of the Black Death on European society in the mid-fourteenth century see McNeill, op. cit., pp. 132-175, and P. Ziegler, The Black Death (Harmondsworth: Pelican Books, 1976), especially pp. 232-259.

36. MacLeod, op. cit., pp. 19 and 98.

37. MacLeod, op. cit., p. 40.

38. Recinos and Goetz, op. cit., p. 115.

39. T. Gage (ed. J. E. S. Thompson), Thomas Gage's Travels in the New World (Norman: University of Oklahoma Press, 1958), p. 263.

40. AGCA, A3.16, leg. 249, exp. 5036.

41. AGCA, A1.14, leg. 386, exp. 8037.

42. AGCA, A3.16, leg. 249, exp. 5036.

43. AGCA, A3.16, leg. 2899, exp. 43049.

44. The monumental work of Sherburne F. Cook and Woodrow Borah has been of primary significance in establishing a model of large Indian populations at Spanish contact experiencing a rapid and precipitous post-contact decline. The Preface to Volume One of their magnificent three-volume Essays in Population History (Berkeley and Los Angeles: University of California Press, 1971, 1974 and 1979), pp. V-XIV, serves as a succinct bibliographical and chronological survey of their painstaking years of research. Other works which establish the existence of large pre-Columbian populations and which support the Cook and Borah thesis of massive post-contact collapse include the following: C. Sauer, Colima of New Spain in the Sixteenth Century, Ibero-Americana No. 29 (Berkeley and Los Angeles: University of California Press, 1948), pp. 59-63 and 93-96; W. M. Denevan, The Upland Pine Forests of Nicaragua: A Study in Cultural Plant Geography, University of California Publications in Geography, Vol. 12 (Berkeley and Los Angeles: University of California Press, 1961), pp. 289-291; C. L. Johanessen, Savannas of Interior Honduras, Ibero-Americana No. 46 (Berkeley and Los Angeles: University of California Press, 1963), pp. 27-47; H. F. Dobyns, "Estimating Aboriginal American Populations: An Appraisal of Techniques with a New Hemispheric Estimate," Current Anthropology, Vol. 7 (1966), pp. 395-416 and 425-435; C. O. Sauer, The Early Spanish Main (Berkeley and Los Angeles: University of California Press, 1966), pp. 65-69, 155-156, 178-181, 200-204, and 283-289; A. W. Crosby, Jr., "Conquistador y Pestilencia: The First New World Pandemic and the Fall of the Great Indian Empires," Hispanic American Historical Review, Vol. 47 (1967), pp. 321-337; C. T. Smith, "Depopulation of the Central Andes in the 16th Century," Current Anthropology, Vol. 11 (1970), pp. 1-12; Gerhard, op. cit., pp. 22-28; MacLeod, op. cit., pp. 37-45; C. H. Lutz, Santiago de Guatemala, 1541-1773: The Socio-Demographic History of a Spanish American Colonial City (University of Wisconsin-

Madison, unpublished Ph.D. dissertation, 1976), pp. 249-317 and 743-752; D. Madigan, Santiago Atitlan, Guatemala: A Socioeconomic and Demographic History (University of Pittsburgh, unpublished Ph.D. dissertation, 1976), pp. 176-206; Veblen, op. cit., pp. 486-494; P. Gerhard, The Southwest Frontier of New Spain (Princeton: Princeton University Press, 1979), pp. 23-30; and W. L. Sherman, Forced Native Labor in Sixteenth-Century Central America (Lincoln: University of Nebraska Press, 1979), pp. 4-6 and 347-355.

9
Demographic Catastrophe in Sixteenth-Century Honduras

Linda A. Newson

In terms of the historical demography of Latin America, Central America is probably the least well-known area, and within that region there is no doubt that the least-researched country is Honduras. This is a reflection of the country's marginal location in the Spanish Empire and of the fragmentary nature of the documentary record for the area. Although there have been a number of estimates of the aboriginal population of the area, they have relied heavily on a small number of published documents and on comparisons with other Central American countries for which more evidence is available. Research on the historical demography of the sixteenth century is also lacking. Although MacLeod and Sherman have published tables of figures for the Indian population in the sixteenth century taken from the documentary record,[1] they have not analyzed the figures or examined the causes of the demographic decline, as this paper will attempt to do.

ESTIMATES OF THE ABORIGINAL POPULATION

The controversy that exists over estimates of the native population in the New World is more difficult to resolve in Central America because of the relative lack of documentary evidence and the speed with which the population declined. Estimates of the size of the Indian population on the eve of discovery range from Kroeber's calculation of 100,000 for Honduras and Nicaragua together

This paper forms part of a more extensive study of the colonial experience of the Indian in Honduras and Nicaragua for which financial support was received from the Social Science Research Council, the Central Research Fund of the University of London, and the Sir Ernest Cassel Educational Trust to all of whom the author wishes to express her thanks.

to Dobyns's estimate of between 10,800,000 and 13,500,000 for Central America.[2] Kroeber maintains that the estimates of early observers were exaggerated, a conclusion which he arrived at after an examination of the demographic history of Indian groups in the United States, particularly California. He assumed that the Indian population had grown at a regular rate since the time of conquest and derived his estimates by projecting the growth rate backwards from figures provided by Humboldt for the end of the eighteenth century. He thus disregarded the devastating impact of newly-introduced diseases and the disruptive effect of conquest and colonization on the economic and social life of the Indians. Steward accepts Kroeber's conclusion that the estimates of contemporary observers were exaggerated and, on the basis of evidence provided by the contributors to the Handbook of South American Indians, he suggests that the population of Central America, excluding Guatemala, was 736,500 of which 392,500 were in Honduras, Nicaragua and El Salvador together.[3] This estimate is somewhat lower than that of Rosenblat, who on the basis of readily available documentary evidence has estimated that the native population of Central America was 800,000.[4] Alternative approaches have suggested that these estimates may be too low. Sapper, who had an intimate knowledge of Mexico and Central America, estimated that on the basis of the climate, resources and Indian technology the native population of Central America was between five and six million.[5] More recently Dobyns has reviewed the literature available for the demographic history of the hemisphere and concluded that insufficient account has been taken of the devastating impact of disease and suggests that the Indian population was between twenty to twenty-five times greater than that recorded at its nadir, which for many Indian groups in Latin America was in the middle of the seventeenth century. For Central America he estimates that the Indian population was 540,000 in 1650 thus giving between 10,800,000 and 13,500,000 Indians at the time of conquest.[6]

These estimates have been proposed on the basis of only a limited reading of the documentary evidence and only recently has archival research by Radell, MacLeod and Sherman begun to provide more detailed information about the size of the Indian population at the time of conquest and its decline during the sixteenth century. These authors are not, however, in complete agreement over the interpretation of the documentary evidence, particularly that relating to the Indian slave trade. Radell has suggested that the population of Nicaragua was over one million at the time of discovery, given that up to 1548 between 450,000 and 500,000 were removed from the country as a result of the slave trade, 400,000 to 600,000 probably died of disease, in war or fled the

province, whilst 200,000 to 250,000 were probably residing in the Central Highlands to be decimated during the
ensuing twenty to thirty years.[7] Denevan adopts this estimate in his calculation of the aboriginal population of
Central America and suggests on the basis of incomplete
comparative evidence that the population of Honduras and
Belize was 750,000.[8] He proposes that the Indian population of Central America in 1492 was 5,650,000. Radell's
estimate of the number of Indians exported as a result of
the slave trade is comparable to the 500,000 and 400,000
Indians enslaved reported by Las Casas and Oviedo respectively,[9] but despite the convergence of estimates Sherman
considers these figures too high.[10] He maintains that
the capacity of the ships was small and that only a small
number of ships were involved in the early years of the
trade, whilst in later years heavy cargo demands for
space reduced that available for slaves. He suggests
that a more realistic figure for the whole period from
1524 to 1549 would be 50,000 and this figure includes Indian slaves exported from the whole of Central America
not just Nicaragua. He estimates that the aboriginal
population of Central America was about 2.5 million. Although MacLeod does not provide an estimate of the Indian
population of Central America, he does suggest with respect to the slave trade that a figure of 10,000 per year
for the decade 1532 to 1542 would appear to be too low
and 200,000 for the duration of the slave trade a conservative estimate.[11] It seems possible therefore that
about half a million Indian slaves were exported from
Nicaragua, although a proportion of those would have come
from Honduras. In addition, some Indian slaves were
shipped from northern Honduras and the Bay Islands to the
Caribbean Islands but the flow was undoubtedly much
smaller than that which passed through the ports of Nicaragua. It will be suggested that between 100,000 and
150,000 Indians were exported from Honduras during the
same period. Unfortunately none of the three authors
proposes an estimate for the aboriginal population of
Honduras and before doing so it is necessary to examine
in detail the evidence available.

THE DOCUMENTARY EVIDENCE

Although numerous archaeological sites have been un-
covered in Honduras, the majority have not been investigated scientifically and it is not possible to estimate
the aboriginal population on the basis of archaeological
evidence, so that the basic source of information is the
documentary record.
Contemporary observers were impressed by the size of
the Indian population in Honduras, although few gave precise estimates. In 1539 the Bishop of Honduras, Cristóbal

de Pedraza, wrote that at the time Gil González Dávila
and Hernan Cortés came to Honduras it had possessed almost as many people as Mexico, and in a later letter he
described the country as having been as highly populated
as Mexico and Peru.[12] In 1541 Benzoni recorded that the
population of Honduras on the eve of conquest had been
400,000.[13] Unfortunately this is the only precise estimate made by a contemporary chronicler. It seems likely,
however, that Benzoni's figure is an underestimate and
this may be due to the late date of the account occurring
after Pedro de Alvarado's brutal conquest of western Honduras and after the Indian slave trade had taken its
heaviest toll. Prior to that time the country had been
highly populated. In 1535 Andrés de Cerezeda reported
that around the town of Naco alone there were 200,000 Indians, who could be of service,[14] whilst further south
the legendary leader Lempira was able to muster a fighting force of 30,000 Indians to resist Spanish conquest.[15]
There were a large number of settlements in Honduras, although the majority did not exceed several thousand
households. Cerezeda reported that all the way from Naco
to the sea were villages with 300 to 2,000 houses,[16]
whilst Stone believes that the abundance of archaeological remains in the Comayagua valley indicates that, "in
pre-Conquest times the Comayagua region must have been a
mass of villages with the population running well into
the thousands."[17] Similarly Gracias a Dios was founded
in "a good area of many villages"[18] and some of them such
as Taloa, Guarcha, Cerquin and Telulocelo possessed 2,000
and 3,000 houses.[19] It is also clear that eastern Honduras had a large population, but little was known about
this unconquered and colonized area at that time, so that
their numbers could not have been included in the early
population estimates. In 1548 when the Indian slaves
were liberated there were said to be 27,000 pans working
gold in the Río Guayape and by the end of the century it
had been revealed that 4,000 to 5,000 Indians were living
between Trujillo and Cabo de Camarón.[20] There were thus
dense populations in Honduras, for although the majority
of settlements were small, what they lacked in size they
made up for in numbers. Benzoni's estimate thus seems
too low especially when the devastating impact of disease
and the Indian slave trade are also taken into account.
An aboriginal population of about 800,000, of which
200,000 were living in the uncolonized areas, seems not
unreasonable and could easily have been supported given
the natural resources and the nature of the Indian economies.[21] This estimate is the highest so far proposed for
Honduras.

By 1539 according to Bishop Pedraza the Indian population of Honduras had been reduced to 15,000, whilst in
1541 Benzoni maintained there were only 8,000.[22] It is
unlikely that either of these accounts took into consid-

eration the Indian population living in the east of the country. Unfortunately there are no more detailed accounts of the Indian population until the 1540s when lists were drawn up for the purpose of tribute assessment.[23] Although the Crown ordered that official assessments or tasaciones should be made in the 1530s and it is possible that some were conducted, the earliest evidence of assessments for Honduras is for 1544.[24] These tasaciones were made by the oidores Rogel, Herrera and Ramírez and although it appears that they covered a large part of the country only the tasaciones for the jurisdiction of Gracias a Dios have been found. These assessments are contained in the residencia of the first Audiencia undertaken by the President of the Audiencia, Alonso López de Cerrato, from 1548 to 1550.[25] Although the assessments do not indicate the number of Indians in each of the sixty-four villages, they do list the number of Indian carriers or tamemes each was to supply, as well as the number who were required to provide "servicio ordinario" (to work as household servants) and render other services such as tending livestock, supplying fish on Fridays and holy days and making pans for washing alluvial gold. Together the sixty-four villages supplied 4,354 tamemes and 373 Indians for other kinds of service. It is assumed that the tamemes were adult males, whether married or single, as were probably the majority of other Indians who provided services. This number thus represents only a proportion of the total Indian population to be found in the area. In addition not all villages were required to provide tamemes or services. As such it is impossible to estimate accurately the total Indian population from these figures, but it seems likely that it would not have been below 15,000.[26] This suggests that the figures for the Indian population given by Bishop Pedraza and Benzoni for 1539 and 1541 respectively were underestimates. When Alonso López de Cerrato became President of the Audiencia in 1548 he reported that the Indians could not pay half of what was due even if they were doubled in number.[27] He thus set about moderating the amount of tribute and personal service which the Indians were required to pay. His reassessments constitute one of the best sources of information about the Indian population in Central America in the sixteenth century.[28] Unfortunately for Honduras the libro de tasaciones only includes the assessments for Comayagua and even then the population of only 38 of the 48 villages listed is included. These villages had a total of 2,745 tributary Indians. Given that the tasaciones regulated the amount of maize to be sown at one fanega per ten tributary Indians, it is estimated that the tributary population for those villages where the population is not stated but where the amount of tribute is indicated was about 485, giving a total for the jurisdiction of 3,230.[29] The term

tributario referred to married male Indians only, for it
was not until 1578 that other able-bodied males such as
widowers and single men were made liable for tribute payment.[30]

There is very little evidence for the size of the
Indian population in the following two decades. Although
general reassessments of tribute were made by the oidores
Alonso Zorita and Tomás López in 1554 and by the oidores
Dr. Mexía and Jufre de Loaysa in 1562, there is no evidence of the number of tributary Indians, only the amount
of tribute they paid. Since the amount of tribute assessed by Mexía and Loaysa was considered to be much
heavier than that of their predecessors it is impossible
to use the tasaciones as indicators of demographic
change.[31] According to Batres Jáuregui, in 1561 the
bishopric of Comayagua contained 145 villages with a population of 10,000 Indians.[32] Unfortunately he does not
cite the source of his information but it may have been
one of these reassessments.

López de Velasco's Geografía y descripción universal
de las Indias is often used by historians to obtain an
overview of the social and economic conditions in Latin
America in the early 1570s, but the population figures he
gives for Central America should be used with caution.
It is almost certain that the figures he gives for individual villages in the jurisdiction of Comayagua were
taken from the tributary lists drawn up in 1549. Only
summary figures are given for other jurisdictions and
their origin is unknown. It is possible that they were
based on other tributary lists which were drawn up at the
same time but which have since been lost, but more likely
they were based on later tasaciones or general estimates.
The figure of 10,000 tributary Indians is the same as
that recorded in an unsigned and undated document in the
Biblioteca Nacional in Madrid and it is clearly a mis-
take.[33]

There is no evidence of other general assessments
until the end of the 1570s, when Lic. García de Valverde
took office as President of the Audiencia and in 1578 ordered a general survey of the conditions of the Indians.[34]
Unfortunately there are no detailed accounts of the numbers of Indians counted during the visita, although one
report from Francisco Cisneros encharged with part of the
visita of Honduras said that in the jurisdiction of
Gracias a Dios there were only 2,400 Indians, whereas at
the time they had been counted by Loaysa there had been
5,000, and that the Indian population of the jurisdiction
of San Pedro had been reduced by two-thirds.[35] Probably
in connection with the visita ordered by Valverde, the
Governor of Honduras, Alonso de Contreras visited the region in the late 1570s and early 1580s. His account
written in 1582 lists the number of tributary Indians in
each village and they sum to 5,106.[36] Another letter

TABLE 9.1
Population estimates for Honduras, 1571-1582

Jurisdictions	1571-74[a] Velasco's account tributarios	1582[b] Governor's account tributarios	1582[c] Bishop's account vecinos naturales	
			(indiv. figs.)	(summary figs.)
Comayagua	2,600	1,723	1,640	1,800
Gracias a Dios	3,000	1,769	2,160	2,100
San Pedro	700	415	330	330
Puerto de Caballos		60	120	120
Trujillo	600	413	590	590
Olancho	10,000	726	460	460
Total		5,106	5,300	5,400

[a]Velasco, op. cit., pp. 307-313.

[b]BAGGG vol. 11, pp. 5-19, Contreras to Crown 20.4.1582.

[c]AGI,AG 164 Bishop to Crown 10.5.1582 and 12.5.1582.

from the Bishop of Honduras written in the same year lists 5,400 vecinos naturales but it is more general giving only the total figures for the jurisdictions.[37] In both accounts many of the figures are fives or tens suggesting rounding or estimation rather than accurate counting.[38]

In 1590 the President of the Audiencia Francisco de Valverde drew up an account of the tributary population of Honduras as part of a proposal to establish a road from Trujillo to the Bay of Fonseca to carry trade to and from Peru. Two accounts exist of the Indian population, one of which includes the number of tributary Indians for each village.[39] With the exception of the jurisdiction of Olancho the coverage is complete and includes Choluteca. In the detailed account there are errors in addition and the more general account, which was probably based on the former, possesses several errors in transcription. The summary figures give a total tributary population of 5,965 with a further 663 in Choluteca.

The most detailed and comprehensive accounts of the Indian population for the end of the sixteenth century is contained in the treasury accounts for that period. In 1591 the Crown introduced a capitation tax known as the servicio del tostón to help pay the costs of defence.[40]

TABLE 9.2
Population estimates for Honduras circa 1590

Jurisdictions	Relación of 1590[a] Indios	Memorial[b] Indios casados tributarios	
		(indiv. figs.)	(summary figs.)
Comayagua	1,061	1,666	2,061
Gracias a Dios	2,188	1,888	2,188
San Pedro	376	376	363
Puerto de Caballos	104	104	104
Trujillo	not given	510	510
Olancho	470	464	469
Total	4,199	5,008	5,695
Choluteca	663	663	663

[a]RAHM 9/4663 No. 15, Relación geográfica, Francisco Valverde, 24.8.1590.

[b]AGI,MEX 257 Memorial de todos los pueblos . . . Francisco de Valverde, no date.

Each tributary Indian was required to pay one tostón a year in two installments of two reales. The treasury accounts list the number of tostones paid by each Indian village and thus they may be used as a rough guide to the size of the tributary population. The figures are an imperfect guide because some Indians only paid for half of the year because they either ceased to pay tribute or became tributary during the year, whilst others avoided payment completely. As such, the figures if anything slightly underestimate the size of the tributary population and it is possible that part of the decline could be attributed to tax evasion. Accounts of the income from the servicio del tostón for Honduras are more or less complete for 1592 to 1602, and are available for the jurisdiction of Comayagua until 1614.[41] Although the income from the servicio del tostón is an imperfect guide to the size of the tributary population, the figures are consistent with other reports of the size of the Indian population already discussed and with a report from the oficiales reales in 1626 in which they complained about the lack of Indian labor for the mines indicating that there were not 3,000 Indians in the country.[42]

With the exception of the figures provided by Valverde, the Indian population in all jurisdictions

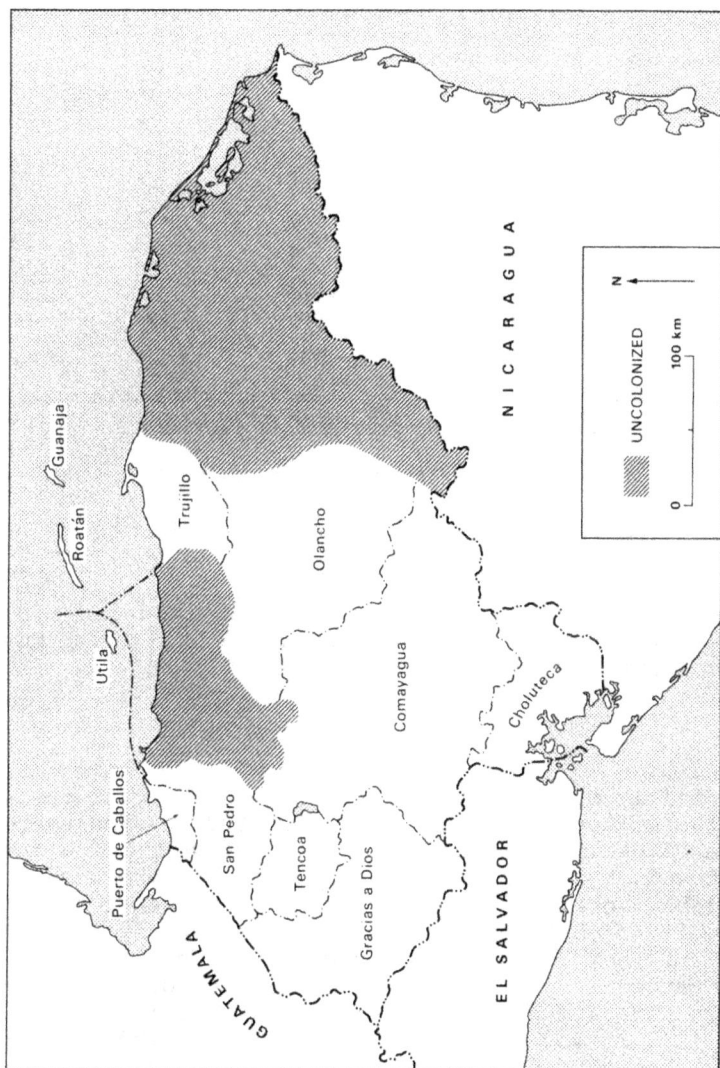

Figure 9.1 Approximate boundaries of jurisdictions and uncolonized areas of Honduras, circa 1600

TABLE 9.3
Population estimates for Honduras, 1582-1602

Jurisdictions	1582[a] Governor's account tributarios	ca. 1590[b] Memorial indios casados tributarios	1592[c] Servicio del tostones	1602[d] tostón
Comayagua	1,723	2,061	1,893	1,325
Gracias a Dios	1,369	1,618	1,088	639
San Pedro	444	620	532½	309½
Tencoa	249	301	205	124
Puerto de Caballos	80	116	88	66
Trujillo	337	436	301	209
Olancho	904	543	627	363
Total	5,106	5,695	4,734½	3,035½

[a] BAGGG vol. 11, pp. 5-19, Contreras to Crown 20.4.1582.

[b] AGI,MEX 257, Memorial de todos los pueblos . . . Francisco de Valverde, no date.

[c] AGI,CO 989, Treasury accounts 1592.

[d] AGI,CO 991A, Treasury accounts 1602.

NOTE: The figures for 1582 and ca. 1590 have been transformed to conform with the jurisdictions delineated in 1592 and 1602 and thus do not correspond with those contained in Tables 9.1 and 9.2.

shows a fairly consistent decline through the last quarter of the sixteenth century (1582 to 1602) at the average rate of decline (ω) of about 2.6% per year and a loss of about 40% of the tributary population. There were considerable variations in the percentage loss of the Indian population between jurisdictions ranging from -17% to -59% but they do not form any clearly identifiable spatial pattern.[43] Taking the jurisdiction of Comayagua for which data are available for a longer period from 1549 to 1612 it would appear that from the third quarter of the sixteenth century the rate of decline slowed down. The rates of decline for these periods are: 1549-1582 = -46.7% at the average rate of decline (ω) of -1.9% per year; 1582-1602 = -23.1% at the average rate of decline (ω) of -1.3% per year; 1602-1614 = -14.1% at the average rate of decline (ω) of -1.3% per year. It should be noted, however, that the decline for the period 1549 to 1582 would have been greater than that recorded, for in

the former year only married male Indians were regarded
as tributary Indians, whereas after 1578 other able-
bodied males were also included in this category. It is
also clear that the jurisdiction of Comayagua experienced
a slower decline than most other jurisdictions in the
country.

It has been shown that at the turn of the century
there were about 3,500 tributary Indians in Honduras,
taking into account some slight underestimation of the
number of Indians as indicated in the records of the servicio del tostón, but they represented only a small proportion of the total Indian population of the country.
There were in addition a large number of Indians who by
virtue of their age, marital status, official status or
physical disability were exempt from tribute payment.
Men paid tribute from between the ages of 18 and 55,
whereas women only paid until the age of 50. The age at
which women began to pay tribute varied considerably.
Initially only married female Indians were required to
pay with the result that many postponed marriage. Later
single women were legally required to pay tribute from
18, but in practice the age at which they commenced payment was extremely variable. Caciques and their eldest
sons were exempt from tribute payment as were those who
held secular and ecclesiastical offices in their communities. Individual Indians could also petition the Audiencia for exemption on the grounds of ill health or dis-
ablement. They could also avoid enumeration by being absent from their villages at the time the tribute lists
were drawn up. The proportion of Indians who were absent
from their villages often living in towns, on estates or
in the mining areas was substantial towards the end of
the seventeenth century, but in the sixteenth century did
not account for a significant number. Some Indians who
lived in these areas paid a reduced amount of tribute as
naborías or lavoríos. These were originally Indians who
worked and lived permanently in Spanish households and
they did not account for more than a very small proportion of Indians who were living within the Spanish settled area.[44] It seems reasonable, therefore, to suggest
that there were about 25,000 Indians in the colonized
area at the end of the sixteenth century, thereby giving
a ratio of tributary to non-tributary Indians of about
1:7. If it is accepted that the aboriginal population of
this area was 600,000 then the depopulation ratio for the
sixteenth century was about 24:1. There were, however, a
large number of Indians who remained outside Spanish control. As has been noted, at the end of the sixteenth
century there were said to be about 4,000 to 5,000 Indians between Trujillo and Cabo de Camarón,[45] and between
1622 and 1623 missionaries working amongst the Paya Indians inland from the north coast managed to settle 700
Indians in 7 villages and to baptise another 5,000.[46]

Although these Indians did not come under Spanish control
during the sixteenth century they had intermittent contact with Spaniards and were thus affected to some degree
by conquest, slavery, disease, and economic and social
disruption. It is possible that the population in these
uncolonized regions was reduced by a half or two-thirds
during the sixteenth century leaving about 65,000 and
100,000 Indians in 1600.

CAUSES OF THE DECLINE

The causes of the decline in the Indian population
were manifold, complex and interwoven. Contemporary observers identified three major factors--the Indian slave
trade, conquest and disease--but the overwork and ill
treatment of the Indians and the severe disruption to Indian economies and societies brought about by conquest
and colonization contributed significantly to the decline
in the Indian population and later miscegenation also began to take its toll. The Indian slave trade and conquest were only significant factors in the first half of
the sixteenth century, whilst the other factors were
operative throughout the period.

THE INDIAN SLAVE TRADE

The largest and easiest profits to be made in Central America in the first half of the sixteenth century
were in the Indian slave trade. The Crown's attitude
towards the enslavement of Indians vacillated throughout
the first half of the sixteenth century as it tried to
reconcile its humanitarian views towards the Indians with
the practical needs of Empire. Finally in 1542 the New
Laws abolished Indian slavery, although the order was not
put into effect in Central America until 1548 when Alonso
López de Cerrato became President of the Audiencia.[47] By
that time, however, there were few Indians left to be enslaved and the trade in Indian slaves had long passed its
peak. Comments have already been made concerning estimates of the numbers of Indians involved in the slave
trade, particularly in Nicaragua, and here it is only
necessary to emphasize its importance in contributing to
the decline in the Indian population in Honduras and to
note that it did not affect all areas equally. The worst
affected areas were the hinterlands of the ports, notably
Trujillo, whilst it was noted that those Indians living
in inland areas were protected by their remoteness from
the coast.[48] When Cortés arrived in Honduras in 1525 the
Bay Islands had already been depopulated as a result of
enslaving raids from Cuba, Española and Jamaica[49] and in
1527, 2,000 Indians from the neighboring coast of Trujillo

and from Olancho were enslaved by the Governor, López de
Salcedo, and taken to Nicaragua for export.[50] In 1530
Andrés de Cerezeda complained that Vasco de Herrera had
made war on Indians in the vicinity of Trujillo and had
enslaved so many Indians that in villages which had possessed 1,000 souls only 30 were left.[51] Thus in 1547
Bishop Pedraza reported that villages of 3,000, 2,000,
1,000, 800 and 600 houses which had existed in the vicinity of Trujillo had been reduced to 150 and 180 people,
whilst one village located five leagues from the town
which had possessed 900 houses had been completely depopulated such that the only survivor was the daughter of
the cacique who had hidden under a boat.[52] The area
around Naco was also badly affected. Bishop Pedraza
maintained that when Andrés de Cerezeda entered the valley of Naco there had been between 8,000 and 10,000 men
but by 1539 there were only 250 left.[53] This was con-
firmed by the Governor, Francisco de Montejo, who reported that Cerezeda had destroyed 27 to 28 villages in the
valley of Naco carrying off the Indians in chains.[54] By
1586 the "great province of Naco" had been reduced to
less than ten Indians.[55] Given this scale of depopulation it is reasonable to suggest that about 100,000 to
150,000 Indians were enslaved and exported from Honduras,
both to the Caribbean islands and Guatemala, as well as
south through Nicaragua to Panama and Peru.

CONQUEST

The conquest of Honduras was a protracted affair
during which innumerable battles were fought and many Indians killed. Conquest was difficult because of the
presence of a large number of Indian groups, which were
not integrated by any political structure through which
the Spanish could achieve control. The whole area thus
had to be conquered piecemeal. No sooner had one group
been pacified than it revolted, often with increased resistance, against the harsh treatment meted out to it by
the Spanish with the result that the whole process of
pacification had to begin again. Meanwhile the rebel-
lious nature of the Indian groups provided justification
for their enslavement. In addition conquistadores moving
south from Mexico and Guatemala and north from Panama met
in Honduras and the country became a battleground for
rival Spanish forces. Efforts to pacify the area were
thus accompanied by battles between the Spaniards themselves and even between rival elements of the same fac-
tion, generally using Indians as fighting forces. Altogether it took the Spanish nearly twenty years to achieve
political control of the area.[56] Conquest and enslavement went hand in hand so that it is difficult to estimate the numbers that were killed in battle as opposed to

those who were enslaved; the impression given is that
conquest was a more significant factor in the decline of
the Indian population in Honduras than it was in the
neighboring countries of Guatemala and Nicaragua, where
political control was more easily achieved using the
existing native political organization.[57] Particularly
disruptive was the conquest of western Honduras in 1536
by Pedro de Alvarado with the help of 3,000 Indian auxil-
iaries from Guatemala known as Achies (or Aches), who
were notorious for looting Indian villages and roasting
people alive. In 1539 Governor Montejo reported that
Taloa only possessed 40 houses whereas when Alvarado arrived there had been 400 and other villages had been depopulated as follows: Carcamo from 500 houses to 20;
Araxagua from 250 to 40; Yopoa from 270 to 30 and Lepaera
from 400 to 70 or 80.[58] As a result of this conquest
Bishop Pedraza maintained that altogether 6,000 Indians
had been killed, enslaved or sacrificed, of which 3,000
had been shipped to Guatemala or sold in the Caribbean
islands.[59] This was only one of the many campaigns that
were conducted in Honduras and as such it seems reasonable to suggest that between 30,000 and 50,000 Indians
were killed as a result of conquest.

DISEASE

     Diseases were undoubtedly a major factor in the de-
cline of the Indian population of Honduras. Epidemic
diseases attracted most attention from contemporary observers but there were other unrecorded diseases, particularly intestinal ones such as typhoid, paratyphoid,
bacillary and amoebic dysentery, hookworm and other hel-
minthic diseases, which took their toll and increased the
susceptibility of the Indians to other diseases. The
first recorded epidemic disease in Middle America was
smallpox, which was introduced into Mexico in 1520.[60] In
1520 and 1521 Guatemala was ravaged by disease but it is
uncertain whether it was smallpox; it has been suggested
that it was influenza.[61] The only reference to disease
spreading further south at this time comes from an account written in 1527, which stated that it was necessary
to introduce slaves to "Panama City, Nata and the port of
Honduras" because smallpox had killed off the Indians
there.[62] In 1531 Guatemala and Nicaragua appear to have
been ravaged by a disease, probably some form of plague[63]
but the only reference to its presence in Honduras comes
from Herrera, who said that two years before the major
outbreak of measles, which was in 1533, "there was a general epidemic of pains in the side and stomach, which
also carried away many Indians." The measles epidemic
appears to have hit Honduras badly. Herrera describes
the epidemic as follows:

> At this time there was such a great epidemic of measles
> in the province of Honduras spreading from house to
> house and village to village, that many people died;
> and although the disease also affected the Spaniards . . .
> none of them died . . . . This same disease of measles
> and dysentery passed to Nicaragua where also many In-
> dians died.[64]

In Honduras Oviedo maintained that the measles epidemic
and other diseases had killed half of the population and
the most susceptible were those who were servants in
Spanish households or workers on Spanish estates.[65]
Since diseases do not act uniformly but are affected by
environmental factors such as population density, the degree of interpersonal contact, sanitation, dietary habits
and immunity, it seems likely that there would have been
great spatial variations in the proportion of Indians
killed by the disease and the estimate of one half of the
population is likely to have been a local maximum. Nevertheless it is clear that a substantial proportion of
the decline in the Indian population can be attributed to
successive waves of disease.

Over a decade later in 1545 an epidemic of either
pneumonic plague or typhus struck Mexico and Guatemala,
but it does not appear to have spread further south at
that time.[66] In fact there is little evidence of either
of these diseases in Honduras throughout the colonial
period and it seems likely that, with the exception of
the west of the country, they were unable to survive in
the warmer climatic conditions. In 1578 there was an
outbreak of romadizo in Nicaragua, generally translated
as catarrh or hay fever, which affected the Spaniards as
well as the Indians.[67] It is possible that the disease
was a mild form of pneumonic plague unable to become more
virulent in the unfavorable climatic conditions.

There is some controversy over the origins of the
tropical diseases yellow fever and malaria, and whether
either was present in Central America in the sixteenth
century. Yellow fever is generally considered to be an
introduction from the Old World. The first agreed epidemic of yellow fever occurred in Yucatán and Cuba in
1648; Ashburn effectively argues that skin coloration recorded in the sixteenth century was the result of starva-
tion rather than yellow fever.[68] Recent zoological and
historical evidence, however, suggests that sylvan yellow
fever may have been present in Latin America in pre-
Columbian times.[69] If this was the case then outbreaks
of the disease in the tropical coastal lowlands of Central America in the sixteenth century cannot be ruled
out. Nevertheless it was only at a later date that these
coasts, and particularly Panama, earned the reputation of
being unhealthy.[70] Similar comments may be made with respect to malaria. It now seems certain that malaria was

introduced from the Old World. This is based on the fact
that Indian populations in Latin America do not produce
polymorphisms resistant to malaria, whereas those in
Africa do, and the fact that the malarial parasites are
relatively unspecialized and have a restricted number of
hosts thus suggesting their recent appearance in the New
World.[71]

ILL TREATMENT AND OVERWORK

As long as the Indian population could be seen to
provide an inexhaustible supply of labor, little attention was paid to its preservation with the result that
Indians were subject to ill treatment and forced to work
long hours in poor conditions on inadequate diets and under threat of punishment for shortcomings. Many of the
tasks in which Indians were employed were strenuous and
contributed directly to illness and death; particularly
important in Honduras were the transportation of goods,
mining, and the manufacture of indigo. Indians were
forced to travel with heavy loads over long distances,
which often traversed climatic zones with the result that
they fell ill and died.[72] In 1547 Bishop Pedraza reported 500 Indians, which had been hired out by the Governor,
Francisco de Montejo, had died and he recorded that generally on the journey from Comayagua to San Pedro and
Puerto de Caballos one half of the Indian carriers did
not return, one third dying or becoming ill on the journey.[73] Despite a ban on the employment of Indians as
carriers in 1541, the lack of paved roads and the difficult communications made the implementation of the order
impossible.[74] Indian bearers were used primarily for
moving goods between the ports, major cities and mining
areas, but in the early years of conquest they were also
used on expeditions to carry supplies. In 1527 López de
Salcedo on an expedition to Nicaragua took with him 4,000
Indian bearers of which no more than 6 returned.[75] Conditions in the mines were sufficiently bad to stimulate
Indian revolts[76] and persuade the Crown to ban the employment of Indians in the mines in 1546.[77] Similarly
Indians were banned from working in the unhealthy task of
manufacturing indigo. The process of indigo manufacture
often required Indians to stand for several hours in vats
of warm water which gave off unhealthy vapors and resulted in them catching colds and other respiratory in-
fections. In addition the rotting leaves which were left
after the manufacture of the dye attracted insects, which
encouraged the spread of disease and earned the obrajes
the reputation of being unhealthy places of work.[78] As a
result, after 1581 repartimiento Indians could not be employed in this work, although they could work there vol-
untarily until 1601 when their employment in indigo

obrajes was banned completely.[79] Other tasks in which
Indians were employed, whilst not contributing directly
to the death rate, were exhausting and with the poor diets that prevailed contributed to the susceptibility of
the Indians to illness and disease. The burden of work
which fell on the Indians was also increased directly and
indirectly by demands made for tribute, the repartimiento,
and other goods and services by encomenderos, royal offi-
cials--particularly corregidores, alcaldes mayores and
jueces de milpas--and priests. Whilst each demand or
exaction may have been small, together they combined to
keep the Indians in continual labor like "frightened
deer" leaving them little time to attend to their own
subsistence needs.[80]

ECONOMIC AND SOCIAL DISRUPTION

    Although very few contemporary observers attributed
the decline in the Indian population to the economic, social, political, and ideological changes brought about by
Spanish conquest and colonization, it is clear that their
effects were considerable. Disruption to the Indian
economy led indirectly to food shortages and famines and
hence to a decline in the Indian population. Many Indians fearing attack and enslavement, or later excessive
tribute and labor demands, abandoned their lands and fled
to the hills, where they attempted to survive on wild
fruits, vegetables, fish and game. Unaccustomed to such
a form of livelihood many of them suffered from malnutrition and some died.[81] Meanwhile those Indians who remained on their lands experienced a decline in food production as a result of a reduction of their land holdings
and a decline in labor inputs, particularly at the time
of sowing and harvest, resulting from heavy demands for
labor services, tribute, and other goods.[82]
    There is some evidence to suggest that the breakdown
in the social organization of Indian communities and the
psychological impact of conquest also contributed to the
decline in the Indian population. Whilst diseases and
famines took their toll on the youngest and oldest sections of the community, enslavement, ill treatment and
overwork largely effected the adult male population probably resulting in an imbalance in the sex ratio. It is
uncertain, however, whether this imbalance effected the
birth rate, but it seems likely that the endless tiring
work which the Indians were forced to carry out would
have dampened their desires to procreate, particularly
since additional children would have placed an increased
burden on already inadequate food resources. In addition
Indians did not wish to bear children that would be born
into slavery. These factors resulted in Indians practicing birth control by abstaining from sexual intercourse

and inducing miscarriages, as well as practicing infanticide.[83] In 1584 the Bishop of Honduras reported that as a result of the overwork of the Indians "mothers kill their children at birth because they say that they wish to free them from the misery they suffer."[84] Apart from infanticide, the infant mortality rate would have increased as a result of malnutrition increasing their susceptibility to the newly-introduced diseases. Unfortunately there are no early accounts of the age and sex structure of Indian communities that could give insights into the effects of a decreased birth rate and an increased infant mortality rate.

MISCEGENATION

Although miscegenation occurred during the sixteenth century it did not make a significant contribution to the decline in the Indian population as it did in succeeding centuries. The degree of miscegenation was dependent on the intensity of contact between the races and was stimulated by the predominance of men amongst the white and Negro elements of the population. Miscegenation was most common in the towns, where Indians were ordered to work and where a substantial number of Indians lived as servants in Spanish households. It was also common in the mining areas of Olancho and later Tegucigalpa to which Negro slaves were imported. In 1543 it was estimated that there had been 1,500 Negroes working gold in the Guayape valley and about 2,000 were employed in mining in the whole country.[85] Although repartimiento Indians could not be employed in the mines, Indians were allowed to work there on a voluntary basis, such that in 1590 there were 200 Negro and Indian peons working in the Guacucarán mines and a further 90 in the mines of Tegucigalpa.[86] Later with the development of agriculture, Negroes and people of mixed race were often employed as domestic servants and overseers on estates where they came into contact with Indians, who worked as free laborers or under the repartimiento, and thus the rural estates also emerged as racial melting pots.

CONCLUSION

It is thus argued that the aboriginal population of Honduras was about 800,000, with 600,000 living in the area which was settled during the sixteenth century and 200,000 in the uncolonized east. This represents the highest estimate for the whole area to have been proposed to date. It has also been demonstrated that during the sixteenth century the Indian population suffered a

decline that was more severe than in many other parts of
Latin America. The depopulation ratio for the settled
area during the sixteenth century was about 24:1, whilst
the population in the uncolonized areas may have been reduced to one half or one third. Whilst the impact of
disease and the general disruption to Indian life probably accounted for the greatest proportion of the decline, in Honduras several other factors contributed
significantly to the mortality rate, which were to a certain degree peculiar to that country. First, the slave
trade took a heavy toll on the Indian population because
the area was discovered, conquered and colonized from an
early date before the New Laws were introduced, which
gave a measure of protection to the Indian population.
Also, and more importantly, there were insufficient Indians in Honduras to form large encomiendas and there
were no other economic incentives in the area to encourage colonists to remain there and preserve the labor supply. As such the country was raided for the only wealth
it possessed--its Indian population. Conquest was also
particularly destructive in Honduras, partly due to the
nature of the native societies, which made political control difficult to achieve, and partly due to the country's location on the boundary of conflicting jurisdictions. As such the Indian slave trade and conquest together probably resulted in the loss of 130,000 to
200,000 Indians. It was a loss from which the Indians
did not recover until the eighteenth century.

NOTES

1. M. J. MacLeod, Spanish Central America: a Socioeconomic His-
tory, 1520-1720 (University of California Press: Berkeley and Los
Angeles, 1973), p. 59; W. L. Sherman, Forced Native Labor in
Sixteenth-Century Central America (University of Nebraska: Lincoln
and London, 1979), pp. 350-352.
2. A. L. Kroeber, "Cultural and Natural Areas of Native North
America," University of California Publications in Archaeology and
Ethnology, Vol. 38 (1939), p. 166; H. F. Dobyns, "Estimating Aboriginal American Populations: An Appraisal of Techniques with a New
Hemispheric Estimate," Current Anthropology, Vol. 7 (1966), p. 415.
3. J. H. Steward, "The Native Population of South America," in
J. H. Steward (ed.), The Handbook of South American Indians, Bulletin of the Bureau of American Ethnology, 143, Vol. 5 (1949), p. 664.
4. A. Rosenblat, La población indígena y el mestizaje en
América (Editorial Nova: Buenos Aires, 1954), Vol. 1, p. 102.
5. K. Sapper, "Die Zahl und die Volksdichte der Indianischen
Bevölkerung in Amerika vor der Conquista und in der Gegenwart," Proceedings of the International Congress of Americanists (The Hague,
1924,), Vol. 1, p. 100.

6. Dobyns, op. cit., p. 415.

7. D. Radell, "The Indian Slave Trade and the Population of Nicaragua in the Sixteenth Century," in W. M. Denevan (ed.), The Native Population of the Americas in 1492 (University of Wisconsin: Madison, 1976), pp. 67 and 75.

8. Denevan, op. cit., 291. Denevan's estimates for the Central American countries are: Guatemala 2,000,000; Honduras and Belize 750,000; El Salvador 500,000; Nicaragua 1,000,000; Costa Rica 400,000; and Panama 1,000,000.

9. Bartolomé de las Casas, Breve Relación de la Destrucción de las Indias Occidentales (London, 1812), pp. 43-45; G. Fernández de Oviedo y Valdés, Historia Natural y Moral de las Indias (Biblioteca de Autores Españoles, Vols. 117-121, Ediciones Atlas: Madrid, 1959), Vol. 4, p. 385.

10. Sherman, op. cit., pp. 4-5. For a full discussion of estimates of the volume of the Indian slave trade see pp. 74-82.

11. MacLeod, op. cit., p. 52.

12. Archivo General de las Indias, Seville (hereafter AGI), Audiencia de Guatemala (AG) 9; and Real Academia de la Historia, Madrid (hereafter RAHM), Colección Muñoz (CM) A/108 4843 ff. 285-8, Pedraza to Crown 18.5.1539; AGI,AG 164, Pedraza to Crown 1.5.1547.

13. G. Benzoni, La Historia del Mundo Nuevo (Biblioteca de la Academia Nacional de la Historia, Vol. 86: Caracas, 1967), p. 163; Johannessen believes that Benzoni was referring to tributary Indians and thus multiplies the figure of 400,000 by three to give a total population of 1,200,000 (C. L. Johannessen, "Savannas of Interior Honduras," Ibero-Americana 46 [University of California Press: Berkeley and Los Angeles, 1963], pp. 29-31).

14. AGI,AG 39; and RAHM,CM A/107 4842 ff. 160-191, Cerezeda to Crown 31.8.1535.

15. F. A. Fuentes y Guzmán, Recordación Florida (Tip. Nacional: Guatemala, 1933), Vol. 2, p. 145.

16. AGI,AG 39; and RAHM,CM A/107 4842 ff. 160-191, Cerezeda to Crown 31.8.1535.

17. D. Z. Stone, "The Archaeology of Central and Southern Honduras," Papers of the Peabody Museum, Vol. 43, No. 2 (1957), p. 9.

18. AGI,AG 39, Cerezeda to Crown 14.8.1536.

19. AGI,AG 49, Celis to Crown 10.3.1535.

20. RAHM, 9/4663 No. 15, Valverde to Crown, no date.

21. Clark and Haswell have estimated that groups practicing shifting cultivation can achieve a population density of 20 persons per sq. km., whilst simple agriculture can only support 10 persons per sq. km. and those dependent on wild food resources only .1 per sq. km. (G. Clark and M. Haswell, The Economics of Subsistence Agriculture [Macmillan: London, 1966], p. 37). Indians in western and central Honduras practiced a form of shifting cultivation, though in some areas agriculture was more permanent in nature and thus may have supported higher densities. In eastern Honduras the Indians practiced agriculture to some degree, but they were also dependent on hunting, fishing and gathering; agriculture appears to have been most poorly developed amongst the Jicaque Indians. Nevertheless there were no Indian groups that were entirely dependent on wild food resources. It is suggested that the population density of the

Jicaque was 1 per sq. km., whilst other Indian groups in eastern
Honduras, the Paya and Sumu, could have achieved densities of 10 per
sq. km. The population supported by different Indians' economies
could thus have been as high as 1,396,858 or even higher for if anything the population density estimates err on the low side, particularly for western and central Honduras.

	sq. kms.	estimated density	estimated population
Western and central Honduras[a]	42,563	20	851,260
Eastern Honduras[b]	52,897	10	528,970
Area occupied by the Jicaque[c]	16,628	1	16,628
TOTAL			1,396,858

---

[a]Departments of Cortés, Santa Barbara, Copán, Ocotepeque,
Lempira, Intibucá, Comayagua, La Paz, Francisco Morazan, Valle
and Choluteca.

[b]Departments of El Paraíso, Olancho, Gracias a Dios, Islas de
la Bahia and half of Colón.

[c]Departments of Atlántida, Yoro and half of Colón.

22. AGI,AG 9; and RAHM,CM A/108 4843 ff. 285-8, Pedraza to
Crown 18.5.1539; Benzoni, op. cit., p. 167.
23. Until the middle of the 1530s the amount of tribute that
could be exacted from the Indians was at the discretion of encomenderos but, due to their excessive demands, the Crown ordered that
official assessments should be made in New Spain and Guatemala in
1533 and 1534. Officials in Central America presented objections to
implementing the order arguing that the income from encomiendas
would decline and as a result encomenderos would leave the area.
Nevertheless, in view of the benefits that had been derived from the
implementation of the order in New Spain, the Crown repeated it in
1536. An order requiring official assessments to be made in Honduras was issued in 1538 but it was not carried out until the 1540s due
to continued warfare, political instability and the reluctance of
royal officials to implement it. (Archivo General de Centroamerica,
Guatemala [hereafter AGCA] Al.23 4575 f. 28v. real cédula 28.2.1536;
Fuentes y Guzmán, op. cit., Vol. 2, pp. 256-258; R. S. Chamberlain,
The Conquest and Colonization of Honduras, 1502-1520 [Carnegie Institution of Washington Publication 598: Washington, 1953], p. 241;
S. Rodríguez Becerra, Encomienda y conquista: Los inicios de la
colonización en Guatemala [Universidad de Sevilla: Sevilla, 1977],
pp. 115-117.)
24. It would appear that tasaciones of parts of Guatemala, San
Miguel, San Salvador and Chiapas were made by the visitador Lic.
Maldonado and the Bishop of Guatemala, Francisco Marroquín, in the
late 1530s but there is no evidence that tasaciones of Honduras were
made at that time (AGI,AG 156, Marroquín to Crown 20.1.1539;
Rodríguez Becerra, op. cit., p. 117).
25. AGI, Justicia (JU) 299, residencia of the first Audiencia
1548 to 1550. It appears that tasaciones were also made of villages

in the jurisdictions of San Pedro and Comayagua (AGI,AG 9, Herrera
to Crown 10.7.1545) but there is no detailed evidence of them.

26. The service of tamemes had been banned in 1541 (AGCA, Al.23
4575 f. 50 reales cédulas 28.1.1541, 31.5.1541). Following a repri-
mand from the Crown in 1546 (AGCA, Al.23 1511 f. 40 real cédula
5.7.1546) in 1547 the service of tamemes was removed from the tribute assessments for villages in the jurisdiction of Gracias a Dios
(AGI,JU 299, residencia of the first Audiencia 1548 to 1550).

27. AGI,AG 9, Cerrato to Crown 28.9.1548.

28. AGI,AG 128, libro de tasaciones 1548 to 1551.

29. This excludes the village of Ynquibiteca for which no tribute assessment is indicated.

30. Recopilación de las Leyes de los Reynos de las Indias (Madrid, 1943), Vol. 2, lib. 6, tit. 5, ley 7, pp. 226-227, 5.7.1578.

31. AGI,AG 9, Audiencia to Crown 25.5.1555. For evidence of
the tasaciones see the amount of tribute paid in succeeding years in
AGI Contaduría (CO) 987 and 988, 1554 and 1562. For comments on the
tasaciones of Zorita and López see L. B. Simpson, The Encomienda in
New Spain: The Beginning of Spanish Mexico (University of California
Press: Berkeley and Los Angeles, 1950), p. 152; A. de Zorita, The
Lords of New Spain (Phoenix House: London, 1965), p. 36.

32. Batres Jáuregui, La América Central ante la Historia (Sánchez y de Guise: Paris, 1920), Vol. 2, p. 367.

33. A. López de Velasco, Geografía y descripción universal de
las Indias (Real Academia de la Historia: Madrid, 1894), pp. 307-313.
The source of his information for jurisdictions other than Comayagua
is likely to have been different from the tasaciones made in 1548 to
1551, since all of those recorded in the libro de tasaciones are included in detail by Velasco; he only gives summary figures for other
jurisdictions. His summary figure of 2,600 for the jurisdiction of
Comayagua does not correspond to the total for the individual villages, which is 1,955. The latter figure is somewhat smaller than
the total of 2,745 found in the tasaciones for 1549, but this is because the population of about one fifth of the villages is not included by Velasco. Where the population of the villages is recorded
in both accounts, it is the same. The document in the Biblioteca
Nacional, Madrid is reproduced in Colección de documentos inéditos
relativos al descubrimiento, conquista, organización de las antiguas
posesiones españoles de América y Oceanía (hereafter CDI) (Madrid,
1864-1884), Vol. 15, pp. 409-572, no author, no date.

34. Simpson, op. cit., pp. 154-155; MacLeod, op. cit., pp. 130-
131.

35. AGI,AG 56, Cisneros to Crown 20.4.1582.

36. Boletín del Archivo General del Gobierno, Guatemala (BAGGG),
Vol. 11 (1946), pp. 5-19, Contreras to Crown 20.4.1582.

37. AGI,AG 164, Bishop of Honduras to Crown. There are two
copies of the same letter with different dates: 10.5.1582 and
12.5.1582.

38. Using the Bishop's account MacLeod, op. cit., p. 59, calcu-
lates the total number of vecinos naturales at 4,840. This is
clearly a miscalculation although it is not possible to identify the
source of the error. Sherman, op. cit., p. 351, gives the total as
5,840. He appears to have erred in transcribing the figure for

Olancho, which he gives as 400 and which is clearly 460 in the document and to have counted Agalteca and Tegucigalpa as separate jurisdictions instead of as parts of the jurisdiction of Comayagua, so
that those areas have been double-counted.

39. RAHM, 9/4663 No. 15, Relación geográfica of Valverde
24.8.1590; and AGI, Mexico (MEX) 257, Memorial de todos los pueblos
. . . Valverde, no date.

40. AGCA, A1.23 1513 f. 719, real cédula 1.1.1591.

41. AGI,CO 989, 990, 991A and 992, Treasury accounts 1592 to
1614. The accounts for the whole country from 1592 to 1602 show a
steady decline in income as follows:

1592	4,734½ tostones	1598	3,302
1593	incomplete	1599	--
1594	4,055½	1600	3,094½
1595	--	1601	2,924½
1596	3,619	1602	3,035½
1597	--		

42. AGI,AG 49, oficiales reales to Crown 23.7.1626.

43. The average rate of decline is calculated using Cook and
Borah's coefficient of population movement ω (See S. F. Cook and W.
Borah, Essays in Population History: Mexico and the Caribbean [Uni-
versity of California Press: Berkeley and Los Angeles, 1971], Vol.
1, pp. 89-91). The regional rates of decline for 1582 to 1602 are:

Comayagua	-23.1% at a rate of decline ω of -1.3% per year.
Gracias a Dios	-53.3%	-3.9%
Tenoca	-30.3%	-1.8%
San Pedro	-50.2%	-3.5%
Puerto de Caballos	-17.5%	-1.0%
Trujillo	-38.0%	-2.4%
Olancho	-40.6%	-2.6%

44. There are no comprehensive accounts of the number of
lavoríos in Honduras in the sixteenth century. However, a detailed
account of the inhabitants of the parish of Tatumbla in 1689 reveals
that they accounted for 3.3 percent of the total population of 2,658
which included men, women, children, Indians and ladinos (Archivo
Nacional, Honduras [ANH], Paquete 4, Legajo 135, padrón 1689).

45. See footnote 15.

46. AGI,AG 371, Fray Joseph Ximénez to Crown 9.9.1748.

47. For a detailed discussion of Indian slavery in Central
America see Sherman, op. cit., pp. 20-82.

48. Colección de documentos inéditos relativos al descubrimiento, conquista y organización de las antiguas posesiones españoles de Ultramar (CDIU) (Madrid, 1885-1929), Vol. 11, p. 400, Pedraza
to Crown, 1544.

49. E. de Vedia, Historiadores primitivos de Indias (Madrid,
1918), Vol. 1, p. 147, Cortés to Crown 3.9.1526.

50. Colección Somoza: Documentos para la Historia de Nicaragua
(CS) (Madrid, 1954-1957), Vol. 1, pp. 293-299, Treasurer of Honduras
to Crown, no date but probably 1527. Of the 2,000 enslaved only 100
arrived in Nicaragua alive.

51. AGI,AG 49, Cerezeda to Crown 31.3.1530.

240

52. AGI,AG 164, Pedraza to Crown 1.5.1547.

53. Sherman, op. cit., pp. 49 and 380 reference to AGI, Patronato 170-145.

54. AGI,AG 39, and RAHM,CM A/108 4843 ff. 239-257; also CDI 24,
pp. 250-297, Montejo to Crown 1.6.1539.

55. Fray Alonso Ponce, Relación breve y verdadera de algunas
cosas que sucedieron al padre Alonso Ponce en las provincas de Nueva
España (Viuda de Calero: Madrid, 1873), Vol. 1, p. 349.

56. The best account of the difficult conquest and colonization
of Honduras is Chamberlain, op. cit.

57. For a comparison of the conquests of Honduras and Guatemala
see S. Rodríguez Becerra, "Variables en la conquista: los casos de
Honduras y Guatemala," in A. Jiménez (ed.), Primera Reunión de An-
tropologos Españoles (Universidad de Sevilla: Sevilla, 1975), pp.
127-133.

58. AGI,AG 39; and RAHM,CM A/108 4843 ff. 239-257; and CDI 24,
pp. 250-297, Montejo to Crown 1.6.1539.

59. AGI,AG 9; and RAHM,CM A/108 4843 ff. 285-288, Pedraza to
Crown 18.5.1539.

60. A. W. Crosby, The Columbian Exchange: biological and cultural consequences of 1492 (Greenwood: Westport, Conn., 1972), p. 47.

61. F. W. McBryde, "Influenza in America during the sixteenth
century (Guatemala: 1523, 1559-1562, 1576)," Bulletin of the History
of Medicine, Vol. 8 (1940), pp. 296-302; J. E. S. Thompson, "The
Maya Central Area at the Spanish Conquest and Later: A Problem in
Demography," Proceedings of the Royal Anthropological Institute of
Great Britain and Northern Ireland for 1966 (1967), p. 24; Crosby,
op. cit., p. 51; MacLeod, op. cit., p. 98; T. T. Veblen, "Native
population decline in Totonicapán, Guatemala," Annals of the Association of American Geographers, Vol. 67 (1977), p. 490.

62. Colección de documentos inéditos para la historia de Costa
Rica (CDHCR) (Imprenta Pablo Dupont: Paris, 1881-1907), Vol. 4, pp.
7-11, Instrucciones a los procuradores de la ciudad de Granada
10.7.1527; Crosby, op. cit., p. 51.

63. MacLeod, op. cit., p. 98 identifies the disease as pneumonic plague but the symptoms of the disease, especially as described
for Nicaragua where the Indians developed swollen glands (AGI,AG 9;
and CS 3, pp. 68-78, Castaneda to Crown 30.5.1531), suggest that it
was bubonic plague.

64. A. de Herrera y Tordesillas, Historia general de los hechos
de los castellanos en las islas y tierra firme del mar oceano (Real
Academia de la Historia: Madrid, 1934), Vol. 10, dec. 5, lib.1, cap.
10, p. 72; Ashburn, The Ranks of Death: A Medical History of the
Conquest of America (Coward-McCann: New York, 1947), p. 91 trans-
lates "cámaras de sangre" as dysentery.

65. Fernández de Oviedo y Valdés, op. cit., Vol. 3, lib. 31,
cap. 6, p. 388.

66. AGI,AG 9; and CDI 24, pp. 442-447, Maldonado to Crown
31.12.1545; H. Zinsser, Rats, lice and history (Bantam: New York,
1965), pp. 194-195; Thompson, op. cit., p. 24; MacLeod, op. cit.,
p. 98; W. H. MacNeill, Plagues and Peoples (Blackwell: Oxford, 1977),
p. 209.

67. AGI,AG 55, Moreno to Crown 8.1.1578.

68. Ashburn, op. cit., pp. 130-134; J. Duffy, Epidemics in colonial America (University of Louisiana: Baton Rouge, 1953), p. 140; MacNeill, op. cit., p. 213.

69. Denevan, op. cit., p. 5.

70. C. O. Sauer, The Early Spanish Main (University of California Press: Berkeley and Los Angeles, 1966), p. 279.

71. F. L. Dunn, "On the antiquity of malaria in the western hemisphere," Human Biology, Vol. 37 (1965), pp. 385-393; C. S. Wood, "New evidence for a late introduction of malaria into the New World," Current Anthropology, Vol. 16 (1975), pp. 93-104.

72. AGI,AG 9; and CDI 24:343-351, Maldonado to Crown 15.1.1545; AGI,AG 164, Pedraza to Crown 1.5.1547; AGI,AG 968B, Pedraza to Crown no date; AGI,AG 44, Cabildo of Gracias a Dios to Crown 16.2.1548.

73. AGI,AG 164, Pedraza to Crown 1.5.1547.

74. See footnote 26.

75. A. J. Saco, Historia de la esclavitud de los indios en el Nuevo Mundo (Cultural: Havana, 1932), Vol. 1, p. 173.

76. For example: CDI 24, pp. 352-381, García to Crown 1.2.1539; AGI,AG 9, Anon 21.2.1546.

77. AGCA, A1.23 1511 f. 40, real cédula 5.7.1546.

78. AGI,AG 10, Audiencia to Crown 4.4.1580; R. S. Smith, "Indigo production and trade in colonial Guatemala," Hispanic American Historical Review, Vol. 39 (1959), pp. 185-186.

79. AGCA, A1.23 1512 f. 594, real cédula 15.5.1581 and AGCA, A1.23 4756 f. 46, Ordinances 24.11.1601.

80. AGI,AG 164, Pedraza to Crown 1.5.1547.

81. AGI,AG 164, Pedraza to Crown 1.5.1547; AGI,AG 968B, Pedraza to Crown, no date; AGI,AG 44, Cabildo of Gracias a Dios 16.2.1548; AGI,AG 56, Contreras to Crown 20.4.1582; AGI,AG 39, Albardez to Crown 29.4.1598.

82. AGI,AG 39, and CDI 24, pp. 250-297; RAHM,CM A/108 4843 ff. 239-257, Montejo to Crown, 1.6.1539; AGI,AG 164, Pedraza to Crown, 1.5.1547.

83. Although there is little documentary evidence for such practices in Honduras, they are well-documented for neighboring Nicaragua and the experience of the two countries, particularly when the Indian slave trade was at its height, is likely to have been similar (AGI,JU 293, and CS 7, pp. 151-224, Petition against the conduct of Castañeda 16.11.1541; CDHCR 6, pp. 199-211, Rodríguez to Crown 9.7.1545; Saco, op. cit., Vol. 2, p. 168).

84. AGI,AG 164, Bishop of Honduras to Crown 20.4.1584.

85. AGI,AG 9, and RAHM,CM A/110 4845 f. 108v; and CDI 24, pp. 343-351, Maldonado to Crown 15.1.1543; RAHM,CM A/110 4845, oficiales reales to Crown 20.2.1543.

86. AGI, Patronato 183-1-16, Antonelli and López de Quintanillas to Crown 7.10.1590.

10
Eighteenth-Century Population Change in Andean Peru: The Parish of Yanque

N. David Cook

      Eighteenth century parish registers in Latin America allow the historical demographer to reconstruct the population history of specific locales, and, as the results of regional studies become available, provide the material to develop a more global view of the evolution of population, and the relationship between population and social, economic and political history. In contrast to the limited number of sixteenth and seventeenth century parish registers remaining in parts of Middle and South America, records of the eighteenth century are abundant, and should furnish ample documentary evidence for comparative analysis.[1]

      Local parish studies are particularly well-advanced in Mexico. There are to date several investigations of parishes which chronologically span more than a century.[2]

      The study of eighteenth century Peruvian population history is, by comparison with Mexico, still in its infancy. General reviews of the subject have been published. Vollmer's compilation of eighteenth century censuses in Spain; Kubler's research in Peruvian archives on the late colonial and national period Indian population; and Robinson and Browning's critical review of the deficiencies of eighteenth century Peruvian censuses introduce the field.[3] Macera has published several volumes of population data for eighteenth and nineteenth century Peru, but Mazet's thorough investigation of the parish of San Sebastián of Lima from 1562 to 1689 is the first modern study of a Peruvian parish series.[4] Unfortunately for our purposes, Mazet's work does not continue into the eighteenth century, although the author is planning on extending the research chronologically. Coleman's study

Investigation in Peru for this project (1977) was funded by the Wenner Gren Foundation for Anthropological Research. My wife, Alexandra Parma Cook, collaborated in all aspects of the study, from the collection of data to the final revisions of the manuscript.

of Trujillo, 1600-1784, which includes population analysis, is based primarily on a series of colonial censuses rather than parish registers.[5] The same is true of Mörner's survey of Cuzco's population.[6] Cushner uses parish registers with great success in his investigation of slave mortality and reproduction on coastal Jesuit haciendas for the period from 1714 to 1767.[7] Population change during a single decade, 1738-1747, in the parish of Yanahuara, the Indian suburb of Arequipa, has been examined by Cook.[8]

Much is to be gleaned from research in parish archives. Although the investigation can at times be tedious, the results enhance our understanding of not only local demographic developments, but also social and economic history at a broader level. The purpose of the present article is to analyze parish data from the Andean highland Indian community of Yanque from 1685 to 1800, in the hope that the study will stimulate others to probe the rich historical data in Peruvian parish archives.

THE SETTING

The community of Yanque, the Spanish colonial administrative center for the control of the Collaguas Indians, is located in the south Peruvian Andes about one-third the distance from Arequipa to Cuzco (Figure 10.1). In the pre-modern era the trip by mule or horse required a journey of several days, although the air distance from Arequipa to Yanque is only about 85 kilometers. Yanque lies on the south side of the Colca River, whose valley provides water and agricultural lands for a series of settlements. The Colca rises on the edges of the snow-capped peaks and windswept puna at elevations from 4000 to 5000 meters, in the direction of Lake Titicaca. It then descends through a break in the mountains as it flows towards the Pacific Ocean. The downward plunge moderates as the Colca enters an elongated intermontane basin at the village of Tuti (3800 m.) until it enters a precipitous canyon west of Cabanaconde (c. 3200 m.) and empties into the Majes River for its brief journey to the sea. The inhabitants of the valley live in a series of villages, more than 50 kilometers in distance east to west (Figure 10.2). The aerial photographs of the Johnson mission provide one of the first twentieth century views of the valley. The viewer is immediately struck by the spectacular terraced hillsides and irrigation canals, and well planned villages in the valley. Until recently, however, access from the outside to the valley has been difficult. The Greater Majes Irrigation project has been responsible, in the last decade, for the construction of a reasonably good all-season road into the region. Relatively reliable bus transportation is now available for

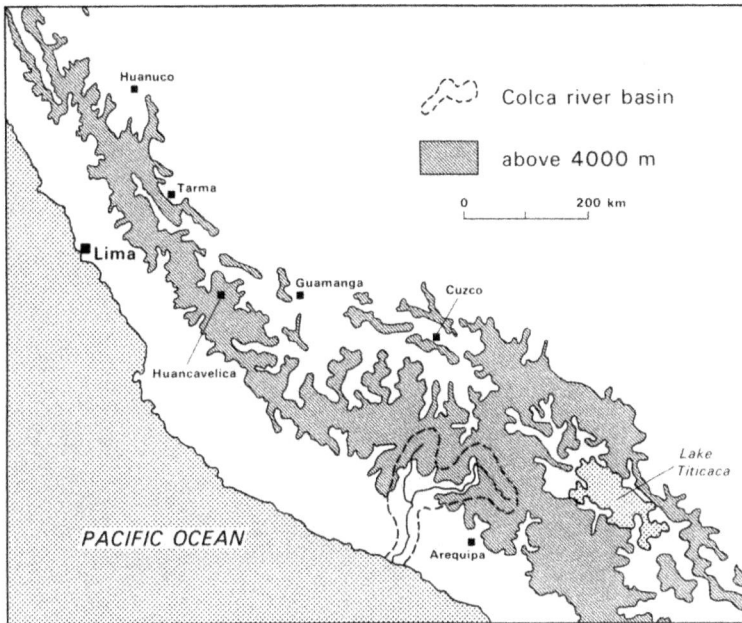

Figure 10.1   The Colca River basin, Peru

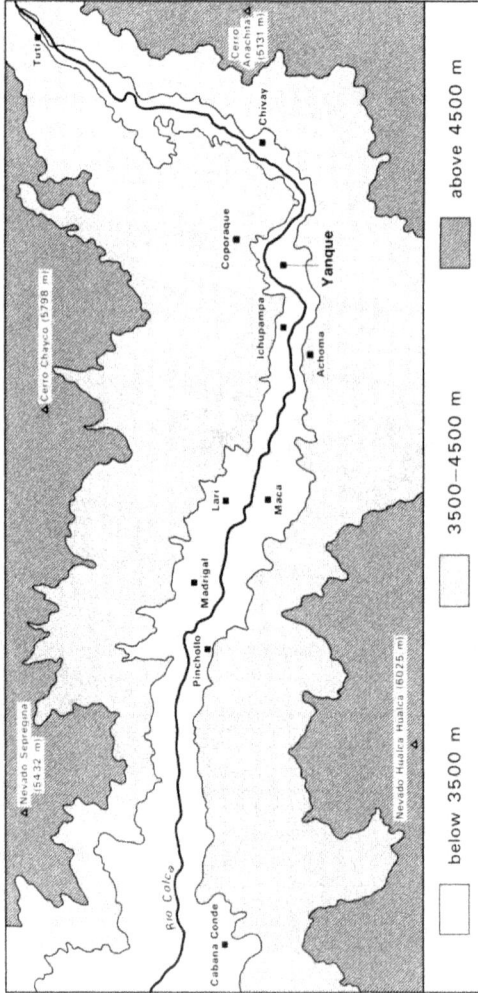

Figure 10.2 Yanque and the middle Colca Valley

villagers who need to make the eight to ten hour trip to
the departmental capital of Arequipa. Change in the valley has consequently rapidly accelerated.[9]
    A late colonial description of the villages and
their agricultural products remains as valid now as it
was when it was written in 1804. The "Memoria de la Santa Iglesia de Arequipa" was authored by Xavier Echeverría
(1748-1826). His description of the parishes in the Colca valley is especially complete. Tisco, the major settlement at the upper end of the valley, is at too high an
elevation for permanent farming. Livestock production,
however, was a major activity from pre-conquest times.
Copper veins were at one period worked extensively. Mer-
cury was discovered nearby at Chununi (between Tisco and
Sivayo), but was unexploited when Echeverría composed his
report. Callalli also was dependent primarily on livestock, although it was warm enough there for the inhabitants to cultivate potatoes, oca and cebada (a type of
barley). The village of Chivay (3693 m.), although cold,
provided potatoes, barley, quinoa and some beans. Coporaque was the first village in the valley in which corn
could be cultivated. Potatoes and livestock were also
produced. The fact that Coporaque was at the upper limit
of corn cultivation and that it was the major center of
preColumbian settlement and political control, suggests a
possible correlation which should be examined in the context of other valley systems.
    Yanque (3417 m.), on the south side of the valley,
and with more land under cultivation, produced corn, potatoes, beans, oca and barley on the surrounding terraced
fields. Inhabitants of Yanque, more numerous than the
villages higher in the valley, transported agricultural
produce to Arequipa, and worked in Spanish vineyards of
the Vitor valley to provide cash to pay tribute and debts.
Just below Yanque a bridge was built across the Colca in
1801, using labor from Yanque and Maca. Maca (3267 m.),
down the valley across the river and around a sharp bend,
produced corn, wheat, potatoes, and alfalfa. Products of
the nearby anexo of Ichupampa appear to have been similar. Across the valley from Ichupampa, and also below
Yanque lies Achoma, at an elevation similar to that of
Yanque, but situated on the edge of a mountain spur, which
was noted as a cold and disagreeable place. The lack of
land resulted in a population more closely linked to
livestock grazing than Yanque or Coporaque.
    Lari, lower in the valley appeared to be a very poor
village by the end of the eighteenth century. Madrigal
(3252 m.), with its anexo Tapay, produced fruits and vegetables and had an extensive trade based on these items.
Cabanaconde produced wheat, corn and potatoes and in a
valley toward the Majes river, some fruit. Two smaller
villages were nearby--Huambo and Pinchollo. The pasture-
lands above Cabanaconde were inhabited by runaway burros,

that were captured and used for transportation in the
valley. Even today, however, man and not animal or ma-
chine, is the most important carrier for the trade which
takes place in the small plazas of the villages of the
valley.[10]

THE SOURCES

    The parish registers of Yanque are not complete.
Franciscan friars, who Christianized the Collaguas region
in the mid-sixteenth century, established their headquarters for the entire province at Yanque, rather than
across the Colca River at the Inca capital of Coporaque.
Yanque is closer to the Spanish colonial administrative
center of Arequipa, than it is to Cuzco. Hence, for most
of the colonial era Arequipa, and not Cuzco, was the primary link with the world of the Coast and the European
invaders. By the end of the sixteenth century the Fran-
ciscans, and the secular clergy who administered to residents further down the valley, were following the Church
injunctions for the careful keeping of parish registers.
But the first full century's records for the village of
Yanque appear to have been lost. The earliest remaining
books for Yanque begin early in 1684, just about a century and a half after the Spaniards entered the Andean
area.
    In the early years separate registers were kept for
the moieties of Yanque. The first baptismal record for
the lower sector (urinsaya) is 10 March 1684, while the
upper moiety (anansaya) entry is for 20 May of the same
year. The moiety structure of Yanque has survived to the
present. There was (and continues to be) little intermarriage between the residents of the two units. One
might think of them as two distinct communities, sharing
the same general living space, but occupying separate
sectors. The Church in the center of the plaza acts as a
focal point for the entire village, yet even the church
is divided, with the residents of anansaya worshipping at
one side, and urinsaya at the other. And the parish registers were kept separately, until at least 1754. That
year the entries for baptisms and deaths begin to be kept
in a single book, with the appropriate moiety, however,
still designated. The ayllu affiliation is recorded on
the respective series, again until the middle of the
eighteenth century when it begins to be dropped from the
registers. Even in the 1680s ayllu connections in the
community of Yanque appear to be in process of decay, and
therefore generalizations concerning the structure and
function of the ayllu cannot be extended to the sixteenth
century on the basis of the community's historical experience in the mid-colonial era.
    The Yanque parish series (Table 10.1) is frustratingly

TABLE 10.1
The Yanque parish series, 1684-1800

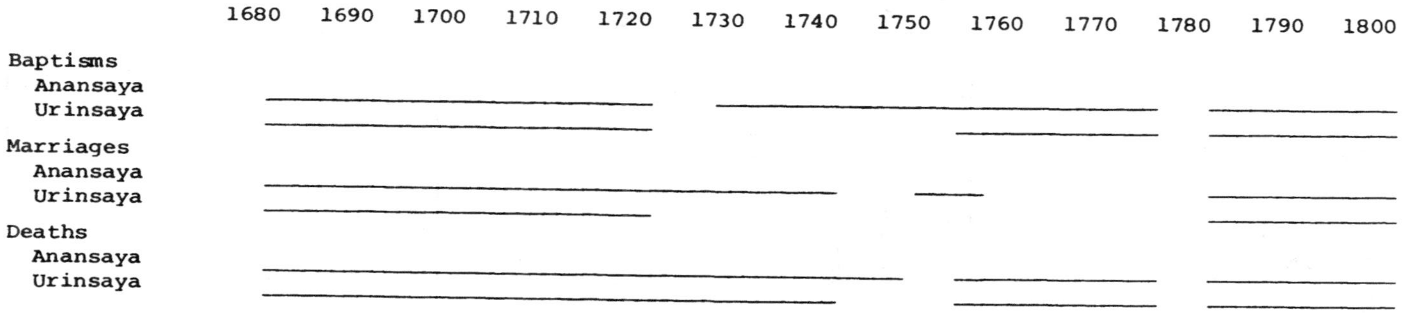

	1680	1690	1700	1710	1720	1730	1740	1750	1760	1770	1780	1790	1800

Baptisms
  Anansaya
  Urinsaya

Marriages
  Anansaya
  Urinsaya

Deaths
  Anansaya
  Urinsaya

incomplete. Between 1684 and 1800 a complete set of the
registers for both moieties runs only for 1684-1722, and
1783 to 1793. Only some forty percent of the full time
period is complete. The largest gap is for urinsaya marriages between 1722 and 1780. A series for Yanque anansaya is only slightly better, with data from 1684 to
1722, 1728 to 1744, and 1780 to 1787. In the anansaya
sector we have a total of 61 of 116 years with a complete
set of marriages, births, and deaths. Thus the question
arises, "What can be extracted from such incomplete
data?" The answer, as will be demonstrated below, is
only partly satisfactory.[11]

THE FLUCTUATION OF BIRTHS

     The rise in births in the community of Yanque, as
calculated using baptismal records, is minor in the period from 1685 to 1720. A slight upward movement is visible in the averages in Table 10.2 but by the mid-
eighteenth century, a major transformation seems to have
taken place. The average number of annual births nearly
doubles by the 1760s, and becomes even higher between
1771 and 1776. But the rapid increase in births appears
to have been sustained only to the end of the 1780s (Figure 10.3). The total births of the last decade of the
century parallels the figures at mid-century. Several
questions arise. Why did the pattern in births appear to
change so sharply between 1720 and 1754? When did the
change take place? Was it rapid, or were there gradual

TABLE 10.2
Averages for numbers of annual births, Yanque village

Years	Number
1685-1690	29.7
1691-1700	30.6
1701-1710	31.1
1711-1720	32.5
1754-1760	59.9
1761-1770	60.8
1771-1776	74.7
1784-1790	72.3
1791-1800	56.5

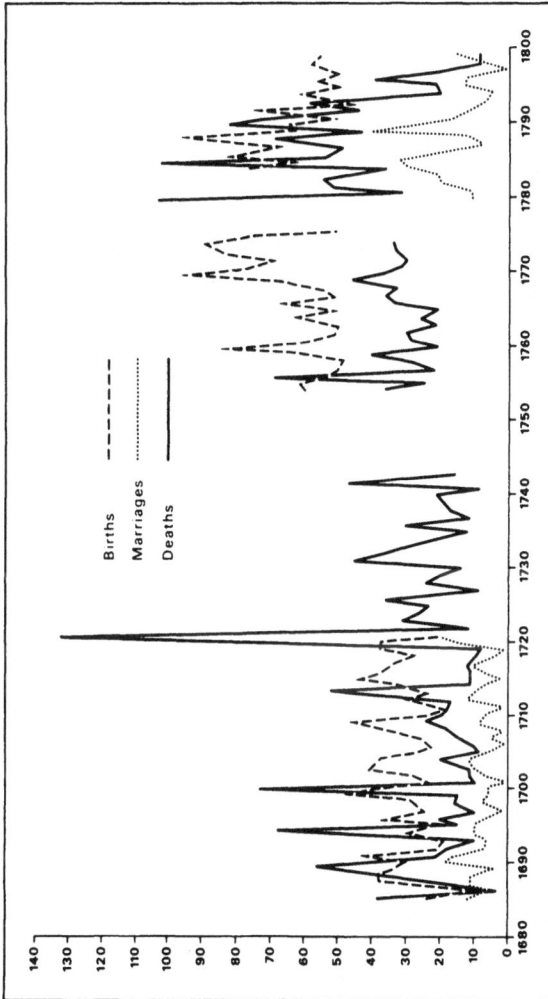

Figure 10.3 Births, marriages and deaths, Yanque, Peru, 1685–1800

transformations during the 45 year period? Also, why were the periods 1771-1776 and 1784-1790 characterized by such a large number of births? And what accounts for the slowdown by the last part of the century? Unfortunately, the extant information cannot provide answers to all such questions. However, it is at least possible to develop a tentative understanding of the changes of the 1720 to 1754 period by looking at one segment of the data which is extant: Yanque anansaya for 1728 to 1753. In the anansaya the gap in the data is far smaller than that of the urinsaya. The anansaya series is listed in Table 10.3. The anansaya information on births suggests that

TABLE 10.3
Average number of annual births in Yanque anansaya

Years	Average
1685-1690	14.8
1691-1700	16.5
1701-1710	18.7
1711-1720	18.6
1731-1740	21.1
1741-1750	21.0
1751-1760	29.1
1761-1770	31.9

the transformation to a higher number of births has been a gradual one, at least until 1750. There is no sharp increase in births, only a slow upward tendency until the 1750s. Then, in a single decade, the break is more abrupt. On average, the number of births each year between 1751-1760 exceeded the previous ten year period's annual totals by eight. During the next decade the upward movement continued but less sharply.

In a small rural Indian parish such as Yanque underregistration of births might be expected. How can one check on potential poor record-keeping and the significance of the problem? One possibility is via the sex ratio at the time of baptism. If large numbers of births were for some reason omitted, a sexual bias, on the part of the priest might be suspected. Is this the case with regard to Yanque? The average sex ratio in the period from 1685 to 1776, for which data are available, is 97.5

TABLE 10.4
Baptismal sex ratios

Years	Male	Female	Ratio
1685-1690	85	94	90.4
1691-1700	143	152	94.1
1701-1710	166	144	115.3
1711-1720	155	170	91.2
1754-1760	209	208	100.5
1761-1770	290	325	89.2
1771-1776	233	221	105.4
Total	1281	1314	97.5

(Table 10.4). The slight excess of females is not enough
to lead to a conclusion that one sex went under-reported.
A higher male than female infant mortality is clear. The
figures suggest that the priests were fairly diligent in
their collection of vital data for the parish. Perhaps
the fact that Yanque was the religious administrative
headquarters for the upper Colca valley explains a relatively complete annual record. Since age at baptism was
recorded by the priests, it is possible to note that most
infants were baptised within a week of birth, many on the
first day itself. We do not, of course, have a record of
stillbirths, nor do we have a count of infants who died
within the first few hours of life. Nor, by the end of
the eighteenth century, are we sure of the true yearly
number who died in the puna before the priest made his
periodic rounds of the chapels to perform his religious
duties. It is evident that not all births were reported,
but even though the total number omitted from the registers is impossible to ascertain, the Yanque series indicate that at least there was little bias between the recording of males and females on the part of the church
record keepers.

THE TREND OF MARRIAGES

The marriage registers are the least complete of the
three series. Combined data for the Yanque moieties are
not available from 1723 until late 1780. In spite of
this long break, it is useful at least to compare the
early series with the latter. For the purposes of analysis, as with births and deaths, the same chronological

TABLE 10.5
Average annual marriages in Yanque

Years	Average
1685-1690	10.2
1691-1700	7.9
1701-1710	6.0
1711-1720	7.3
1781-1790*	22.2
1791-1800	10.1

*Forastero marriages are included, but not Spanish-Indian or Mestizo-Indian unions.

divisions will be made.

At first glance, it is evident that the average number of marriages in the first two decades of the eighteenth century did not match the number in the last part of the previous century (Table 10.5). But most striking is the very large average of the 1780s, then a decline in the 1790s to a level very similar to the decade of the 1680s. Variations in the annual number of marriages (Table 10.6) are greater than the variations in the births. Once again, the more complete series for the anansaya permits a closer view of changing marriage patterns.

In Yanque anansaya we see a marked increase in the number of marriages in the decade of the 1720s (Table 10.7). This level is roughly maintained until 1749. Then, if we carry the average for the three years 1751 to 1753, the number for anansaya slightly exceeds 10 per year. In the birth series for Yanque anansaya we also noted a sharp increase in the 1750s.

THE DEATH SERIES

The most complete sets of data, for both anansaya and urinsaya, relate to deaths. The only gaps which exist are between 1743-1754 and 1774-1780. The mortality statistics demonstrate vividly both general trends and the periodic devastation wrought during epidemic years. For analysis of the death patterns the results of both the moieties have been combined. In the last decade of the seventeenth century and first two decades of the eighteenth century, the average yearly number of deaths ranged in the low to mid-twenties. Then, in the period

TABLE 10.6
"Normal" monthly patterns of marriage in non-epidemic years*

Month	Average number
January	0.7
February	1.6
March	0.3
April	1.0
May	0.6
June	1.8
July	1.4
August	1.1
September	0.8
October	1.6
November	1.5
December	0.8

*Based on the experience of 1701, 1702, 1704, 1706, 1708, 1781, 1784, 1791, and 1792.

TABLE 10.7
Average annual marriages, Yanque anansaya

Years	Number
1685-1690	4.7
1690-1700	2.9
1701-1710	3.0
1711-1720	4.3
1721-1730	5.9
1731-1740	5.4
1741-1750*	6.0

*No marriages listed for 1745 and 1746.

from 1720-1729 the figure nearly doubled. This large increase was predominantly the consequence of the 1720-1721 epidemic period. The number of deaths of the following decade, the 1730s, is more similar to the earlier years of the century. Between 1754-1774 the average number of annual deaths in Yanque seems to have risen to the low thirties. Then, by the last two decades of the eighteenth

256

century the numbers increase. Part of the reason for the
elevated figure for the 1780s lies in the fact that there
were several years of high mortality: 1780, 1785, and
1788. In both 1780 and 1785, 102 Yanqueños died.
  In the years between 1685-1800 for which data are
available, we can pinpoint the years of exceptional mortality: 1689-1690, 1694, 1700, 1713, 1720-1721, 1731,
1742, 1756, 1769, 1780, 1785, 1788, and 1790-1791 (Figure
10.3 and Table 10.8). The surge in deaths can often best
be seen when the epidemic year is compared with the year

TABLE 10.8
General Andean epidemics, 1685-1800, and Yanque*

Year	Epidemic
1687	Various, plus general contagion
1689	Yanque
1692-1694	Measles, (Cuzco, 1693), Yanque, 1694
1700	Yanque
1708	Lima, perhaps smallpox
1713	Yanque
1719-1720	Various: Smallpox, influenza, yellow fever, exan-thematic typhus, pneumonic plague, Yanque 1720-21
1731	Yanque
1742	Influenza, Yanque
1746	Tabardillo, Lima
1749	Smallpox, Lima
1756	Smallpox, Mainas, Yanque
1764	Smallpox, Lima
1769	Yanque
1779	"Bone-Breaker" (influenza?)
1780	Yanque
1781	Typhus (yellow fever?) Callao
1784	Measles, Lima
1785	Yanque
1786	Measles and croup
1788	Yanque
1789	Measles--to Peru from Bogotá
1790	Croup and measles, smallpox, Lima
1790-1791	Yanque
1795	Measles, Lima, or scarlet fever
1796	"Tabardillos," Andaguaylas

*The major periods of mortality at Yanque are noted, but no symptoms
are given in the parish registers. Based on Dobyns and Lastres (see
notes).

preceding and following. For example, ten died in 1693, fifteen in 1695, and 68 in 1694. The figures for the 1700 epidemic are similar: 73 that year, opposed to fifteen the preceding year and ten the following. The most devastating epidemic occurred in 1720-1721, with 62 and 132 deaths respectively, but only eight in 1719 and twelve in 1722.[12]

In the epidemic period of 1720 we find one of the few mentions of disease symptoms. On 11 December, 26-year old Miguel Trujiano died, "without receiving the sacraments, having fallen dead from the peste." On 3 February 1721, a 60 year-old female passed away, also without sacraments because the peste did not allow time. On 9 June of the same year the priest noted that during the epidemic death came very quickly. In this case the victim was a thirty year old male.

Parish registers of the seventeenth and eighteenth centuries rarely record the cause of death. However, some unusual circumstances of death are listed. Often, the victims of lightning are noted by the parish priest. For example, on 20 February 1721, a sixteen year old boy, Sebastián, was hit and killed by a lightning bolt while on the road to Arequipa. On 20 October 1717 a ten year old boy died after being dragged by a horse. One of the worst accidents befell the community on 24 March 1715, when four men working on the bridge across the Colca canyon connecting urinsaya agricultural areas, fell into the

TABLE 10.9
Average annual number of deaths, Yanque Community

Years	Number
1685-1690	33.7
1691-1700	26.7
1701-1710	15.0
1711-1720	21.2
1721-1730	31.9
1731-1740	24.5
1754-1760	34.4
1761-1770	31.2
1771-1774	32.3
1781-1790	57.1
1791-1800*	31.5

*Separate book added in 1791, includes the puna surrounding Yanque, then apparently the sole book after 1793. Figures for this decade are questionable.

river and drowned.

Some other causes of death are occasionally noted. For example, on 5 August 1782, a 35 year old woman of anansaya died during childbirth; on 3 November of the same year, one Manuel Arequipa, a twenty year old from Vincocaya, was discovered with his throat slit in a ravine of one of the nearby hills.

In order to calculate the monthly cycle of mortality to distinguish seasonal fluctuations among the annual averages (Table 10.9), the experience of several non-epidemic years has been utilized. I believe this provides as close to a "normal" pattern for Yanque as is possible, given the nature of the evidence (Table 10.10). The small numbers involved provide an inadequate base for definitive generalizations. But there are, clearly, sharp variations from month to month in the series. March, April and May appear to be the months of lowest mortality. These months follow the heavy rains, and are the period of highest agricultural productivity, when food is most abundant. December, January and February are months of normally high rainfall, and certain diseases associated with warmer weather and higher precipitation might be expected. The reason for the high number of average deaths in June and September is less clear from the historical record.

The average age of death for adult members of the community (aged twenty or more) has been calculated for

TABLE 10.10
"Normal" monthly patterns of mortality in non-epidemic years, Yanque community*

Month	Average Number
January	1.8
February	2.5
March	1.4
April	1.4
May	1.4
June	2.9
July	1.6
August	1.7
September	3.1
October	1.5
November	2.2
December	2.8

*Based on the following years: 1701, 1702, 1704, 1706, 1708, 1781, 1784, 1789, 1791 and 1792.

TABLE 10.11
Average age at death for those twenty and above, Yanque*

Period	Males	Females
1691-1700	51.1	42.1
1781-1790	49.4	55.1

*For 1691-1700 there are a total of 36 males, 56 females, and for 1781-1790, 130 male deaths opposed to 118 female.

two periods: 1691-1700 and 1781-1790 (Table 10.11). These two decades were chosen so as to see if significant changes take place in the century-long span. The parish registers are usually inexact in their report of age at death. In most cases the age is listed as within the decades ninety, seventy, sixty or forty and so on. Such approximations appear with much greater frequency than an exact numeric age, such as 57 or 63. This is a similar pattern to that found in the colonial visitas, or padrones. Exactitude is impossible, but comparative generalizations, if carefully made, do shed light on major developments. The results are here analyzed by sex, so that at least the outlines of differential mortality can be seen. Most striking is the large number of deaths of women who were in their twenties and thirties in the 1690s. It is much rarer to find male deaths in these age categories. The obvious cause is a relatively high rate of mortality associated with childbirth. In the 1690s the average age of death for males is 51.1, for the females it is 41.2. In the 1780s a major difference occurs. The average age of death for men is slightly lower than before: 49.4, yet for women it is 55.1, which is significantly higher than the previous century. Why did this change take place? Was it true only for the single decade? Unfortunately the answers are not to be found in the data.

YEARS OF CRISIS

Periods of demographic crisis occur with some regularity during the eighteenth century. By far the worst was the period 1720-1721. Review of such crisis periods presents common patterns which help illuminate the demographic experience of the Yanque region. Some crises may be of solely local importance, others may extend to wider areas.

The crisis of 1685 began in late March, and continued

through July. All deaths were of children, under the age of seven. In 1689 an epidemic began in March, but lasted only until the end of May. Most victims were the old people of Yanque. In 1694 an epidemic commenced in August and ended in November. Most who died were under ten years of age, plus a handful of young adults. The disease could have been measles, which was recorded for Cuzco in 1693. The 1700 crisis extended from June through August and affected children under seven. In 1713 another epidemic peaked in October and November, with most of those who succumbed being children, with a few elders. The crises of 1695, 1689, 1700 and 1713 are not noted in the standard epidemic references for Peru as being years of exceptional mortality, yet it is evident that these were disastrous for the residents of Yanque.

The years 1719-1720 are critical for Peru's population growth. George Kubler's generalization that the first major epidemic to affect the aboriginal population of the Andean region occurred then is obviously incorrect, nonetheless 1720 was a year of major crisis. Dobyns suggests the disease was multiple, which my research tends to confirm. A general epidemic was reported in Huánuco from 1714 to 1718. Smallpox was noted in Socabaya in 1718 and Argentina in 1720. Influenza afflicted Andean residents simultaneously. It is also possible as Lastres posits, that a major component of the 1720 series is typhus. Dobyns suggests pneumonic plague or severe influenza but discounts the likelihood of typhus.[13] On the basis of the parish evidence of Yanque, two epidemics struck the community. The first occurred in January of 1720, in which almost all the victims were children. Perhaps this was an epidemic of smallpox. The next epidemic began in November 1720, and continued through June of 1721. This disease affected all elements of the population, but especially the older members of society. Large numbers between the ages of fifty and ninety succumbed. Only those in their twenties appear less likely to fall victim to the devastating epidemic.

The 1731 crisis was brief, and relatively insignificant reaching a peak in November and December. There was a stronger shock which hit Yanque in June and July of 1742, with 17 residents dying in the former month. Here most deaths were of children under six, but a few adults also died. Influenza was noted elsewhere in Peru that year. In November and December of 1756 a short but severe epidemic passed through. A total of 28 recorded deaths were listed in November. The vast majority of these were children. Perhaps the epidemic was of smallpox, recorded for Mainas in 1756 in Peruvian epidemiological research.

The single month with the highest number of deaths in Yanque was July of 1780, when 51 members of the community died. An epidemic began in May and continued at least through July, and almost all who died were children under six. Might this be influenza, which was recorded elsewhere in 1779? Next, a crisis took place from August through December of 1785. In the month of August, adults were the victims, but from September to the end of the period children predominated. November was especially bad, with 29 people dying. Measles is noted in Lima for the preceding year. In December of 1787 and January of 1788 another crisis took place. In these two months all age sectors of Yanque's population were afflicted. Measles and croup are recorded elsewhere in Peru the previous year. The 1790 crisis was prolonged, from June to the close of November. At peak mortality, children were the primary victims. Measles, croup and smallpox are noted in Lima the same year.

What monthly patterns are visible in the figures? October, November and December are bad months for years of demographic crisis in Yanque. During the normal years high mortality commences in September, with a lull in October. These are the last of the dry months of the local agricultural cycle. The rains which provide the moisture for the planting season begin in earnest, normally late in December. Daily rains continue until April to May. This is Yanque's main growing season, and beginning in March it is also the period of generally lowest mortality. There are exceptions to the pattern: the 1720-1721 epidemic clearly breaks the normal pattern. Table 10.10, based on average monthly deaths of ten nonepidemic years of the century, gives a general, if not exact illustration of this pattern.

What else do we learn from the Yanque death registers? First, the standard works on Peruvian epidemic history are incomplete, at least insofar as local histories are taken into consideration. To have a more comprehensive picture of eighteenth century epidemics, several local studies should be undertaken, in diverse geographical regions of the Andes, which are composed of different ecological systems. It would be useful to compare these results, not only with each other, but with local studies of other regions of eighteenth-century Hispanic America.

Further, it is quite clear from the death registers that in reality we know little of the true causes of death of the residents. On rare occasions the parish priest did note the cause of death, but eighteenth century notations in Yanque are unusual. The diagnosis of measles in Lima in 1784 does not necessarily mean that Yanqueños suffered the disease the following year. Furthermore, one must be extremely cautious of any of the eighteenth century diagnoses in even a major city of Spanish South America.

262

MIGRATION AND MISCEGENATION

Yanque parish registers provide information on the
geographical and social background of individuals. While
data are included within the three record groups, the
marriage registers give us the best picture of the origin
of adult, working aged inhabitants. The marriage series
provides some tentative views of migration to the community during the years from 1685 to the end of the following century.

Of the slightly more than forty marriages which take
place from 1685-1689, six local males married females
from outside the village. Three were from nearby Achoma,
two from Chivay, and one from Yauri in Cavanas. In only
three cases did outside men marry local women. Here the
origins were more dispersed: Arequipa (San Lázaro),
Cayma, and Quiquixana. And in three marriages, both par-
ties were from outside Yanque: one couple from Pucara in
Lampas, a man from Cibayo and a woman from Andaray, and
a male of the neighboring Coporaque who married a woman
from Arequipa (San Lázaro). There were apparently no
mixes between anansaya and urinsaya during the five
years.

During the decade of the 1690s approximately ninety
weddings occurred in Yanque. Of these only two were outside the moiety: one anansaya male with an urinsaya female, and another case in reverse. In several cases male
immigrants took local brides: one male from nearby Tisco,
another from Cibayo, one from Coporaque. Females who
married into the community were from Tisco, Ichupampa,
Guasacache, Coporaque, and Lari. The outsider who had
come from the most distant region was a male from Copaca-
vana, on the shores of Lake Titicaca. He claimed to be
of the parcialidad of the Incas. In one case a Spaniard
married an Indian: on 23 August 1696 Francisco de
Lastarría married Teresa Casqui, an Indian from the village of Chachas.

In the following decade a remarkable change in the
number of marriages outside the moiety takes place. In
ten cases out of sixty, marriage was moiety exogamous.
The anansaya females married outside more than males (six
cases opposed to four). Three females were from Achoma,
one from Ichupampa, another from Coporaque, one from
Arequipa, and another from Tiquillaca. Two male immigrants married within the community. One of the immigrants was from Tuti, and the other originated in the
village of Yacamaque.

The ten years beginning in 1710 saw about sixty-five
marriages celebrated. Of this group of unions, six were
outside the moiety. Two were of anansaya males with urinsaya women, but four were the reverse. Females from
Monopata, Lari, and Pichigua married local men while
Yanque males married women from Achoma, Viuñas, and

Chivay. In one marriage both were outsiders; a male from urinsaya of Caylloma married a female of anansaya Chivay. Then, on 17 September 1715, a Spaniard from Potosí, a widower named Sebastián Vasconcelos married a widow of anansaya, Rosa Cuadra. She had been married to Pedro Suri, and the marriage was included in the urinsaya register.

By the last part of the century, in the 1780s, marriage patterns indicate a relatively similar pattern of migration. About 210 couples united during the decade, of these only two marriages were between members of the opposite moieties. If anything, the moiety structure seems tighter in the later part of the century than it was before. Numerically more outsiders enter the community. Four males from Caylloma married into the village; there were two from Arequipa; two from Tisco; two from Juliaca; the same number from Cabinilla and Tuti; and one each from Coporaque, Langui in Cuzco, Cibayo, and Yauri. Fewer outside females entered; one each from Lari, Cibayo, Chivay, Sicuani, and Cabinilla. A large number of marriages were also celebrated in the puna. During the decade eleven marriages took place between residents of upland Ranran, nine from Casca and nine from Chuca, eight from Pulpería, six from Chalguanca, four from Coito, three from Rayo, two from Tocra, and one from Vincocaya. There were also several marriages between partners of different puna districts. The marriage records suggest dispersal of the residents of Yanque to the surrounding upland region during the final part of the century. Four cases of Spaniards marrying Indian women also occurred during the decade. In all but one instance the female was from urinsaya.

About 115 marriages took place during the closing decade of the century. Of these, five were moiety exogamous; in four of the cases the males were of urinsaya. Three men entered the community via marriage from neighboring Coporaque; two were from Tuti, with one each from Cibayo, Caylloma, Umachiri and Hacarí. Female migrants were from Umachiri, Tuti, and Pichigua. Several marriages were celebrated in the punas: six at Casca, three at Ranran, and one at Coito. One union was between a male of Ranran and a female from the punas above Lari. An indication of the complexity of late eighteenth century Yanque society can be seen in some of the combinations which took place. On 17 September 1795 a Spanish couple was united in Yanque, with don Jacinto Sánchez, from downstream Cabana marrying doña Paula Adrian from nearby Coporaque. Then, on 8 February 1796, Diego Caseres, a Spaniard living in Yanque anansaya, married María Perales, an illegitimate española of urinsaya. On 25 November 1795, a Spanish orphan of Yanque, named Domingo Bernedo, married Rosa Checa. Then on 27 January 1796, one Felipe Visa married a widow, Jacoba Suico.

This marriage is unusual for two reasons. In the first
place, there is cause to suspect Felipe was a <u>mestizo</u>.
As the priest states, there is some question as to whether Visa "is Indian as implied, or mestizo as he appears
by the aspect, and for other reasons . . . ." The marriage took place with the bishop's dispensation which was
allowed to Indians within the third degree of consanguin-
ity. Perhaps the most interesting marriage of the decade, and an indication of the growing social complexity
of even rural areas by the end of the century, was the
marriage on 14 April 1795, of Alexo Corrales and Melchora
Olmedo. The groom's mother was Ignacia Otanula, and the
bride's parents were Antonio Felejo and María Carmen
Gonzalez. Alexo was an illegitimate from Ichupampa but
residing in Yanque. Melchora had come to the valley from
Lima two years earlier. Both were slaves of the subdele-
gate of the <u>partido</u>, Don Joachím Miguel de Arnaco.
    For the decades with data on the origin of marriage
couples, the percentage of outsiders marrying within the
community remains relatively constant. In about ten percent of the marriages, at least one of the partners is
from another community. The periods 1685-1690 and 1710-
1719 have averages which are higher, at about twenty-five
percent for the earlier of the two, and fifteen percent
for the latter. Male immigrants generally outnumbered
female. Most migrants were from the nearby villages of
the Colca valley: Coporaque, Cibayo, Chivay, Achoma,
Pichigua, and Ichupampa. The number of migrants from beyond was relatively small. There are not even many who
come to Yanque from the Spanish administrative center of
Arequipa. Data are extant which suggest the eighteenth
century flow of Indian migrants to the Arequipa region
from the Colca valley was relatively strong, but obviously the information on the extent of this flow will be
found in the Arequipa parish books, and the registers of
suburban Indian communities such as Yanahuara and Cayma.[14]
One factor stands out clearly and persistently in the
Yanque registers: moiety endogamy. With the exception of
the period from 1700 to 1719, when the number of moiety
exogamous marriages roughly equals the number of unions
outside the community, marriages between members of anansaya and urinsaya were quite unusual. Marriages between
Spaniards and Indians were also rare. Only seven such
marriages took place in the years 1685-1719 and 1780-1799,
with four of the seven celebrated in the 1780-1789 decade.
    In the last decade two marriages were recorded be-
tween Spaniards, a Spanish-Indian and Mestizo-Indian
match, and a case of negro slaves uniting in matrimony in
the Yanque church. What is most striking from such local
evidence is the apparent stability of the community for
the period from 1685 to 1800. Both moiety and racial exogamy are quite rare. The village remains essentially
Indian in spite of the occasional influx of outsiders at

various times during the period.

Yet the situation is not that simple. There is a remaining register for Spanish baptisms which covers the period 1685 through 1722. About 112 baptisms are recorded for the period, of these 51 occur in 1694, 1695, and 1713. From the data most of the entries appear to be Indians, not Spaniards. But some intermixture was noted. Permanent Spanish residents of Yanque were rare. A few examples provide an illuminating glimpse of the complexity of late seventeenth century society, as well as the specific experience of individuals. One case is that of Juan Gonzalez de Huelva and his wife María Veronica, who had one daughter in 1685, and a second in 1688. In 1685, two women, one definitely an Indian, had illegitimate daughters. The fathers were probably Spanish. In the following year, Pedro Cid, a Yanque resident (vecino) had an illegitimate daughter with one Tomasina Córdova, from Chincheros. Nicolás Martínez de Montoya and his wife had a son in 1687, but Nicolás had an illegitimate daughter by an urinsaya widow the next year. Miguel Pérez Romero had an illegitimate daughter by Juliana Angulo in 1688, and a son by an anansaya female, María Ana de Saavendra in 1689. Martín Pérez Romero appears to have had a stable union with his wife María Vasconcelos with children in 1688, 1689, 1690, 1691, and 1693, and 1696. In 1704 Don Alfonso Tinco and his wife Doña Bernardina Mendiguren y Buytrón had a daughter. In June of the same year Sebastián Joseph Romero and Gregoria Gonzalez, mulato slaves of the corregidor's wife, Doña Francisca Zaraya y Zarate, also had a daughter. Though legal unions between racial groups did take place, interracial liaisons outside marriage were much more typical; many illegitimate children appear in the baptismal lists, and abandoned infants are frequently reported.

THE TRENDS

The three series, side by side, illustrate if not the total population of the community of Yanque at a given point in time, then the gradual evolution of its population over a number of decades. The series of births, marriages and deaths elucidate the evolution of one moderate-sized, and relatively isolated south Andean village through the eighteenth century. The trends are important because they may have broader applicability. What are these trends?

During the last decades of the seventeenth century and the early years of the eighteenth century community growth was in all likelihood minimal. The difference between births and deaths was marginal. In fact, in the 1685-1690 period, deaths exceeded births. During the first decade of the eighteenth century the excess of

births increases, but the epidemic period of 1720-1721
probably wiped out the gains of the previous decade. The
twenty year period between 1754-1774 shows a very wide
divergence in the excess of births over deaths. Yet the
1780s brings a narrowing of that margin, with a surplus
of births similar to the early part of the eighteenth
century. The 1780s was a period of exceptional mortality; though the number of births was high, the number of
deaths that decade was much higher than earlier or later.

The community of Yanque was probably larger in 1799
than it was at the start of the century. Yet, demographic growth within the region was not continuous. Negative
growth in the 1685-1690 period gave way to a gradually
enlarging population. Growth accelerated in the 1710s,
but the gains were subtracted by the impact of the 1720-
1721 epidemic period. The years 1754-1774 are ones of
continuous and accelerated population expansion for
Yanque, but the epidemics of the 1780s, with several
years of large numbers of deaths, again deplete the ranks
of the village. The situation improves only slightly, if
at all, in the last decade of the century (Table 10.12).

The eighteenth century was the world of Malthus.
The era of improved medicine did not reach isolated communities of the Andean area until the introduction of
smallpox vaccination. The campaign against smallpox began in Lima late in 1805, with the arrival of nine

TABLE 10.12
Baptisms, marriages and deaths, Yanque community

Period	Marriages	Baptisms	Deaths	B - D
1685-1690	10.2	29.7	33.7	-4.0
1691-1700	7.9	30.6	26.7	3.9
1701-1710	6.0	31.1	15.0	16.1
1711-1720	7.3	32.5	21.2	11.3
1721-1730	--	--	31.9	
1731-1740	--	--	24.5	
1754-1760	--	59.9	34.4	25.5
1761-1770	--	60.8	31.2	29.6
1771-1774	--	74.7[a]	32.3	42.4
1781-1790	22.2	72.3[b]	57.1	15.2
1791-1800	10.1	56.5	31.5	25.0

[a] 1771-1776 average

[b] 1784-1790 average

containers of vaccine from Buenos Aires. Vaccination
reached Lambayeque, Huamanga, Piura and probably Cuzco,
Ica and Arequipa in 1806. But the eradication of smallpox from Peru was not completed until the twentieth century.[15] Other diseases, such as measles, influenza, typhus, took their toll each time the susceptible population became large enough.

Unfortunately, we lack a series of eighteenth century censuses for the community of Yanque. The tribute
records, with repartimiento data for the whole of the repartimiento of Yanque anansaya and urinsaya obviously include the other communities which made up the administrative unit: Callalli, Chivay, Coporaque, Maca, Achoma, and
Ichupampa. There is, however, one count of Yanque which
dates from the early nineteenth century, probably 1804.
That year 885 residents were recorded in Yanque itself,
with 1194 residing nearby, but counted within the administrative unit. Crude birth, marriage and death rates,
using a three-year average for 1803, 1804, and 1805, give
the following figures: births, 22.5 per thousand; marriages, 4.7 per thousand; and deaths, 10.7 per thousand.
The resulting annual growth rate (obviously excluding migration) is 1.2 percent for the early years of the nineteenth century. By twentieth century standards, these
figures are quite low, and there is clearly underregistration of vital data. But the growth of Yanque's population was destined to be limited. The community's urban
and rural sectors (the puna surrounding the village) included a total of 2,079 in 1804, fell to 1,876 in 1843,
then 1,578 at the time of Peru's first national census
(1876), rose to 2,530 in 1940, then 2,545 for the third
census of 1961, then declined to 2,170 for the most recent (1972) national count.[16] What is the meaning of
these figures? Did the low point of the population curve
of Yanque occur in the late nineteenth century? Why has
there not been a very rapid increase in Yanque's population in the most recent half-century? Further research
is required to shed light on the answers to such questions. It is evident that external and internal economic
factors were influencing the community's growth during
the eighteenth century and beyond. There was an obvious
shift of population away from Yanque's "urban" core in
the eighteenth century. Increasingly economic surplus
became associated with the puna livestock grazing. An
earlier era of forced Spanish urban concentration gave
way to a more traditional Andean pattern of dispersed
settlement. The precise dates for this transformation
are not yet clear, but it should be possible to place the
movement in its chronological context. In the nineteenth
century, economic control of the puna resources was chal-
lenged, and it appears community Indians waged a losing
battle as they faced the encroachments of private landholders. The outlines of the conflict are well estab-

lished by the mid-nineteenth century. Then, the concentration of economic power shifted away from Yanque. The mining center of Caylloma drew both outside capital and talents. Even nearby Chivay, by 1940, was larger than Yanque. Chivay's growth accelerated as Yanque declined. By 1961, Chivay, geographically more conveniently situated where the road from Arequipa enters the Colca valley, was about half again as large as Yanque, and the disparity had widened by 1972. Whatever the internal population growth taking place within Yanque in recent times, it appears to have been siphoned off via emigration, to more active economic centers such as Chivay, or perhaps more important, Arequipa. The explosive urban growth of that Peruvian city since 1940 has been fed by the escape of not only Yanqueños in search of an elusive better life, but also other villagers of Arequipa's hinterland.[17]

The population history of Yanque may not represent the experience of all South Andean communities in Peru in the eighteenth century, but the results are at least suggestive of parallel developments elsewhere. Epidemics were not restricted to one locale. If disease struck Yanque in 1700, then it is highly likely that the same epidemic afflicted a much wider area. Similar patterns of mortality were shared by neighboring Indian communities. The movement of deaths followed weather and agricultural cycles. The demographic experience of Yanque reflects that of nearby native settlements in other ways. Droughts, earthquakes and other major disasters had a concurrent effect over a broad section of the south Peruvian Andes. Further, Indians in the southern section of Peru migrated to the colonial urban administrative center of Arequipa in the centuries following the foundation of the city. Yanque may also provide a good example of the social structure of south Peruvian Indian villages. The moiety was a distinctive characteristic of Yanque's organization. The strength and persistance of moiety endogamy is a feature which was probably shared by many Indian communities in the region. Further, the ayllu was an important part of the social organization of Yanque, but was in process of decay and atrophy in the eighteenth century. Yanque provides a clear glimpse of the demographic experience of the south Peruvian Andes during the period from 1685 to 1800. But the view is incomplete. Future research in other parish registers will assist in developing a truly comprehensive vision of the historical demography of the region.

NOTES

1. Several general works on parish research in Latin America
are available. See Nicolas Sánchez-Albornoz, "Les registres parois-
siaux en Amérique Latine. Quelques considerations sur leur exploita-
tion pour la démographie historique," Revue Suisse d'Histoire 17
(1967), pp. 60-71; and Claude Morin, "Los libros parroquiales como
fuente para la história demográfica y social novohispana," Historia
Mexicana 21 (1972), pp. 389-418.

2. Thomas Calvo, "Démographie historique d'une paroisse Mexi-
caine: Acatzingo (1606-1810)," Cahiers des Ameriques Latines, 6
(1972), pp. 7-41; Claude Morin, Santa Inés Zacatelco (1646-1812)
(Mexico City: Departamento de Investigaciones Históricas, INAH,
1973); Elsa Malvido, "Factores de despoblación y de reposición de la
población de Cholula (1641-1810)," Historia Mexicana, 23 (1973), pp.
52-110; David A. Brading and Cecilia Wu, "Population Growth and Crisis: León, 1720-1860," Journal of Latin American Studies, 5 (1973),
pp. 1-36; Michael M. Swann, "The Spatial Dimensions of a Social
Process: Marriage and Mobility in Late Colonial Northern Mexico," in
David J. Robinson (ed.), Social Fabric and Spatial Structure in
Colonial Latin America (Syracuse University: Dellplain Latin American Studies, 1979), pp. 117-180; and the studies of David J.
Robinson, Linda Greenow, and John K. Chance in this volume.

3. Günter Vollmer, "Bevölkerungspolitik und Bevölkerungsstruktur
im Vizekönigreich Peru zu Ende der Kolonialzeit, 1741-1821," (Ph.D.
dissertation, University of Köln, 1965); George Kubler, The Indian
Caste of Peru, 1795-1940, Smithsonian Institution, Institute of Social Anthropology, No. 14 (Washington, 1952); David G. Browning and
David J. Robinson, "The Origin and Comparability of Peruvian Population Data: 1776-1815," Jahrbuch für Geschichte von Staat, Vol. 14
(1979), pp. 199-222.

4. Pablo Macera, Tierra y población en el Perú, siglos xviii-
xix (4 vols., Lima: Seminario de Historia Rural Andina, 1972);
Claude Mazet, "Récherches Historiques sur le Pérou: la Population de
Lima aux XVIe-XVIIe siècles: parroquia San Sebastián (1562-1689)"
(M.A. thesis, University of Nice, 1975); and the same author's "Pop-
ulation et société à Lima aux XVIe et XVIIe siècles," Cahiers des
Amériques Latines 13/14 (1976), pp. 51-102.

5. Katherine Coleman, "Provincial Urban Problems: Trujillo,
Peru, 1600-1784," in Robinson, Social Fabric, pp. 369-408.

6. Magnus Mörner, Perfil de la sociedad rural del Cuzco a fines
de la colonia (Lima: Universidad del Pacífico, 1978).

7. Nicolas P. Cushner, "Slave Mortality and Reproduction on
Jesuit Haciendas in Colonial Peru," Hispanic American Historical Review, 55 (1975), pp. 177-199.

8. Noble David Cook, "La población de la parroquia de Yanahuara,
1738-47. Un modelo para el estudio de las parroquias coloniales
peruanas," in Franklin Pease (ed.), Collaguas I (Lima: Universidad
Católica, 1977), pp. 13-34; and the same author's "Recent Research
Trends in Peruvian Historical Demography," Latin American Population
History Newsletter, 1 (1978), pp. 3-9.

9. The Colca valley, well photographed by air in the famous
Johnson expedition of the National Geographic Society presents one

of the most spectacular series of irrigated terraces of the south
Peruvian Andes. In spite of this glimpse of the area almost a half
century ago, the region has stimulated little scholarly investiga-
tion from the outside world. See George R. Johnson, Peru from the
Air (American Geographical Society, Special Publication No. 12,
1930); Philip Ainsworth Means, Fall of the Inca Empire and the Span-
ish Rule in Peru, 1530-1780 (New York, 1932); and Handbook of South
American Indians, Vol. 2, Plates 4 and 85. See also Máximo Neira
Avendano, "Los Collaguas," (Ph.D. dissertation, University of
Arequipa, 1961).

10. Francisco Xavier Echeverría, "Memoria de la Santa Iglesia
de Arequipa," in Victor M. Barriga (ed.), Memorias para la historia
de Arequipa (Arequipa, 1952), 4, pp. 80-104.

11. In spite of incomplete data, much useful information can be
taken from the parish registers for social history. Peter Laslett
presents a good argument for attempting the task in E. A. Wrigley
(ed.), An Introduction to English Historical Demography from the
Sixteenth to the Nineteenth Century (New York: Basic Books, 1966),
pp. 1-13.

12. Henry F. Dobyns, "Andean Epidemic History to 1720," Bulletin of the History of Medicine, 37 (1963), pp. 493-515; and Juan B.
Lastres, Historia de la medicina Peruana (Lima: San Marcos, 1951),
2, pp. 174-180, 299-303.

13. See N. David Cook, "La población indígena en el Perú colonial," Anuario de Investigaciones Históricas, 8 (1965), pp. 73-110.

14. For generalizations on migration from the Collaguas to
Yanahuara see N. David Cook, "La población de la parroquia de Yanahuara, 1738-47," in Collaguas I, pp. 13-34.

15. Lastres, Historia de la medicina, 3, pp. 20-34.

16. The 1876, 1940, 1961 and 1972 census results have been published by the Peruvian government. See the appropriate returns for
Caylloma, Yanque and Chivay in these volumes.

17. I was brought into close contact with the present-day residents of the Colca valley in 1974, through Dr. Franklin Pease, then
director of the Museo Nacional de la Historia in Lima. The Museum
had in its archive a nearly complete visita of the urinsaya half of
the repartimiento of Yanque Collaguas, which was prepared by colonial officials in 1591. This census provides an excellent panorama
of the late sixteenth century Indian world of the middle and upper
Colca valley. A group of Dr. Pease's students at the Universidad
Pontifícia Católica del Perú transcribed the document and prepared
studies based on the rich data it contains. Through the support of
the Peruvian Office of the Ford Foundation, Dr. Pease, a group of
students, professors of the Universidad Nacional de San Agustín of
Arequipa, and myself, were able to conduct preliminary field research in the valley in October of 1974. For an outline of the
project see N. David Cook and Franklin Pease, G.Y., "New Research
Possibilities in Los Collaguas, Peru," Latin American Research Review, 10 (1975), pp. 201-202. Father Pablo Hagan and Sister Antonia
Kayser of the parish of Yanque provided, both times my wife and I
were in the village, support and hospitality without which the research would have been difficult if not impossible. My thanks also
to Dean Robert FitzGeral of the University of Bridgeport who
assisted with University travel funds in 1979.

Index